English in the International Context

Discourse Across Cultures

Strategies in World Englishes

ENGLISH IN THE INTERNATIONAL CONTEXT

Series Editor: BRAJ B. KACHRU

Members of the Advisory Board

Eyamba G. Bokamba (Urbana)

Charles A. Ferguson (Stanford)

Andrew B. Gonzalez (Manila)

Sidney Greenbaum (London)

Michael A. K. Halliday (Sydney)

R. Parthasarathy (Delhi)

Other titles in this series

Sidney Greenbaum (ed.)
The English Language Today

Braj B. Kachru
The Alchemy of English

See also:

Braj B. Kachru (ed.)
The Other Tongue: English Across Cultures

Larry E. Smith (ed.)
Readings in English as an International Language

Christopher Brumfit (ed.)
English for International Communication

Discourse Across Cultures

Strategies in World Englishes

Edited by

LARRY E. SMITH

East-West Center,
Institute of Culture and Communication,
Hawaii, USA

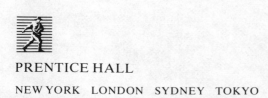

PRENTICE HALL

NEW YORK   LONDON   SYDNEY   TOKYO

First published in 1987 by
Prentice Hall International (UK) Ltd
66 Wood Lane End, Hemel Hempstead,
Hertfordshire, HP2 4RG
A division of
Simon & Schuster International Group

© 1987 Prentice Hall International (UK) Ltd

Printed and bound in Great Britain by SRP Ltd,
Exeter.

Library of Congress Cataloging in Publication Data

Discourse across cultures.

(English in the international context)
Papers presented at a conference organized by the
Institute of Culture and Communication in 1983,
revised and updated.
Includes index.
1. English language – Variation – Congresses.
2. English language – Foreign countries –
Congresses. 3. Intercultural communication –
Congresses. 4. Communication, International –
Congresses. 5. English language – Study and
teaching – Foreign speakers – Congresses.
I. Smith, Larry E. II. Institute of Culture and
Communication (East-West Center). III. Series.

PE2751.D57 1986 420 86-15090
ISBN 0-13-215005-0

British Library Cataloguing in Publication Data

Discourse across cultures: strategies in
world Englishes. – (English in the international context)
1. English language – Social aspects
2. Intercultural communication
I. Smith, Larry E. II. Series
302.2′2 PE1073

ISBN 0-13-215005-0

ISBN 0-13-215005-0

1 2 3 4 5 91 90 89 88 87

Contents

PART III TEXT, CONTEXT AND CULTURE   85

PART IV THE BILINGUAL'S CREATIVITY AND CONTACT LITERATURES IN ENGLISH   123

PART V CULTURE AND THE LANGUAGE CLASSROOM   167

Foreword

IN focusing upon discourse, we are not recommending yet another 'method' of learning English – still less an alternative to learning English. Effective discourse depends upon a sound mastery of lexical and syntactical fundamentals: this is not in question. No, what we are concerned with is rather a *goal* in language learning; and this does, of course, have a welcome and highly valuable mediating effect upon the teaching materials and the language learning methodology.

But the effect is still more profound. As soon as we home in on successful interpersonal discourse as our strategic goal in teaching and learning English, we come face to face with those aspects of communication that demand more than a dutiful knowledge of lexicon and grammar. As soon as we use English in an international context (an American speaking to a Thai, an Indian writing to a Korean), we are using it in an *intercultural* context. The types of impact that cross-cultural factors must have on our discoursal strategies are richly illustrated and insightfully scrutinized in the present volume. The cultural contrasts may be very great – as those between China and America examined by Xu Guo-zhang. Or they may be superficially small – as those between the neighbouring and ultimately cognate cultures of Germany and England examined by Michael Clyne. But the principle is the same: language and culture have to be studied together, and have to be brought into interactive relation in successful discourse.

As a member of the International Advisory Committee serving the East-West Center, I am glad to note another welcome feature of this book. In our advance towards recognizing the essential cultural component in our use of English for international purposes (however mundane and practical a given purpose may be), we must increasingly recognize too that a society's culture is often most exquisitely represented in its literature. This present volume deserves special attention because it focuses on two unique functions of English. It not only discusses the role of English as an international language as an exponent of different cultural values, but it also presents the international uses of English in various literatures around the world. It is evident that these two functions are remote from those that were carried by English before it became a language of international communication.

RANDOLPH QUIRK

Series Editor's Foreword

THIS volume, third in the series 'English in the International Context', brings together thirteen commissioned papers addressing major theoretical and applied issues concerning discourse strategies used in World Englishes. One might ask: Is there a paucity of scholarly papers and book-length studies on this topic? This question is particularly relevant since the past two decades have been very fruitful in the study of formal and functional characteristics of discourse. The answer is that the primary focus of such research has been on the native varieties of English: the language used in the Inner Circle, e.g. Britain and the USA. The number of studies focusing on the Outer Circle (e.g. West Africa, South Asia, Southeast Asia, the Philippines) is very limited indeed. And within that small number, only a few studies address the issues which are raised in this volume.

Discourse Across Cultures: Strategies in World Englishes, therefore, is most welcome, as it adds an important cross-cultural and cross-linguistic dimension to ongoing research on discourse analysis, discourse strategies, and stylistic innovations. The papers in this volume attempt to answer and further elaborate several issues that were first raised in two conferences held in 1978: one at the East-West Center, Honolulu (1–15 April), and the other at the University of Illinois, Urbana-Champaign (30 June–2 July). In both these conferences it was strongly felt that a fresh approach was needed for understanding the uses and users of English in the world context.

That there was a need for a new perspective became evident in the several conferences and colloquia which followed the Honolulu and Urbana conferences. Larry Smith of the East-West Center and I organized these conferences in conjunction with the 1980–6 annual conventions of the Teachers of English to Speakers of Other Languages (TESOL).

The chapters in this volume, as Larry Smith says in the Preface, were originally presented at yet another conference at the East-West Center in 1983. In this conference there was stimulating interaction among participants representing over a dozen cultures and more than a dozen countries. All the participants had a shared interest: a commitment to teaching and research in various aspects of English studies across cultures. Each paper was discussed with unusual candour. The multi-cultural implications of each presentation were discussed by a group of participants with rich teaching and research experience in Australia, China, India, Japan, the Philippines, Sri Lanka, the UK, and the USA, to name just a few countries.

However, this volume does not purport to present proceedings of the conference. It represents only a selection of conference presentations, and each selected paper has been substantially revised and updated. The comments by conference participants and the external reviewers have been taken into consideration. The Editor and the Series Editor have tried to provide an overall structure and cohesiveness to the contents.

The five parts of this volume represent five major areas of concern and research on English in the world context. In the thirteen chapters an attempt is made to present the theoretical and classroom implications of intercultural communication, the bilinguals' creativity, and the relationship of text, context and interpretation. These issues are of interest in several interdisciplinary fields of knowledge. However, in this volume these issues are specifically related to English, and the illustrations are drawn from diverse types of texts – literary and interactional – from various English-using parts of the world.

We are grateful to the Institute of Culture and Communication, the East-West Center, for organizing the 1983 conference on such an important aspect of English around the world. Again, much credit goes to Larry Smith for initiating such projects at the Center. As a participant in several conferences, as a Research Fellow of the Institute of Culture and Communication, and as a member of the Center's International Advisory Committee on English since 1978, I have personally experienced the excellence and the significance of the cross-cultural dimension of these conferences.

The theme of this volume and its individual contributions will no doubt go a long way in fulfilling the goal of this series: the study of English in its international and intranational contexts.

BRAJ B. KACHRU

Preface

Discourse Across Cultures: Strategies in World Englishes is the outcome of a cross-cultural and cross-linguistic conference held at the East-West Center, Honolulu, in 1983. This conference was part of a series of meetings which began in 1978 on the topic of English as an international language (EIL).

The EIL concept, as introduced almost a decade ago (Smith, 1976), is based on the premise that English is the property of its users, native and non-native, and all English speakers need training for effective international communication. The core argument of EIL is that non-native speakers do not have to use English the same way native speakers do; indeed it may be actively counterproductive, in terms of effective communication, for them to do so.

There are still many people who have never heard of EIL, or who are confused by it. There are those, for example, who think it to be a kind of English for special purposes (ESP) or to be the same as English as a second or foreign language (ESL/EFL). EIL is not English for special purposes with a restricted linguistic corpus for use in international settings, nor is it the same as EFL and ESL. In EFL and ESL, English is regarded as the sole property of its native speakers and the focus is on international communication between a native speaker and a non-native speaker. It is assumed that the non-native English speaker should work towards a native speaker's communicative competence. In ESL/EFL there is no attention given to cross-cultural communication between native speakers from different countries, and little attention given to international communication between non-native speakers.

The theory of EIL asserts that linguistic competence equivalent to that of a native English speaker is not enough to ensure successful international communication. Most native speakers have yet to realize that if they are going to be effective cross-cultural communicators, they must learn how other cultures structure information and argument, as well as how they use English to do things such as make refusals, compliments, suggestions, etc. This includes those other cultures whose first language is also English. Britons and Americans have had many cross-cultural communication problems with one another even though they share a common language.

Equally important, the theory of EIL argues that non-native users of English must be prepared to interact with one another as well as with native speakers, and that this implies the need for more than a study of basic English. It has been assumed in the past that problems in cross-cultural communication hinge primarily on linguistic ability; and that if the relevant parties speak or write English competently (i.e. like a native speaker) the communication problems will be solved. What usually happens in ESL/EFL courses is that non-native speakers are trained to interact with a group of native speakers assuming that if they can interact well with them, they will be able to interact successfully with all other fluent (native and non-native) users of English.

ESL and EFL generally fail to take into account the fact that today there are more non-native users of English than there are native users, and more and more frequently international interactions in English take place between non-native speakers. EIL recognizes that different language groups have different ways of speaking. These create different discourse patterns which are carried over, in part, into their use of English.

Users of English in international contexts must be prepared to deal with diversity and not to expect that all English users will communicate in ways similar to their own.

This volume should serve as a step towards understanding these complex issues which are involved in a discourse across cultures using the many Englishes of the world.

The book is the result of the co-operation and support of many people. I am grateful to Dr Mary G. F. Bitterman, Director of the East-West Center's Institute of Culture and Communication, under whose direction and supervision I work; to Professor Braj B. Kachru for his encouragement and support throughout the conference and preparation of this volume and for including it in his series 'English in the international context'; to Sir Randolph Quirk for his foreword to the volume and for his support and advice; to Jean D'souza of the University of Illinois, Maureen O'Brien of the East-West Center and Sandra Tawake of the University of Hawaii for their expert editorial assistance; and to the University of Hawaii Graduate School of Library Science for their help with the index. It has been my pleasure to work with these fine people.

LARRY E. SMITH

Reference

SMITH, L. E. (1976) English as an international auxiliary language. *RELC journal* 7: 2.

Contributors

CHRISTOPHER N. CANDLIN is Professor of Linguistics in the School of English and Linguistics at the MacQuarie University, Sydney. He has published extensively in the areas of second language curriculum design, sociolinguistics, discourse analysis and pragmatics, and language learning. His latest publications include *Language Learning Tasks*, *Computers in English Language Teaching and Research*, and *The Communicative Teaching of English*.

MICHAEL CLYNE is Associate Professor in the Department of German at Monash University, Victoria. He has published on various aspects of applied linguistics, culture and discourse structure, and multilingualism. His publications include *Transference and Triggering*; *Perspectives on Language Contact*; *Forschungsbericht Sprachkontakt*; *Multilingual Australia*; *Language and Society in German-speaking Countries*; and *Australia, Meeting-Place of Languages*.

REUEL DENNEY is an advisor to the Humanities Forum of the East-West Center and Professor Emeritus of the University of Hawaii, Honolulu, Hawaii. He is the author of *The Astonished Muse* and co-author (with David Riseman and Nathan Glazer) of *The Lonely Crowd*. He has published three volumes of poetry. His research interests include sociology of culture and language and communication.

WIMAL DISSANAYAKE is Assistant Director and Research Associate at the Institute of Culture and Communication, East-West Center, Honolulu, Hawaii. He was head of the Department of Mass Communication, University of Sri Lanka, before joining the East-West Center. His research interests include communication theories and literary communication, and the literary traditions of South Asia. His publications include *Critical Communication*; *Continuity and Change in Communication Systems* (co-editor); and *Communications Research and Cultural Values* (co-editor).

ANDREW GONZALEZ is President of De La Salle University, Manila. He has published extensively on Philippine languages (especially Kapampangan), English in the Philippines, language policies, and bilingualism.

BRAJ B. KACHRU is a Professor of Linguistics and of Education and English, and Director, Division of English as an International Language at the University of Illinois, Urbana, Illinois. He was head of the Department of Linguistics at the same university from 1969 to 1979. His publications include *The Other Tongue: English Across Cultures* (ed., 1982); *The Indianization of English: The English Language in India* (1983); and *The Alchemy of English: The Spread, Functions and Models of Non-Native Englishes* (1986). He is co-editor of *World Englishes: Journal of English as an International and Intranational Language*, and series editor of 'English in the International Context', published by Prentice Hall International.

YAMUNA KACHRU is a Professor of Linguistics and of English at the University of Illinois, Urbana, Illinois. Her research and teaching focus on syntax, semantics, South Asian languages, and discourse analysis. Her publications include *An Introduction to Hindi Syntax* (1966), *Aspects of Hindi Grammar* (1980), and papers in professional journals on syntax, semantics, pragmatics, and discourse.

VIRGINIA LoCASTRO is currently a lecturer at the University of Tsukuba. Before joining the university she was the Academic Director of the Simul Academy of International Communication in Tokyo. Her academic background is in French/linguistics and applied linguistics. Before going to Japan in 1980, she taught at the American Language Program and Teachers College, Columbia University. Her interests and publications are in cross-cultural communication and in the teaching of English as a second language.

MIMI NICHTER has a multi-disciplinary background in applied linguistics, communication, and anthropology. Her past research and publications have focused on language and communication, women and health, and development communication.

R. PARTHASARATHY is an Assistant Professor of English and of Asian Studies at Skidmore College, Saratoga Springs, New York. He is the author of *Rough Passage* (1977), a long poem, and has edited *Ten Twentieth-Century Indian Poets* (1976), both published by Oxford University Press, Delhi, where he was, until recently, senior editor. *Rough Passage* was the runner-up for the Commonwealth Poetry Prize, 1977. He has translated into modern English verse the *Cilappatikāram* (The Epic of the Anklet) from the Classical Tamil of South India.

LARRY E. SMITH is Research Associate in the Institute of Culture and Communication, East-West Center, Honolulu, Hawaii. His research interests include the international intelligibility of English, English for cross-cultural communication, and applied linguistics. He has edited *English for Cross-cultural Communication*, *Readings in English as an International Language*, and is co-editor (with Braj Kachru) of the journal *World Englishes: Journal of English as an International and Intranational Language*.

PETER STREVENS is Director-General of the Bell Educational Trust, Cambridge, and Fellow of Wolfson College, Cambridge University. He has held professorships at the University of Leeds and the University of Essex, where he established programmes in applied linguistics. His publications include *New Orientations in the Teaching of English*, *The Teaching of English as an International Language*, and (with others) *Reference Manual of the Essential English for International Maritime Use: SEASPEAK*.

ELAINE TARONE is Associate Professor in the Department of Linguistics, University of Minnesota, Minneapolis, Minnesota. She has published extensively in the area of second-language acquisition, focusing on the pronunciation, strategic competence, and style-shifting characteristic of second-language learners.

HENRY G. WIDDOWSON is Professor of English for Speakers of Other Languages, University of London. He was previously British Council Officer and Lecturer in the Department of Linguistics, University of Edinburgh. He is a founder editor of *The Journal of Applied Linguistics*. His publications include *Stylistics and the Teaching of Literature*, *Teaching Language as Communication*, *Explorations in Applied Linguistics I* and *II*, and *Learning Purpose and Language Use*.

XU GUO-ZHANG is Director, School of Linguistics at the Beijing Foreign Studies University. He was educated in China and at Oxford University, Oxford. He has published extensively in linguistics, language teaching, and teacher training.

GEORGE YULE is Associate Professor in the Linguistics Program, Louisiana State University, Baton Rouge, Louisiana. His research interests include theoretical and applied linguistics. He is author of *The Study of Language* and co-author, with Gillian Brown, of *Discourse Analysis*, *Teaching the Spoken Language*, and *Teaching Talk*.

Introduction: Discourse Strategies and Cross-cultural Communication

LARRY E. SMITH

THERE is no doubt that a good command of English grammar, lexis, and phonology is helpful in effective cross-cultural communication. What is not so commonly realized is that this is not enough (Krishnaswamy and Aziz, 1983). Recognition is needed that such things as the place of silence, appropriate topics of conversation, forms of address, and expressions of speech-acts (e.g. apologies, requests, agreement, disagreement, etc.) are usually not the same across cultures and that these are perhaps more important to effective cross-cultural communication than grammar, lexis, or phonology.

Everyone's use of English is based on cultural presuppositions about the kinds of language behaviour that are appropriate for particular situations and the expectations people have regarding effective structuring of information. These presuppositions are taken for granted and are usually at a low level of awareness. An incident which illustrates a contrast between Japanese and American use of apologies may help to demonstrate how cultural assumptions determine what is considered to be appropriate language behaviour.

> An American woman went to Japan to marry a Japanese man and was stopped at Haneda airport because there was a problem with her visa. In the ensuing confusion she did not fill out a form for her unaccompanied baggage.
>
> When her baggage arrived at Osaka Port several weeks later, she couldn't get it out of customs without this form. Her husband was told she should write an apology and send it, with her passport, to Tokyo.
>
> She was incensed at the idea of having to apologize for something she was convinced was not her fault, since the Haneda authorities were to blame for not giving her the appropriate form. However, her husband told her to write the apology any-way, which she did, and promptly received her baggage with no further trouble; except that this American woman felt she had been made to shoulder the blame for what she felt was Japanese incompetence (Naotsuka, 1978: 11).

The communication problem was due not to the language code, but to different cultural assumptions about what language behaviour was appropriate. To the Japanese an apology was appropriate; to the American, it was not. The problem was caused by the American being unaware (and her husband being unable to explain to her) that in Japan apologies are not only an admission of fault as they usually are in the United States, but also a social

1

lubricant, where both parties in any interaction accept mutual responsibility for the content as well as the tone of the interchange.

Communication problems like this are not limited to interactions involving non-native speakers. They also occur frequently between native English speakers who do not share the same culture – between English people and Americans, for example, or between Americans and Australians. When this happens, the cause of the problem can be difficult for the interactors to diagnose, because language usage is not usually thought of as a likely culprit. For this reason the work of Renwick (1983) is of special interest: he writes about communication barriers between Americans and Australians; and though his research appears to deal almost exclusively with male subjects, his observations are an important contribution to the field. For example, he writes (p. 119):

> Americans tend to like people who agree with them. Australians are more apt to be interested in a person who disagrees with them; disagreement is a basis for a lively conversation. Americans assume that if someone agrees with them, that person likes them; disagreement implies rejection. Australians assume that someone's disagreement with them has little to do with that person's attitude toward them. Disagreement, in fact, can indicate real interest and respect ('The fellow cares enough about me to really disagree with me').

Thus Renwick argues that Americans may not always find they like Australians very much, and may feel rejected by them. He further suggests that most American men, in ordinary business or social intercourse, are inclined to let their achievements and position speak for them. The 'average Australian', however, wants to probe the American's wit and resilience. While the American is seeking a topic to chat about, the Australian is seeking a partner to spar with. Thus the American finds the Australian intrusive, and the Australian finds the American boring. In order to evoke some definite opinions or other tangible reactions, the Australian often becomes more self-assertive, while the American is more inclined to withdraw. These frustrations do not have as much to do with the language code as they do with cultural assumptions about what is appropriate for particular situations.

An example to illustrate the problems regarding expectations about the structure of information and argument may also be useful. Naotsuka (1978: 8) reports that Japanese often approach a subject in a spiral way, while Westerners use more linear, straight-line logic. This can present a problem when, for example, Japanese business people try to explain things to Britons. The Japanese will tend to take into consideration all conceivable facts and ideas, many of which may seem irrelevant from a Western viewpoint, before focusing on the subject. Their British counterparts, after hearing only the first few sentences, will complain of their irrelevance, then take the conversational lead away from the Japanese and try to 'get to the point' in ways more logical to themselves.

In this volume (Chapter 6) M. Clyne, with examples from Germany and Australia, points out how the presentation of an argument that sounds fluent and elegant in one culture may be regarded as clumsy and circular by members of another culture.

It is clear that using a common language such as English does not change the interactors' cultural assumptions and expectations about what is and is not appropriate language behaviour in particular situations. People involved in cross-cultural communication should neither expect the discourse strategies in English to be the same as their own, nor be quick to interpret a language behaviour as they would if they themselves had done/said the same thing. In all intercultural situations a negotiation of meaning is necessary (Candlin, 1981).

This negotiation of meaning can perhaps be done by taking into account what I have called the five senses (Smith, 1983b): (1) a sense of self; (2) a sense of the other; (3) a sense of the relationship between self and the other; (4) a sense of the setting/social situation; and (5) a sense of the goal or objective.

Knowing self is a dynamic, lifelong process. Race, gender, nationality, age, and socioeconomic status are important factors one must remember, but they are rather simple, basic things. What about belief system and values? How are honesty, loyalty, freedom, harmony, generosity, competition, wealth, power, faith, and pleasure, rank ordered? When there is a conflict between or among any of these, which one is more powerful? Which is more important, facts or feelings? Are style and form as important as content? How important is work to our identity? How do we determine success? Is it better to be direct or indirect when expressing ourselves? Is one accent better than another? We need to know these things about ourselves and also to realize that in using English across cultures there is no reason to act as though we are somehow different than we are. One's ethnic, religious, and political background is an important part of one's identity, and there is no need to pretend that these change somehow when one is using English. We certainly want to use English well, but this should not require us to try to change our identity. It is true that language and culture are inextricably tied together, and that it is not possible to use a language without a culture base. However, one language is not always inextricably tied to one culture. English already represents many cultures and it can be used by anyone as a means to express any cultural heritage and any value system. Using English does not make one a different person. There is no need to become more 'Western' or 'Eastern' in order to use it well. One's morals and dedication to family traditions need not change at all. People interacting with members of their own culture do not usually need to have a verbalized awareness of their individual values and styles of communication because they are shared within the culture. However, when one communicates across cultures, a clear sense of self is crucial in negotiating meaning.

The second sense is a sense of the other. In order to communicate most effectively with anyone, we need to know as much about him or her as possible. The more we know and understand someone, the greater our chances are for effective communication. That does not mean that once we are familiar with someone we will never misunderstand him or her, but it should mean that we are better able to cope with misunderstandings and correct them more easily. In the use of English, one needs to know something about the discourse strategies of the prospective other. People who work with Thais need to know that they are more subtle and indirect than Americans, and that a Thai audience is not as likely to be impressed by facts and figures as they are with form and style. We must learn as much about our prospective audience as is possible. Of course, the best way to get this knowledge is through personal experience, but much of it will have to come from reading about the other in works of literature. Chapters 7, 9, 10, and 12 illustrate how this can be done.

The third sense is a sense of the relationship between self and other. The degree or affiliation of distance between sender and receiver will help to determine the discourse strategies that are used. We do not speak to a stranger and an old friend in the same way. The status of our interactor relative to our own status and the social distance between us are very important factors to keep in mind as we negotiate for meaning. We must remember that relationships, like people, are dynamic not static, and that although blood relatives remain so for life, our relationships with them often change dramatically over time. Relationships between friends can be strained or improved by the communication strategies that are used, and addressing someone as a friend when he is obviously a stranger will not make that person a friend. An accurate (i.e. agreed on by the parties involved) assessment of the relationship between the self and the other will perhaps do more to determine the discourse strategies to be used than any other sense, and may thus have the greatest impact on the negotiation of meaning across cultures.

The fourth sense is a sense of the setting and/or social situation. No one should expect to find English being used in the same ways in London and Los Angeles, in Manila and Melbourne, in Tokyo and Toronto. As we negotiate meaning across cultures we will, no doubt, want to take the geographic setting and the social situation into account. We do not talk the same way at a funeral as we do at a wedding or at a racetrack. An argument in an American bar will not usually be the same as a debate in a public congressional hearing, even if the participants are identical. There are formal and informal occasions that each of us participate in, and we must be prepared to adjust our discourse strategies for different settings and social situations if we are to be effective cross-cultural communicators.

The fifth sense is a sense of the goal or objective to be accomplished. No matter what the relationship or setting, we do not use the same verbal and non-verbal behaviour when we want to show interest as we do when we want to express disappointment. The objective may be very specific (e.g. to borrow money or to refuse to loan money) or more general (e.g. to make a good impression or to keep the conversation alive), but it must be kept in mind if we are going to achieve it. There are often multiple goals (e.g. to show concern for the feelings of the other while at the same time refusing a request), and sometimes conflicting ones (e.g. to show that we are all comrades but also to demonstrate that one person is in control). As crucial as this seems, the sense of the goal/objective is often the one least clearly perceived. It is frequently said and thought to be one thing but observed to be something else. Important general goals and objectives are commonly at a subconscious state of awareness and require effort to verbalize. Having a clear understanding of the goal/objective is essential if we are to negotiate meaning successfully across cultures.

It is generally accepted that if we increase the involvement of the body senses in the learning process, we will be more successful. The same is true, I believe, of the five senses as they are related to cross-cultural communication. The greater the involvement and understanding of self, the other, the relationship between self and the other, the setting/social situation, and the goal/objective, the greater the possibility of genuinely negotiated meaning which is acceptable to all parties involved.

Problems in cross-cultural communication in English which involve discourse strategies usually are the result of accepting one of the following erroneous hypotheses:

(1) When using a second or foreign language, a speaker will use the discourse strategies of his mother tongue. For example, a French speaker will use the same patterns of discourse in English as he or she does in French. There is, therefore, no need to study French people using English. One need only study how the French use French, then one can be confident that they (the French) will use English in the same ways.
(2) There is only one correct set of strategies for discourse in English and everyone using English attempts to use that set. This hypothesis leads one to believe that when English is the common language, one can expect the words, sentences, and discourse to have common meaning across cultures. One may then interpret what is said by an interactor of another culture in the same way it would be interpreted had it been said by a fellow national.

The chapters in this book deal with these issues and demonstrate that communication across cultures in English is a complex topic which requires a greal deal more research – research which is empirically based (Chapter 4) and goes beyond description to explanation (Chapter 2). Several things are clear from the work which has been done:

(1) Discourse patterns from the first language do not carry over entirely into the second language (Chapter 8).
(2) Using a common linguistic medium (English) does not mean that the discourse strategies are shared (Chapter 5 and 6).
(3) A great deal can be learned about discourse patterns from newspapers, the study of literatures (Chapters 7, 9, 10, 11 and 12), and poetry (Chapter 3) written in English from around the world.
(4) Care should be taken so that literary works are not treated as if they were ethnographic data (Chapter 1).
(5) English language classrooms can benefit from discourse studies as well as become research sites for them (Chapter 13).

Discourse Across Cultures: Strategies in World Englishes is divided into five sections:

Literature, conventions, and explanation;
Discourse expectations and cross-cultural communication;
Text, context, and culture;

The bilinguals' creativity and contact literatures in English;
Culture and the language classroom.

Each section is preceded by an introduction which attempts to summarize the
main ideas and arguments and show how the papers relate to one another.

It has taken much longer than it should have for comparative discourse to be
studied in the way that comparative phonology and comparative syntax have
been studied. It is my hope that this volume will serve as a step towards
understanding the issues which are involved in discourse across cultures using
the many Englishes of the world, will stimulate discussion, and will encourage
further research on discourse across cultures.

References

CANDLIN, C. N. (1981) Discoursal patterning and the equalizing of interpretive opportunity. In
Smith (1981), pp. 166–199.

KRISHNASWAMY, N. and A. S. AZIZ (1983) Understanding values, TEIL and the Third World.
In Smith (1983a), pp. 95–101.

NAOTSUKA, R. (1978) *Mutual understanding of different cultures*. Osaka, Japan: Educational
Science Institute of Osaka Prefecture.

RENWICK, G. W. (1983) If Australians are arrogant, are Americans boring? If Americans are
boring, are Australians arrogant? In Smith (1983a), pp. 117–123.

SMITH, L. E. (ed.) (1981) *English for cross-cultural communication*. London: Macmillan.

SMITH, L. E. (ed.) (1983a) *Readings in English as an international language*. Oxford: Pergamon
Press.

SMITH, L. E. (ed.) (1983b) The five senses of teaching/learning English as an international
language. *PASAA Journal* **XII**(1): March.

PART I

Literature, Conventions and Explanation

INTRODUCTION

THIS section introduces some fundamental questions with a cross-cultural perspective for understanding and explaining conventional and literary discourse for both prose and poetry. The issues raised here provide a context for understanding the sections which follow in the volume. The three chapters are provocative, and therefore controversial.

Widdowson assumes that discourse can be studied through literature (an assumption not shared by everyone), and that we must have a theoretical framework which relates discourse studies and literary criticism. He offers a programmatic proposal and establishes the distinction between representation and reference: representation with literature and reference with 'normal' discourse. He claims that the relationship between literary tradition and the current customary practices in conventional discourse is a complex one. In Widdowson's terms the complexity has to do with the way iconic representation (literature) relates to indexical operations of language in normal referential use. Widdowson argues that it cannot be assumed that literary writing directly reflects customary practices in ordinary discourse. Some distortion always exists and it is crucial to establish the nature of such distortion. In his view literary works should not be treated as if they were so much ethnographic data, i.e. the same as the evidence of ordinary social encounters. In his framework he claims that there is a continual adjustment of literary conventions to contemporary practices and beliefs; a constant realignment of representation to reference.

Candlin, in Chapter 2, deals with spoken cross-cultural discourse. He argues for an explanatory stance rather than a descriptive one. He draws upon a view of pragmatics which regards discourse as a means of learning the value-systems held by the participants. His position is that discoursal patterns reveal values and beliefs held to be 'natural' in the cultures of the participants. He believes an explanatory analysis provides more powerful insights into the potentially conflicting value systems of cross-cultural interactants than does a quantifying description. Candlin claims that critical moments of communication in social life between representatives of different ethnic groups offer rewarding research sites for the study of spoken, cross-cultural communication problems

7

and that such studies require a foundation in social theory if they are to explain discourse rather than merely describe it.

Chapter 3, by Denney, deals with another type of creativity – poetry. He discusses the formal discourse structure of poetry written in English. His analysis demonstrates that literature can provide insight for the study of discourse. It has generally been claimed that a poem is differentiated from other utterances by rhyme. In Denney's view, poems, phrase by phrase and clause by clause, draw on common speech-acts which help to contextualize the poem and give it meaning. He argues that speech-act analysis shows, for example, the special effects arising out of the use of the performative in poetry. In poems by Rilke and Ashberry, he says the perlocutionary performative is a key strategy; and its use in each separate case provides clues to the poetic stance of the writer.

The three chapters together provide refreshing insights for the understanding and analysis of conventional and literary discourse.

1

Significance in Conventional and Literary Discourse

HENRY G. WIDDOWSON

THE central argument of this chapter is that there is an essential difference between the way meaning is achieved in literature and the way it is typically achieved in conventional uses of language. This difference has to do with significance in two senses. First, it can be described by invoking certain distinctions between types of sign, and in this case significance can be glossed as modes of signifying. Second, this difference can be related to how language has been defined as an object of analysis by linguists and as a subject by language teachers. In this case significance can be glossed as relevance. What I shall seek to show, therefore, at the end of the chapter, is how the first significance provides a basis for the second: how the use of language to signify meaning in literature is significant for the practices of language description and learning.

I want to begin with the assumption commonly made by linguists that the linguistic signs which they identify as the proper object of their analysis are basically the same as those signs which the language users employ in the contexts of actual communicative activity. It is assumed that the necessary idealization process removes certain accidental and contingent features of signs, contracted by their association with context, but their fundamental, essential character survives. So it is that sentences, the analytic constructs of linguists, are said to *underlie* utterances, the actual instances of language use, and it is only various incidental circumstances that prevent performance from being a direct projection of competence, which the linguist characterizes as the knowledge of language which determines behaviour. Against this I should like to suggest that the decontextualization of language does not strip it down to its bare essentials, leaving its basic nature intact, but actually changes it into something else. I want to suggest that the methodology of idealization alters in quite crucial ways the data it is designed to account for.

The dissociation of elements of language from their context has the effect of forcing attention on how they signify as formal isolates, both in denoting general types of particular instances and in contracting sense relations with other items as terms within systems. To specify the denotation and sense of linguistic items thus separated out from context is to show their signification as symbols. The complex rules which define these systems and which determine the ways in which signification is given formal expression are the business of the grammarian to describe. Thus given a particular sentence:

He came back into the kitchen.

Signification can be specified by indicating that *he* denotes a singular male person, that it enters into sense relations with *she* and *they* as terms within the pronoun system and contrasts with the former in gender and the latter in number. It can be shown how *came* contrasts with *has come*, *is coming* and so on within the tense/aspect systems of English; it can be demonstrated how the whole combination of symbols as a sentence enters into paradigmatic relations with other sentences. And so on. All this is a matter of describing the signification of symbols and so accounting for the knowledge of the native speakers of English which enables them to assign a meaning to the sentence as an isolated expression. What it cannot account for, of course, is what might be meant by anybody actually uttering such an expression. We cannot know, without a context, what the signs are intended to *refer* to. Knowledge of the signification of signs is only a means to an end for the language user, not an end in itself. It is knowledge which has to be exploited: it cannot simply be invoked. And it is exploited by treating linguistic signs not as symbols with self-contained and invariant meanings defined by the conventions of the code, but as a set of indications as to where meaning is to be found in the contextual circumstances of the utterance. The linguistic sign in the sentence functions as a *symbol*: its meaning is stable and subject to specification. It works by a kind of centripetal attraction of attention to itself, and the discovery of what it signifies is a matter of *deciphering*. The linguistic sign in the utterance functions as an *index*: its meaning is unstable and unspecifiable depending, as it does, on the user relating it successfully to aspects of the context in which it occurs. The index works centrifugally and points away from itself; the discovery of what meaning is indicated depends on *interpretation*.

It will be clear from this distinction that to detach a linguistic sign from context and to consider it in isolation is to radically alter its character from index to symbol. It is perfectly possible to decipher an expression symbolically and still be incapable of interpreting it indexically. If there is no context for the signs to point to, the symbols cannot be converted into clues. They simply direct attention into a void. A knowledge of what symbols signify is obviously crucial as a source of information but communication has to be achieved by plotting a course of interpretation which involves taking bearings both on this knowledge and also on aspects of the immediate context, including what is known apart from language by those engaged in the interaction.[1]*

The description of linguistic signs as symbols defines what has been codified as grammatically possible within the systems of a particular language. We may say that this description accounts for linguistic competence. But, as Hymes (among others) has pointed out, this is only one kind of knowledge which the language user draws upon in assessing the effect of utterances. Hymes (1972:

*Superscript numbers refer to Notes at the end of the Chapter.

281) proposes four kinds of judgement which a communicatively competent speaker of a language is capable of making, namely:

> Whether (and to what degree) something is formally *possible*;
> Whether (and to what degree) something is *feasible* by virtue of the means of implementation available;
> Whether (and to what degree) something is *appropriate* (adequate, happy, successful) in relation to a context in which it is used and evaluated;
> Whether (and to what degree) something is in fact done, actually *performed*, and what its doing entails.

Hymes indicates here the kinds of knowledge which are brought to bear in *identifying* a particular expression as manifesting varying degrees of normality. It seems reasonable to suppose, however, that the same kinds of knowledge are engaged in realizing the communicative effect of utterances. Relating these criteria for assessment to the conditions for achieving meaning that I have previously referred to, we can associate the formally possible with the symbol and appropriacy with the index. An expression in English, for example, which is decipherable as a sentence but which relates to no context can be assigned a signification as a combination of symbols. Only when such an expression is associated with a context can it function indexically and be appropriately interpreted. Interpretation then involves providing a symbolic variable with a particular indexical value. But this process can be disrupted by the intervention of the other conditions of acceptability which Hymes mentions. An expression can be formally possible but be relatively unfeasible. A notorious case of this is the nesting construction where recursion results in increasing incomprehensibility, as in this commonly cited example:

> This is the cat the dog chased.
> This is the rat the cat the dog chased killed.
> This is the malt the rat the cat the dog chased killed ate.

And so on.[2]

A reduction in feasibility makes it difficult to recognize what the symbols signify and so creates a deciphering problem. The degree to which something is done, actually performed, on the other hand, is a factor in case of interpretation since the sign in this case is called upon to make an unusual indexical connection. In short, possibility and feasibility are features of the symbol; and appropriacy and frequency of performance are features of the index.

Now, in the normal circumstances of language use, conformity to the co-operative principle, as formulated in Grice (1975), would bring these various conditions into alignment. That is to say, the performance of an appropriately indexical expression would realize those resources for meaning which were symbolically coded in the language as formally correct and would avoid constructions which, though permissible, were difficult to process. Conventional uses of language, by definition, make use of conventional means to engage schematic knowledge of a conventional kind. What is actually done is appropriate, and what is appropriate is formally possible and feasible. It is only under such conditions of normality that the efficient conversion of symbol to index can occur. For the index, in the way I have defined it, serves to mediate between the known symbolic categories within the language system and the known schematic structures which organize reality outside language.[3] If the context is not in some degree familiar as a frame of reference, then it cannot be used as a bearing on meaning and indexical value cannot be realized. Similarly, if the symbols are (in Hymes's terms) impossible, they create types for which there are no tokens and no match can be made with context; and if they are unfeasible, the consequent difficulties of deciphering will provide no secure linguistic basis for interpretation.

The linguistic sign as used indexically in conventional discourse then *refers* the user to pre-existing knowledge as formulated in the categories of language and in the schematic frames of reference and behavioural routines which make particular contexts familiar. Such reference is a function of the convergence of the four factors that Hymes refers to and which provide therefore the required conditions for effective communication in conventional discourse.

The question now arises as to what happens when these conditions do *not* converge. Consider, for example, cases where expressions are formally correct (i.e. possible) and create no difficulty for deciphering (i.e. feasible) but do not normally occur. The following would be examples:

> The sailors sailed the seas with seven sisters.
> This small secluded shop sells smart socks and scarves.

There is nothing in the rules of English which prevents this dense accumulation of sibilants, and their occurrence does not make the symbols difficult to process. The meaning of each sentence is perfectly plain. But they have a very odd ring to them and any native speaker of English would recognize the oddity, and would generally avoid such phonological effects in performance.[4] But effects of this kind *are* found in actually attested instances of language use:

> When to the sessions of sweet silent thought
> I summon up remembrance of things past,
> I sigh the lack of many a thing I sought,
> And with old woes new wail my dear times' waste. . .
>
> (Shakespeare)

> What passing bells for those who die as cattle?
> Only the monstrous anger of the guns,
> Only the stuttering rifle's rapid rattle
> Can patter out their hasty orisons . . .
>
> (Wilfred Owen)

Here, however, the clustering of sound segments gives direct support to the meanings conveyed by the syntax and lexical choice, and the abnormality is recognized as appropriate. We understand the two expressions (*The sailors sailed . . .*, *This small secluded shop . . .*) as two separate sentences whose symbolic character is evident and calls for no superimposed phonological pattern. We identify them, therefore, as devices for presenting and practising these sounds. The sounds themselves have no significance. But in the lines of poetry they obviously do have a signifying function and are an essential part of the meaning. How, though, is this meaning to be characterized? The signs here are not really indexical: they do not mediate a shared knowledge of language structure and a familiar state of affairs: they go beyond the requirements for reference so that we do not interpret what is said by recognizing how the signs indicate something in reality outside themselves. They actually create their own reality: they do not refer to experience, they *represent* it.

The phonological patterns in these poems carry meanings which are not sanctioned by the language codification which defines the symbol. They have significance without signification, because they exploit a potential within the language which is not formally incorporated into the code, but which is available for exploitation should the occasion require it. If it is used, however, the resulting expressions will necessarily be recognized as relatively unacceptable in respect of the norms of actual performance (Hymes's fourth criterion) and so they cannot be interpreted in the normal way of converting symbols to indices. Interpretation must achieve not reference but representation: the signs take on an *iconic* character.[5]

Similar consequences follow from a failure to conform to the other conditions that Hymes mentions. Consider, for example, cases of attested utterances which are symbolically deviant in that they would fail a test of formal possibility:

Not, I'll not, carrion comfort, Despair, not feast on thee;
Not untwist-slack they may be – these last strands of man
In me or, most weary, cry *I can no more*. I can;
Can something, hope, wish day come, not choose not to be . . .

(Hopkins)

The structural non-conformity of these lines, the detachment of the negative particle *not*, the fragmentation of the syntax, create meanings which cannot be expressed within the confines of the established code. They do not refer to but represent a struggle with despair, and the meaning would be drastically altered if the expressions were adjusted to meet the conditions of normal reference:

I will not feast on thee, carrion comfort, despair;
these last strands of man may be slack but I will not untwist them . . .

We should note that the normalized version improves on the feasibility of the original. Hopkins's lines present us with deciphering problems. But again, it is appropriate that they should, for they are an attempt to give expression to emotional disturbance and our difficulty engages us directly in the poet's struggle for coherence. An increase in feasibility diminishes the representation. It would not be appropriate to this particular communicative purpose.

In Hopkins's lines the particle *not* is detached from its normal structural dependency to represent a kind of insistent refusal to succumb to despair. In the following example from E. E. Cummings, this detachment serves a very different function:

Pity this busy monster, manunkind,
not. Progress is a comfortable disease:

The deviation from formal possibility here has the effect of causing us to process what is said, to make it feasible, in two different ways. The end of the metrical line suggests a closure, and we are led to suppose that the statement is complete and that we are being enjoined to be pitiful. The appearance of *not* at the start of the next line abruptly cancels this injunction and forces us to an opposite interpretation. But because the negation is not incorporated in the normal way into the first expression, it only works retrospectively so that in effect we have two expressions of equal force contradicting each other, both incorporated within the same grammatical structure. The formally impossible lexical item *manunkind* can now be seen as the element which fuses these contradictions. The abnormally positioned *un* negates the normal noun *mankind* just as the abnormally positioned *not* negates the whole expression which precedes it. We should note, however, that *manunkind* is not a part of that expression: it is structurally detached, as the commas make clear, so that its oddity is given particular prominence. If we now separate out the normal from the abnormal features of these lines, we can associate them in the following way:

> Pity this busy monster, mankind
>   not   un

A referential gloss on this might run something like:

> Pity mankind, but to the extent that mankind has become a monster, man*un*kind, then do not pity him.

But this is a poor substitute for the lines of the poem which fuse these contradictions into one coherent expression and so directly represent meanings which can only otherwise be imperfectly indicated by the referential device of paraphrase. Paraphrase necessarily resolves the paradox which Cummings represents by deviating from the norms of possibility and feasibility. We are meant to puzzle over what is said: that is the point of the poem.

   In the examples we have considered so far, departures from the norms of normal possibility have also reduced feasibility. But this is not a necessary consequence: such departures may leave feasibility unimpaired, even improved. The formation of reported speech, for example, is not only a fairly cumbersome operation, but it frequently causes deciphering problems because of the formal requirements of possibility (in the technical sense of Hymes). Thus the following sentence contains unresolved ambiguities:

> She said that she was watering the garden.

The expression being reported here could be any one of the following:

> I am watering the garden.
> I was watering the garden.
> She is watering the garden.
> She was watering the garden.

The structural changes required by the code neutralize the distinctions of pronoun and tense and reduce feasibility accordingly. Now, in fiction we very often find reported speech which in part dispenses with such changes to yield what is usually referred to as free indirect speech. Here is an example from Dickens's *Bleak House*:

> Name Jo. Nothing else that he knows on. Don't know that everybody has two names. Never heard of sich a think. Don't know that Jo is short for a longer name. Thinks it long enough for *him*. *He* can't find no fault with it. Spell it? No. *He* can't spell.

The present tense of direct speech is retained but there are recurrent shifts from third person (e.g. *he knows, thinks*) which marks indirect speech to first person (*Don't know*), which is the normal feature of direct speech. This hybrid form is not reported speech in the conventional sense. It seeks to capture the immediacy of the speaking voice, to make it actual even though it cannot possibly be present. It is, in short, *represented* speech.[6]

The examples I have cited of literary uses of language are meant to show that when normal conditions for reference in respect of feasibility, possibility and performance are flouted in the interests of appropriacy (that is to say, when such deviations are communicatively motivated) then a non-conventional mode of meaning is achieved. This I have called representation, and it is this, I would claim, which is the essential feature of literary discourse.[7] The language of literature is not used to refer to a familiar and verifiable reality but to represent a reality of a different and alternative order which has no direct counterpart in the conventional world. It follows that the linguistic sign as used in literature has a distinctive character of its own which warrants a distinctive term: the icon.[8] It is not a symbol, since it figures in actual use, and contracts relations with context, but it is not an index either, since it does not point to any token instance of which the symbol is the type. Its nature is such that the realization of its meaning depends on the kind of deciphering usually associated with the symbol, but directed towards the kind of interpreting usually associated with the index.

In representation, therefore, attention is directed at the resources for making meaning, the rules and conventions which control the formation and use of language are brought into prominence, focused upon, as they are in linguistic analysis. But this prominence, or foregrounding,[9] is done not in dissociation from context but as a force in its creation. Consider, for example, the expression cited at the beginning of this chapter:

> He came back into the kitchen.

As I indicated earlier, to decipher this as a sentence requires us to concentrate on each symbol and the manner of its combination with others in order to assign signification to the whole. We cannot interpret it as an utterance, however, since we have no context so that the normal indexical function of the signs *he* and *the* is not activated. But of course if the expression were to occur in a context, these signs would be interpreted in relation to a previously established reference, so that there would be no need to actually decipher them as symbols by invoking their sense and denotation. We do not realize pragmatic use by syntactic and semantic analysis.

But this expression happens to occur at the beginning of a short story by

Somerset Maugham, so there is no possibility of reference to any context. In this case, attention is directed at the meanings contained within the signs themselves, as if they were symbols, but this is done in order to create a context, so the signs are interpreted as having prospective significance. *He* – who is he? *The kitchen* – which kitchen? The reader is projected forward in quest of information which will enable him to formulate some kind of context which will enable him to find his bearings, and to understand the scene that is represented here:

> He came back into the kitchen. The man was still on the floor, lying where he had hit him, and his face was bloody. He was moaning. The woman had backed against the wall and was staring with terrified eyes at Willi, his friend, and when he came in she gave a gasp and broke into loud sobbing . . . (*The Unconquered*)

Notice that this passage leaves a good deal to be desired as far as feasibility is concerned; it flouts the Gricean maxim of quantity by giving too little information, so in spite of the signalling of definite reference we have no definite idea about who *the man* or *the woman* might be. And it is not very easy on first reading to sort out the links between the various third person masculine proforms (Is Willi the friend of the man on the floor or the man coming from the kitchen? Could Willi perhaps be the man on the floor himself?). But although in conventional discourse this could be counted as referential failure, here it is representationally appropriate since it sets up the conditions of forward projection whereby context is created within the literary work itself.

Representation, then, draws attention to symbolic meanings, while putting them to context-creative use. In this respect the meaning potential inherent in the language system is given a fuller realization than is required by conventional reference. Herein, I think, lies the particular relevance of literature to the description and learning of language.

Consider the question of description first. The linguist sets out to account for the user's competence, defined as knowledge of the codified forms of a language and their signification. There are two difficulties about validating the account against actual data. Firstly, the user may not need to give explicit expression to his knowledge in order to achieve required indexical meaning. This is because of the contextual factor previously discussed. So the utterances that are actually produced may in effect only partially realize the meanings inherent in the corresponding symbols. So what users do with their language does not correspond with what they know of their language. Symbolic meaning is not derivable from indexical meaning. Secondly, what has been codified in the language, and described by the linguist, does not by any means exhaust meaning potential. If it did there would be no way of accounting for the interpretability of literature, or for the ordinary language user's capacity for representation (see Note 7) or, indeed, for the natural process of language change. What literature can offer the linguist is a source of attested use which exemplifies a fuller realization of the meaning potential as it is codified in the language systems he seeks to describe. At the same time, it challenges him to extend the scope of his description *beyond* codification to account for the abundant examples of representation which depart from the canons of formal possibility and which exemplify imminent meaning potential in the language.[10] To limit attention to what has been codified, and can be exemplified by well-formed sentences, is to account for only part of language as a resource for conceptualization and communication.

Representational uses of language reveal that users have a capacity for language which cannot be confined within competence, even when that concept is extended to cover a knowledge of norms which Hymes indicates with his four factors. So literature is not only relevant to the study of what is possible and feasible in usage, but also to what is appropriate and customarily done in contexts of use. It is a requirement of representation, as I have defined it, that contexts are internally created. It follows that the conditions that determine illocutionary and interactive function have to be recoverable from the text itself. Consider, in view of this, the problems discussed in Labov and Fanshel (1977) in interpreting the communicative significance of what is said in therapeutic interviews. To get at this significance they have to resort to what they call 'expansions' of the given utterances, and this involves drawing evidence about shared knowledge from outside the interactions. In literary interpretation (which the work of Labov and Fanshel, and ethnomethodological analysis in general, quite closely resembles) the evidence is drawn from within the created context and is in principle, therefore, more readily accessible. Furthermore, since this context is created and represents reality which does not conform to convention, literature provides insights into how communication would be achieved in the abnormal circumstances of the fictive world. It, again, reveals a capacity for realizing meaning which is potential in the user but not generally called upon in the routine interactions of ordinary social life. In brief, literature constitutes data of language use which those concerned with the description of language cannot afford to ignore. The traditional concerns of linguists and literary scholars are, properly understood, in a very crucial sense complementary.[11]

The relevance of the reference/representation distinction for language teaching can be indicated by a kind of paradox. Language learners are commonly encouraged to produce instances of language which can only *function* appropriately as representation, and they are discouraged from producing instances of language which function appropriately as reference but take a representational *form*.

The point about functional representation can be illustrated by the expression previously cited:

> He came back into the kitchen.

Learners are commonly called upon to produce pieces of language like this as sentences, strings of symbols, often in paradigmatic association with other strings. But as sentences, detached from context, they can have no referential value. They can only take on communicative function if they are understood as representations, as context-creating expressions of a literary kind, and in this case attention is directed at the syntactic and semantic particularities of the signs in order to realize their full import as icons. So learners can be made aware of the signification of linguistic forms, as they are with sentences, but in order to realize a communicative significance. Instead of presenting the expression we are considering with others which demonstrate its symbolic character as a sentence, e.g.:

He came back into the kitchen.
She came back into the room.
He went back into the room.

we could present it with others which directed attention to its meaning potential as representation:

He came back into the kitchen. The man was still on the floor. His face was bloody. He was moaning, etc. [12]

Finally, the point about representational form. Learners frequently produce expressions which are entirely feasible and appropriate, in that they are communicatively effective in context, but which are not possible in respect to codified rule. Such expressions are generally characterized as errors, and the teacher's usual inclination is to correct them and impose conformity. But it should be noted that such expressions, which are assumed to have referential function, take on a form which is indistinguishable from that of deliberate representations. [13] It seems reasonable to suppose that what is revealed in these erroneous utterances is the exercise of capacity for realizing the conceptual and communicative resources inherent in both the first and the second language. If this is so, then there would seem to be a case for relating these uses to literary representations rather than forcing them back into the codified forms of competence, and allowing correctness to emerge as a function of appropriate reference. In other words, would one seek to convert one kind of use into another rather than inhibit use by imposing the constraints of standard usage? It is after all the capacity for realizing the resources of a language and not just conformity to code which we are trying to develop in the learners. We cannot both require them to acquire native-speaker mastery and at the same time deny them the exercise of the capacity that provides for its achievement. Nothing is more frustrating for an advanced learner than to be corrected when he knowingly produces an expression which aptly represents his intended meaning *because* it does not accord with convention.

The significance of literature, then, for the study and teaching of language is that it reveals the capacity of the language user for realizing the concealed resources of language to achieve meaning. Grammarians have traditionally been concerned with idealized language, with the linguistics of systems and their symbolic constituents. Discourse analysis deals with conventional uses of language, with the linguistics of reference and indexical function. I would argue that literary uses of language provide data for a complementary linguistics of representation which would seek to account for the user's ability to make the language mean what he wants it to mean, and which focuses on the essential capacity for creativity which cannot be confined within competence and which informs both works of literature and the developing interlanguage of learners.

Notes

1. '. . . information' directly expressed 'by sentences cannot always be equated with the information available to the comprehender. Comprehenders do not simply store the information underlying sentences, but instead use linguistic inputs in conjunction with other information to update their general knowledge of the world. . . . One may have knowledge of language and yet fail to understand utterances unless one is able to activate appropriate alinguistic knowledge' (Bransford and McCarrell, 1974: 204). Cf. 'Creating a referential bridge must always be a function of both the available contextual information and the form of the particular sentence which is being processed' (Sanford and Garrod, 1981: 98).
2. Notice that relative feasibility is not necessarily a function of syntactic complexity; cf. 'Simple syntax may actually hinder comprehension by forcing S's to do too much of the integration. And more complex structures (like some forms of embedding) may actually facilitate comprehension by explicitly expressing easily codable semantic integrations of ideas' (Bransford and Franks, 1972: 245).
3. These schematic structures have been given a variety of names by scholars: schemas, scripts, scenarios (see Beaugrande, 1980 for an attempt to give conceptual distinctions to the terms). My own preference is to use schema to denote the general category of cognitive structures which organize experience in long-term memory; frame, or frame of reference, to denote structures which order propositional information, and routine to denote those which order sequences of acts and actions into conventional patterns of occurrence.

   Sanford and Garrod's 'scenario' would seem to be a combination of frame and routine as defined here. At all events, their definition of it will serve as a particularly clear formulation of which schematic knowledge is meant to be: 'The scenario is an information network called from long-term memory by a particular linguistic input . . . in all cases the basic principle is one of enabling the knowledge of the reader to be used in such a way as to allow for direct interpretation of entities or events predicted by this knowledge. To the extent that any text conforms to the predictions, it is readily interpreted, to the extent that it does not, it will be more difficult to understand' (Sanford and Garrod, 1981: 127). The linguistic sign is indexically effective (in my terms) to the extent that it provides access to such scenarios.

   The referential process, as I conceive it, may be shown diagrammatically thus:

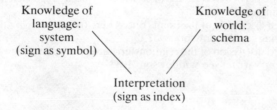

   Knowledge of
   language:
   system
   (sign as symbol)

   Knowledge of
   world:
   schema

   Interpretation
   (sign as index)

4. They are avoided because if they have no warrant in respect to appropriacy they can have the effect of reducing the seriousness of the message rather than enhancing its point. William Whewell, for example, in his *Treatise on Mechanics* (1819) unintentionally produced the following:

   There is no force, however great, can stretch a cord, however fine, into a horizontal line, which is accurately straight.

   This is quoted in Butler and Fowler (1971), who noted that the passage was omitted from a later edition after the lines had been recited in an after-dinner speech.
5. I have borrowed the terms *symbol*, *index* and *icon* from J. S. Peirce via Hawkes (1977) and Lyons (1977). I am not sure how far my use of the terms is in accord with Peirce's original conceptualization, but I would claim a broad agreement. In my terms the symbol relates sign to reality by *denotation*, the index by *reference* and the icon by *representation*.
6. There has been a good deal of critical discussion on the phenomenon of 'free indirect speech' as a device for representing both the supposed speaking voice and the inner speech or 'stream of consciousness' of characters in fiction. See, for example, Page, 1973; Pascal, 1977;

Leech and Short, 1981 (where the *Bleak House* passage is cited) and Banfield, 1982. Banfield, incidentally, also uses the term *representation* in a sense consistent with mine but defined more specifically to mean the conveyance of subjective impressions of here and now.

7. This does not mean that representation as a mode of meaning is exclusive to literature. It occurs in ordinary everyday uses of languages also as a kind of secondary resource for regulating interaction and for providing for individual expression within conventional norms. But in literature it has constitutive status as a defining principle.

   It should be noted too that I include within literature such speech events as jokes and ritual insults. The latter, as described by Labov, are a particularly good example of representation: there are prescribed rules which control how things are said, and which block what would otherwise be quite unacceptably offensive reference. There is a 'fundamental opposition between ritual insults and personal insults' (Labov, 1972: 152). This opposition is between what I have called representation and reference.

8. The use of the term 'icon' in reference to literature naturally calls to mind the title of Wimsatt's book *The Verbal Icon* (Wimsatt, 1954). The note on the title provided by Wimsatt suggests that his meaning for the term corresponds quite closely with mine, although his meaning for symbolic is clearly quite different. The relevant part of the note runs as follows: The verbal image which most fully realizes its verbal capacities is that which is not merely a bright picture (in the usual modern meaning of the term *image*) but also an interpretation of reality in its metaphoric and symbolic dimensions. Thus: *The Verbal Icon*.

9. Foregrounding is a translation of the Czech term *aktualisace*. The concept was put forward by the Prague School as a fundamental principle of artistic expression (see Garvin, 1964).

10. The term 'meaning potential' is borrowed from Halliday. But Halliday seems to conceive of it only as a resource which is codified within the systems of a language (see, for example, Halliday, 1979: 39, 112).

11. There have been sporadic attempts within linguistics to extend the scope of competence grammar to account for expressions which reveal the capacity to realize meaning potential beyond what has been codified. See, for example, the papers by Chomsky and by Katz in Fodor and Katz, 1964 and Lakoff and Johnson, 1980. It is interesting to compare these efforts with the work of literary scholars which seeks to describe the representational function of language (e.g. Empson, 1930; Davie, 1955; Brooke-Rose, 1958). The study of representation is the particular business of stylistics, typically regarded as peripheral to the main concerns of linguistic analysis.

12. For a more detailed discussion of the points raised here on the pedagogic value of literature for language teaching see Widdowson, 1982.

13. For a more detailed discussion of the relationship between the language learner's creativity and that of the literary writer see Widdowson, 1983.

References

BANFIELD, A. (1982) *Unspeakable sentences*. London: Routledge and Kegan Paul.

BEAUGRANDE, R. de (1980) *Text, discourse and process*. London: Longman.

BRANSFORD, J. D. and J. J. FRANKS (1972) The abstraction of linguistic ideas: a review. *Cognition* **1**: 211–250.

BRANSFORD, J. D. and N. S. McCARRELL (1974) A sketch of a cognitive approach to comprehension: some thoughts about what it means to comprehend. In Weimer and Palermo (1974).

BROOKE-ROSE, C. (1958) *A grammar of metaphor*. London: Secker & Warburg.

BUTLER, C. and A. FOWLER (eds) (1971) *Topics in criticism*. London: Longman.

CLARKE, M. A. (ed.) (1983) *On TESOL '82*. Washington, DC: TESOL.

COLE, P. and J. L. MORGAN (eds) (1975) *Syntax and semantics*, vol. 3: *Speech acts*. New York: Academic Press.

DAVIE, D. (1955) *Articulate energy: an enquiry into the syntax of English poetry*. New York: Harcourt Brace.

EMPSON, W. (1930) *Seven types of ambiguity*. London: Chatto and Windus.

FODOR, J. A. and J. J. KATZ (eds) (1964) *The structure of language: readings in the philosophy of language*. Englewood Cliffs, NJ: Prentice Hall.

GARVIN, P. L. (trans.) (1964) *A Prague school reader on aesthetics, literary structure and style*. Washington, DC: Georgetown University Press.

GRICE, P. (1975) Logic and conversation. In Cole and Morgan (1975).

HALLIDAY, M. A. K. (1979) *Language as social semiotic*. London: Edward Arnold.

HAWKES, T. (1977) *Structuralism and semiotics*. London: Methuen.

HINES, M. and W. RUTHERFORD (eds) (1982) On TESOL '81, Washington, DC: TESOL.

HYMES, D. (1972) On communicative competence. In Pride and Holmes (1972).

LABOV, W. (1972) Rules for ritual insults. In Sudnow (1972).

LABOV, W. and D. FANSHEL (1977) *Therapeutic discourse*. New York: Academic Press.

LAKOFF, G. and M. JOHNSON (1980) *Metaphors we live by*. Chicago: University of Chicago Press.

LEECH, G. N. and M. H. SHORT (1981) *Style in fiction*. London: Longman.

LYONS, J. (1977) *Semantics*. Cambridge: Cambridge University Press.

PAGE, N. (1973) *Speech in the English novel*. London: Longman.

PASCAL, R. (1977) *The dual voice*. Manchester: Manchester University Press.

PRIDE, J. B. and J. HOLMES (eds) (1972) *Sociolinguistics*. Harmondsworth: Penguin.

SANFORD, H. J. and S. C. GARROD (1981) *Understanding written language*. New York: John Wiley.

SUDNOW, D. (ed.) (1972) *Studies in social interaction*. New York: Free Press.

WEIMER, W. B. and D. S. PALERMO (eds) (1974) *Cognition and symbolic processes*, Hillsdale, NJ: Lawrence Erlbaum.

WIDDOWSON, H. G. (1982) The use of literature. In Hines and Rutherford (1982)

WIDDOWSON, H. G. (1983) Competence and capacity in language learning. In Clarke (1983).

WIMSATT, W. K. (1954/1970) *The verbal icon*. London: Methuen.

2

Beyond Description to Explanation in Cross-cultural Discourse

CHRISTOPHER N. CANDLIN

Multi-racialism in the United Kingdom has resulted in a greater fluidity of boundaries between previously distinct communities. This fluidity imposes considerable burdens on the communication skills of ethnic minority members, as Jupp *et al.* (1982) have shown. There is a greater potential for miscommunication in a society where there is increasing mutual dependence among citizens who share neither the same language nor the same world-view. Such misunderstanding may have unintelligibility as an immediate cause but more particularly derives from uninterpretability, itself stemming from alternative, and at times conflicting, systems of value and belief. (For the distinction between intelligibility and interpretability see Candlin, 1982.) Such misunderstandings are frequent in the many gatekeeping encounters which characterize life in an industrial society, as has been illustrated in Gumperz (1982) and in Smith (1977), HMSO (1978), Erickson (1976), Tannen (1981) *inter alia*. Successful living depends on individuals' capacities to negotiate successfully these varying encounters. Going to a doctor or to a solicitor, drawing supplementary benefits, seeking places on workschemes or training courses, all require that minority groups accommodate in the United Kingdom to the communicative conventions of the majority. For particular examples see Candlin *et al.* (1980) and Thorp (1981). Verbal adaptability is consequently at a premium. For those unable to cope we offer very little, despite the pioneering national work of the National Centre for Industrial Language Training and its local affiliates (see Jupp *et al.*, 1982, and references therein). In the midst of an increasing hardening of social and ethnic group differences in language use, we cannot even appeal to some generalizable set of communication strategies (for details see Faerch and Kasper, 1983) guaranteed, as it were, to avoid critical moments of communication. Majority and minority communities are not at the same line, between and among themselves. Diversification of language use is on the increase, and becomes the more difficult to chart as groups and sub-groups adopt modes of talking, not now in some consciously differentiating way, but inherit them as naturalized and unremarkable phenomena. (For some illustrative discussion from one setting, see Sayers, 1983.) In such an atmosphere, critical moments of misunderstanding and breakdown rapidly translate themselves into antagonisms as sub-group members take exception to each others' choices of communicative expression. This often occurs with little mutual understanding of what may have served as the local linguistic trigger for prejudiced confrontations of conflicting values and beliefs (see e.g. Scollon and Scollon, 1981, 1983 and the papers in Gumperz, 1982).

If we are to understand the social bases of cross-cultural discourse, at least in the United Kingdom, we have to view minority use of the majority language, or non-metropolitan varieties (see Kachru, 1982; Smith, 1983) not just in linguistic and textual terms but also in terms of the ways in which such use displays particular strategies of communication and interpretation seen by those minority groups as relating to their purposes and goals, yet also accommodated to the needs in general of public life. To do this we need to begin from a standpoint of variability: firstly, in terms of cultural assumptions about encounters and the communicative behaviour deemed appropriate to them – in particular, matters such as norms of interaction and interpretation, degrees of explicitness and directness, patterns of politeness, constituents of a convincing argument or case; secondly, in terms of the variety of means of structuring information and argument in what one might call social rhetoric, exploring what is held to be 'logical' or 'rational' in the (sub)-culture in question, emphasizing locally conventional sequencing and presentation of information (for valuable discussion see Kaplan *et al.*, 1982); thirdly, in terms of different modes of speaking and writing, emphasizing variability in language use within particular encounters at all 'levels', linguistic, semantic and pragmatic, and in their interconnection. For examples and discussion see Candlin (1981, 1982).

Studies of such variability reveal that groups are able to be distinguished against a range of criteria in language use, both in terms of performance features and in terms of modes of interpretation. This variation can be explored in order to discover and highlight complex differences of underlying ideology among the groups whose language is under investigation. For some examples in the context of written discourse see Fowler *et al.* (1979), and more generally de Souza (1983), Pateman (1981). Indeed, maintaining such variation is a powerful way in which the group itself learns and maintains its ideology, and ultimately maintains itself, as Therborn (1976) and Pecheux (1982) discuss theoretically, and Riccardo (1983) documents. If we are to understand ethnic and cultural differences as a necessary preliminary to any programme of amelioration or harmonization of relationships, we must determine our position on the *approach* we take to language, the *encounter-types* we wish to study, and the *research methodology* we wish to adopt. These are, of course, interdependent choices.

On language, what has already been said concerning interpretability directs us towards a study of meaning in pragmatic rather than semantic terms. We are not only concerned with Leech's (1983) phrase 'meaning by' instead of merely 'mean', but Haberland and Mey's (1976) phrase 'How did this utterance come to be produced.' A similar direction is given in Habermas (1970) where he argues as follows in favour of a pragmatic approach to meaning:

> the analyst's understanding owes its explanatory power to the fact that the clarification of a systematically inaccessible meaning succeeds only to the extent that the origin of the faulty or misleading meaning is explained . . .

Or, more generally, in cultural terms, in Hall *et al.* (1980). As such our attention becomes focused on directive and personal activity; communication aimed, if you like, by X on Y. Activities where participants place a premium on the successful negotiation of meaning, but where, typically, one or other of them places himself or herself at risk during the communication itself. At risk, because of possible injury from the encounter, whether physically, socially or psychologically. Such encounters, as we have indicated, typify those between minority and majority groups.

This stance on language argues against a traditionally descriptive view of the *text as object* where one is concerned only to document variation in terms of a set of idiosyncratic surface features. Dialectology (and, we could say, correlational sociolinguistics of the traditional 'static' type) is not revelatory of those strategies of communication and their motivation that we have been anxious to foreground, although, as is clearly shown in the work of Milroy (1980) in Belfast, such sociolinguistic studies that are premissed on links with social networks can serve as powerful indicators of group membership. We need to augment the formal, determinate and, to an extent, arbitrary study of text with one which examines discourse as the skilled accomplishment of participants in the service of some social goal. Such an approach is interpretive, not merely descriptive, and offers a way in which we can assess the degree to which participants achieve or fail to achieve their conversational goals. (For illustrative examples see Labov and Fanshel, 1977 and McKnight, 1976, in the context of psychotherapeutic discourse.) Our stance on language here is an indirect one in which mappings are indeterminate, constrained by varying principle, purpose and event. Unpacking such discourse gives us important insights into motive and intent, and goes beyond description in offering some interpretation of why people say what they say and what inferential schemata they employ. Nonetheless, as Fairclough (1982) and de Souza (1983) indicate, it will always remain inadequate, since if we are to satisfy the demands set upon us by my characterization of the social context of cross-cultural discourse study, we need not only to correlate but also to explain. We need, through what is said and meant, to infer and explore the social conditions which govern particular performances and interpretations. Such a study will need to accommodate not only the distinct perceptions of the participants of the nature, purpose and proceedings of the encounters they engage in, but understand that, in addition, discourse regularly naturalizes participants' values and beliefs in an unconscious manner. By this I mean that we take for granted and see as transparent ways of talking which actually serve as powerful indicators of social view and group values. They are insidious metaphors for particular ideologies. Indeed, they may not be revealed even by traces in the discourse or by participant comment (in the manner documented by Gumperz, 1982) but be significantly absent in that it is not what is said but what is not said that offers the clues explanation seeks. To that extent such absences are both beyond description and perhaps also beyond interpretation, in that participants do not regard them as worthy of post hoc comment or elucidation. They are not noticeable, as Candlin *et al.* (1980, 1983) point out in the context of medical discourse. The existence (or significant absence) of such phenomena requires an explanatory approach to discourse, one which problematizes and critiques that which participants hold to be natural. It is the thrust of this chapter that such explanatory unmasking is necessary if we are to probe the deep-seated assumptions and, as in this case, prejudices about personalities and behaviours held by the social members whose interactions we are studying. For a valuable discussion of the role of shared knowledge in such a debate see Kreckel (1982).

This explanatory approach to the study of cross-cultural discourse rests on the assumption, therefore, that participants use language, employ strategies of communication, and infer particular meanings often without any conscious awareness of how such usages, in particular social conditions, act to betray sectional interests, beliefs and values. In so far as these beliefs and values are representative of the powerful and majority culture, reference to and realization of them, however direct or indirect, constitutes an exercise of power. For some illustration in the context of police-witness interviews see Candlin *et al.* (1982), Thomas (1983a) and Candlin (1983a). Indeed, we may wish to delve further and say that the organization of the encounters themselves, and the roles they enforce upon participants, acts to produce the unconsciousness of signals and meanings that I have been referring to. In a world of illusion, description and interpretation take on distinct and very untraditionally linguistic aspects. Yet if we are to understand cross-cultural communication, or indeed any communication at all, we have, in my view, to make this unconsciousness plain (see Candlin, 1981).

To summarize: an explanatory approach to discourse analysis seeks to demystify the hidden presuppositions and world-views against which meanings are co-constructed by participants. This approach does so by subjecting the use of particular terms, the choice of phonological and lexico-syntactic realizations, the conversational strategies and routines, the speech act values and the understandings by the participants of the norms of interaction and interpretation in encounters, to analysis and critique. In so doing, this approach seeks to illustrate the degree to which our use of language and our meaning-making, as well as our perceptions of role relationships, are determined by the properties of the social situation, its unstated values and interests, its economy; and from this the degree to which such use confirms the status quo and determines the values of the conversational 'goods' which are being exchanged. I quote from Fowler *et al.* (1979), cited in de Souza (1983):

> Anyone who can give orders without even acknowledging this in the surface of his utterance has access to an insidiously powerful form of command. For instance, someone who can say 'the door is open' and be interpreted as saying 'close the door' has issued an imperative which has been totally deleted yet is fully effective. The person who obeys accepts the reality of the power that has not been claimed, which has been completely mystified into the form of an apparently neutral, factual observation.

It is this attempt to see discoursal features and pragmatic markers characteristic of particular types of encounter (here cross-cultural ones) as being socially and culturally produced, reflective and reproductive of social relationships between participants, and, importantly, between groups, which marks off an explanatory approach to discourse analysis from one which is merely descriptive or even interpretive.

Much of what has been said above concerning the critique of the ulterior purposes and goals of the participants suggests a focus on research sites where minority and majority group representatives meet at critical moments of communication. Such moments maximize the opportunities for breakdown and miscommunication and thereby offer openings for the explanatory analysis I have been advocating. Gumperz (1982) offers a variety of such examples. It is likely, too, that 'bureaucratic' (Gumperz) and institutional sites will prove useful because communication is there at a premium. Attitudinal and instrumental goals may be in conflict; perceptions of the event and a person's role in it may be at variance; power differences are likely to be heightened; and possibilities of face-threat are enhanced. For general discussion on the pragmatics of such encounters see Brown and Levinson (1978) and for an illustrative example in the context of black–white interaction in South Africa see Chick (1983). It is not difficult in practice to identify many such sites, although it may be more problematic to localize problems without begging the question of who does the identifying and who determines the terms in which the problems are to be described. From what has already been said we must assume that different participant ideologies and social views will produce a plurality of norms against which utterances are to be judged: breakdowns in communication and pragmatic failure are relative not absolute matters. Nonetheless we might look to the following sites for likely instances of significant cross-cultural data:

  (i) Doctor/dentist–patient consultations (see, e.g., Sexton, 1976; Candlin *et al.*, 1980; Tannen, 1981).
 (ii) Lawyer–client interviews and examinations (see, e.g., Harris, 1980; Gumperz, 1982).
(iii) Police–witness interrogations (see, e.g., Candlin *et al.*, 1982; Thomas, 1983b; Candlin, 1983a).
 (iv) Social security–client interviews (see, e.g., Jupp *et al.*,1982).
  (v) Counsellor/social worker–client interviews (see Candlin and Lucas, 1986).
 (vi) Trainee–manager interviews (see, e.g., Thorp, 1981).
(vii) Applicant–employer interviews (see, e.g., Jupp *et al.*, 1982).
(viii) Worker–manager negotiations (see, e.g., Etherton, 1975; Sayers, 1983).

Within each of the above we can identify particular discoursal actions, for example challenging co-participants' views, requesting 'goods', repairing misunderstandings, criticizing performances, mitigating demands, etc. For some detailed examples see Thomas (1981, 1983a), Candlin *et al.* (1980, 1983).

It follows from what was said in the first section of this chapter that in each of the above sites and discoursal actions we would need to carry out an explanatory ethnographic study with the object of asking what the circumstances of the carrying out of the action in question were, and the purposes to which it was directed, much in the manner suggested by Corsaro (1980) and

Cicourel (1978), but with the added need to go beyond the data as presented in the pursuit of explanation. Such questions will at least demand an understanding of the comparative ethnicity of the participants; their mutual perceptions of attitude, motive and purpose; their feelings of co-membership in the action; their relationships of power, distance and imposition (see Brown and Levinson, 1978); and the variance and (in)compatibility of goals. Such features need in turn to be set against 'established' and normative characteristics of the action in question, seen from the perspectives of both participants, and evaluated against both communities, perceptions of what counts as 'good' and 'successful' behaviour. (For discussion see Candlin *et al.*, 1980.)

Our ethnographic study will no doubt permit us to formulate a number of hypotheses which we can test against data, to provide some experimental basis for our *descriptive* accounts. It will, of course, be the extended ethnographic investigation which will warrant our *explanations* since these, by their nature, are not open to experiment in the same way. In what follows I identify, on the basis of discussions at Lancaster (see Note 1), a number of such hypotheses relevant to the study of cross-cultural discourse, and offer some brief textual illustration.

(i) Majority group members control the topic and resist attempts by minority group members to shift topic.
(ii) Challenges by minority group members are rejected or minimized.
(iii) Majority group members demand explicitness of minority group members.
(iv) Majority group members control the overriding illocutionary force of the discourse.
(v) Majority group members declare what is to be counted as 'shared knowledge'.
(vi) Majority group members will use greater directness of utterance.
(vii) Minority group members will exhibit greater self-effacement, will comply more and frequently abandon positions taken.
(viii) Majority group members will expect minority group members to conform to act sequences the former have initiated.
(ix) Majority group members will determine the turn-taking system of the encounter in question.
(x) Majority group members will determine which utterances are to be sanctioned as permissibles in the interaction.

The above is by no means a complete list. As exemplification, let me examine some data relevant to (ii), (vii) and (ix).

(ii) The data are drawn from Candlin *et al.* (1980) and relate to dentist–patient communication in the context of general practice, where a merchant seaman is receiving treatment from a dentist whom he has never met before:

D: alright
P: yep
D: youre having trouble are you

P: yeah the back ⎰ one I had a filling I had a filling in
                    ⎱   but it all came
                    ⎱ which side
P: out ⎰ and it started to er   (   )
D: ⎱ oh I see   just you rest your head
((8 seconds))

Here the patient describes an event which took place in the recent past (the break-up of his filling) which he believes to be the cause of the problem which he is presently experiencing. The consultation continues:

D: now is it eh left side bottom   the very back one
   mm youve got
P: mm hm
D: two that are quite bad there   this one further forwards not hurting
D: you   no no pain when I touch that   just open fairly wide
P: no

The dentist's observation 'mm youve got two that are quite bad there' makes no reference to the patient's own diagnosis that one of his fillings started to 'break up' and 'come out'. In other words, the dentist ignores and rejects the patient's analysis of the problem: the patient never learns whether he is correct or not in attributing the pain to a crumbling filling.

(vii) Here the example is drawn from Sexton (1976) and the data in question derive from some studies of patient–patient and doctor–patient communication in a ward for young schizophrenics in a psychiatric hospital (see also McKnight, 1976). In this extract the doctor in question is criticizing patient behaviour:

D: similarly this morning, X, I had to call you three times before you got out of bed
P: yes
D: mind you youre not the only culprit as far as thats concerned
P: how do you mean culprit
D: well youre not the only one who does that
P: no

Note how the blame is simply accepted, the patient backing down before the doctor's criticism. A further example indicates how the patients efface themselves by accepting decisions, in this case relating to which patients should be permitted to go home for the weekend:

D: I think in all fairness, Y, we should wait until we hear what your mum has to say really
P: yes
D: whether she can have you home
P: yes
D: whether she can actually afford it you know
P: yes
D: so would you be agreeing to that then, Y, that we left it till we heard from your mum
P: yes

(ix) The final example is drawn from work on a police–client interview (see Candlin et al., 1982; Candlin, 1983a) where the allocation of turns is firmly in the hands of the powerful party in the interaction, namely the police. The context of the interaction is that the woman in question (W) has made a complaint of rape. In the first example, the policeman (C) interrupts and seizes the turn from the woman.

```
C:                          listen very carefully
W:              I dont want
C:  what Ive got to say      listen carefully what Ive got to say
```

In the second example the woman takes a turn which acts to threaten the face of the police (in that she suggests that the police should investigate a suspected case of rape even in the absence of a formal complaint); the police immediately act in consort (participants B and C) to seize the turn and interrupt the woman's argument:

```
W:  what if what if someone doesnt make a complaint but you believe there is a rape
B:        ⎰ we dont do anything because . . .
C:        ⎱ we cant do anything about it because . . .
```

In examining these and other cross-cultural data themselves we will have need to focus on features drawn from different levels of description, specifically from:

(i) *Pragmatic features* (of which the following are examples)
degrees of indirectness of utterances (cf. Leech, 1983);
upshots and conversational reformulations (cf. Thomas, 1983b);
indicators of macro speech acts (cf. van Dijk, 1977);
markers of deference and politeness (cf. Leech, 1983).

(ii) *Discoursal features* (again, some examples)
turn allocation;
turn length;
topic control (cf. Candlin *et al.*, 1980);
relationships between agents and events (cf. Trew, 1979).

(iii) *Linguistic features* (again some examples)
stress placement and key choice (cf. Brazil *et al.*, 1980);
alterations in voice quality (cf. Labov and Fanshel, 1977).

It would be inappropriate to see these features as operating in an independent way. Features combine and co-occur polysystemically to signal particular discoursal and rhetorical choices. These linked choices may themselves mark differences between groups, as may the discoursal patterns they are intended to mark. Prosodic patterns combine with syntactic choice to signal discourse boundaries; thematization, for example, links with stress placement to focus important matters to the speaker, much in the manner illustrated by Brazil *et al.* (1980). Given the multiple signalling available to speakers, it is crucial that we examine how speakers from different ethnic groups co-select features in particular encounters and utilize such patterns to realize particular conversational strategies (see Gumperz, 1982).

Recent work at Lancaster has focused on powerful versus powerless talk shows. For example, how at moments of conversational crux (i.e. where the powerless has an opportunity of threatening the face of the powerful) the powerful participant simultaneously marshals resources at different levels – phonological, lexico-syntactic, kinesic, discoursal – to ward off the challenge.

For an illustration of this in the context of a police-witness interview, see Candlin (1983b) where a woman (W) having made a complaint of rape has her fears of being attacked by the rapists in question if she lays a formal complaint dismissed by the policeman (B) who is accompanied by his colleague (C). The policeman's dismissal of her challenge is, we may surmise, due to his desire to resist the implication that if the attack were to take place, he would be responsible, and also to close the interview as rapidly as possible now that he and his colleague have persuaded the woman in question not to pursue the charge.

C: we'll take a statement off you and then you're quite free to
M: right   mm   hh   I don't want to end up in the river
C: leave the station all right like
B: this is Reading nineteen eighty its not bloody Starsky and Hutch end up in the river
    whats the matter with you (leaves)

Notice here how the woman's frame of reference (that she might be murdered) is revalued by the policeman. Her time (now) is regarded as being time then, her world (real) is regarded as being imaginary (*Starsky and Hutch*, a TV police serial), she is moreover regarded as being psychiatrically disturbed (whats the matter with you). Discoursally, the policeman interrupts, seizes the turn, reformulates dismissively what she says and performs in a bald-on-record fashion (Brown and Levinson, 1978). Lexico-syntactically, the above strategies of the policeman are reinforced by the thematization of 'Reading 1980' and the intensifier 'bloody', while phonetically there is a rapid dismissive fall on both 'Hutch' and 'end up in the river'. To these co-occurrent features can be added the abrupt kinesic dismissiveness of arm movements and the sudden departure of the policeman while the woman is still speaking. In this way a variety of signals is used interdependently and in a mutually reinforcing manner to block the challenge of the powerless. Such 'concentrated effects' in discourse may also be a feature of cross-cultural communication, especially at moments of crisis.

From the argument so far in this chapter my overall intention has been to indicate that the study of cross-cultural discourse requires reference to what Cicourel (1978) refers to as a 'broader organizational setting' if it is to relate to the systems of value and belief underlying linguistic and pragmatic choice. At the same time it will be necessary to illustrate how the methodology reflects one's view of how the data are created and interpreted by the participants. Finally, it will be necessary to resist the extreme positivist position that the researcher can ever be free from theory, or that the object of research can (or should) be uncontaminated by the presence of the researcher (see also Willis, 1980 and Candlin, 1983b).

These preliminaries suggest a methodology which is both 'top-down' and 'bottom-up'. 'Top-down' in the way that it involves reference to what Cicourel (1978) calls 'higher-order predicates', such as participants' general and particular goals in the interaction in question, beliefs, views on co-participant relationships, all set within a socio-cultural and ethnographic account of the groups in question within the society in which they are. 'Bottom-up' in its focus on such features as have been outlined in the previous section of this chapter:

pragmatic, discoursal, lexico-syntactic, and phonological. At the same time, however, one needs to be cautious in not always attributing 'lower-level' features to macro and higher-order predicates when they may be the 'product' of some local interaction. In part this danger, identified by Cicourel (1978), can be averted by always siting focused examples of talk in the context of an emerging discourse, thus allowing participants themselves the 'conversational space' to clarify or indicate how utterances are to be valued. To that extent one can hope for significance to emerge, as it were, from the record. At the same time, the need to denaturalize compels the researcher to offer expansions for participant comment which, presumably, derive from his/her understanding of the global picture as well as the particular frame of the encounter in question. Such a 'bottom-up' orientation has the merit of permitting all concepts and views to be included which may enrich the interpretation. The danger here, of course (and it is one incipient in discourse analysis which moves away from text alone), is that we cannot easily determine where the significant data stop.

There is, however, a middle road; one in which the ethnographic and sociocultural information acts as a potential explanatory mechanism for a study which is focused on the schemata participants follow in pursuing particular conversational plans and goals, schemata which are realized by poly-systemic choices from the code. Here a research methodology concentrates on participants' perceptions of each other and the event in question and the consequences on the attainment and the non-attainment of variable goals (see Candlin *et al.*, 1980).

The above may yet obsure certain current and overarching problems for the approach to the analysis of discourse advocated in this chapter. Let me identify four:

(i) What specific kinds of ethnographic and sociocultural information ought researchers to invoke in accounting for data, and how normative will this process be, and how culturally specific?

(ii) When should appeals be made to higher-order predicates and what bounds do we place on critical revelation?

(iii) To what extent do researchers fit incoming data into pre-existing schemata in their attempt to study an event in progress?

(iv) How do we record this complex of data in systems which do not themselves prejudice how the data will be 'read'?

Concealed in the above discussion is a recognition that the research methodology I am advocating must be both quantitative and qualitative. We need to seek for strong evidence, both from the text and from what Garfinkel (1967) and Cicourel (1978) refer to as 'triangulation', obtaining all parties' perspectives on the data, but we need to resist what Willis (1980) refers to as 'contamination phobia'. If we can sustain both these then we create a relation-ship of tension between the researcher, the text and the participants which is likely to reveal precisely those values that the participants and the researcher have both naturalized, and, as a consequence, often ignore. It is here, with Gumperz and Willis, that we can ask data-forcing questions concerning the reasons for the asking of X or the answering of Y, or the motivations for the openness of A or the dissembling of B. We can also ask why are the things happening as they appear to be, and why certain areas of the discourse remain obscure to the researcher. Moments of contradiction and crisis in interpretation are no longer disturbances to a 'well-oiled' analytical process (Willis, 1980) but opportunities for precisely the explanatory approach to discourse analysis that I am advocating in the cross-cultural context. Such a reflexive research methodology both confirms the presence of a pre-existing theory in the researcher as well as opening up possibilities for critical and revelatory moments in the interpretive process. It also compels researchers to warrant their interpretations in terms which participants can understand, since not to do so closes off the very opportunities for demystification of language upon which the long-term demolition of prejudice depends.

Let me conclude by summarizing some of the tenets of an explanatory methodology in discourse analysis:

  (i) It is important to study cross-cultural discourse in actual settings against a background of social theory and ethnographic account.
 (ii) Participants' abilities to make use of a range of interdependent features to signal plans and goals have to be offset by the presence of naturalized and 'unconscious' linguistic choices, themselves, when critiqued, revelatory of values and beliefs.
(iii) As a consequence of the above, there is a need for researchers to adopt a stance of concurrent analysis of different 'levels' of language and discourse and to seek a reflexive relationship with the participants, the data and with themselves.
 (iv) A quantitative methodology must be supplemented by a qualitative one in which experiment is augmented by ethnographic and explanatory accounts in which researchers are in a social relationship with their informants.
  (v) To do so requires a variety of imaginative data collection techniques.
 (vi) The described, interpreted and explained data ought to be returned to those from whom it came in a form and manner which they can understand and debate.

The figure which follows is intended to summarize the interdependence between the 'linguistic' and the 'interactional-social' (cf. Brown and Levinson, 1978, for comment), the link to descriptive, interpretive and explanatory approaches to discourse analysis and the importance of setting these against an ideological background in the quantitative and qualitative analysis of data from crucial research sites.

Note

1. Many of the arguments in this chapter have profited from seminars with graduate students in the Department of Linguistics and Modern English Language at the University of Lancaster following courses in Discourse Analysis, in particular Leo van Lier and Jenny Thomas. They also in part stem from working meetings of the research group on 'Unequal Encounters' in the Department led by Norman Fairclough and myself.

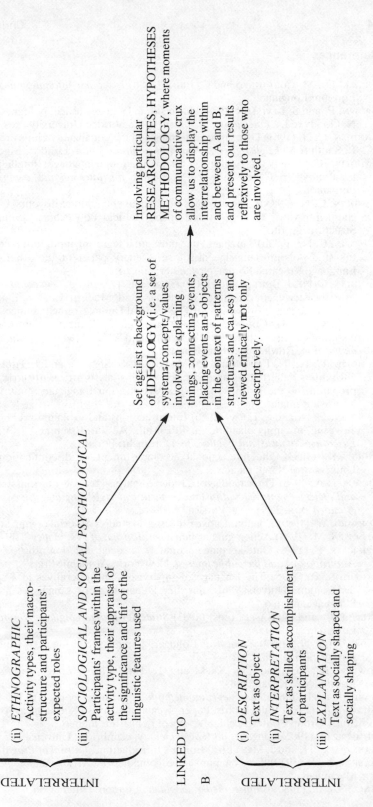

A

INTERRELATED

(i) *LINGUISTIC*
Linguistic/Discoursal/Pragmatic features

(ii) *ETHNOGRAPHIC*
Activity types, their macro-structure and participants' expected roles

(iii) *SOCIOLOGICAL AND SOCIAL PSYCHOLOGICAL*
Participants' frames within the activity type, their appraisal of the significance and 'fit' of the linguistic features used

LINKED TO

B

INTERRELATED

(i) *DESCRIPTION*
Text as object

(ii) *INTERPRETATION*
Text as skilled accomplishment of participants

(iii) *EXPLANATION*
Text as socially shaped and socially shaping

Set against a background of IDEOLOGY (i.e. a set of systems/concepts/values involved in explaining things, connecting events, placing events and objects in the context of patterns structures and causes) and viewed critically not only descriptively.

Involving particular RESEARCH SITES, HYPOTHESES METHODOLOGY, where moments of communicative crux allow us to display the interrelationship within and between A and B, and present our results reflexively to those who are involved.

Figure 1

References

BRAZIL, D., M. COULTHARD and C. JOHNS (1980) *Discourse intonation and language teaching*. London: Longman.

BROWN, P. and S. LEVINSON (1978) Universals in language usage: politeness phenomena. In E. N. Goody (ed.), *Questions and politeness*. Cambridge University Press.

CANDLIN, C. N. (1981) Discoursal patterning and the equalizing of interpretive opportunity. In L. Smith (ed.) *English for cross-cultural communication*. London: Macmillan.

CANDLIN, C. N. (1982) English as an international language: intelligibility versus interpretability. In C. Brumfit (ed.), *English for international communication*. Oxford: Pergamon.

CANDLIN, C. N. (1983a) The language of unequal encounters: discoursal features in a police–client interview. Paper delivered at the Hatfield Polytechnic Conference on Discourse Structure, April.

CANDLIN, C. N. (1983b) Three into one must go: integrating input, interaction and inference in the study of interlanguage discourse. Plenary paper at the 5th Los Angeles Second Language Research Forum, November: mimeo.

CANDLIN, C. N., J. BURTON and H. COLEMAN (1980) *Dentist-patient communication*. University of Lancaster Department of Linguistics and Modern English Language/Institute for English Language Education for The General Dental Council: mimeo.

CANDLIN, C. N., H. COLEMAN and J. BURTON (1983) Dentist-patient communication skills: communicating complaint. In N. Wolfson and E. Judd (eds), *Sociolinguistics and language acquisition*. Rowley: Newbury House.

CANDLIN, C. N., N. FAIRCLOUGH, M. MAKOSCH, S. SPENCER and J. THOMAS (1982) Unequal encounters: alternative approaches to the analysis of asymmetrical discourse. Paper prepared for the British Sociological Association Language Study Group Conference. Lancaster: mimeo.

CANDLIN, C. N. and J. LUCAS (1986) Interpretations and explanations in discourse: modes of 'advising' in family planning. In T. Ensink, A. Van Essen and T. Van der Geest (eds), *Discourse Analysis and Public Life*. Dordrecht: Foris.

CHICK, K. (1983) The interactional accomplishment of discrimination in South Africa. University of Natal: mimeo.

CICOUREL, A.(1978) Three models of discourse analysis: the role of social structure. In *Language and society: cognitive, cultural and linguistic aspects of language use. Sozialwissenschaftliche Annalen*, Vol. 2. Vienna: Physica.

CORSARO, W. (1980) Communicative processes in studies of social organization. *Text* 1, 1.

de SOUZA, M. (1983) Action-guiding language. *Journal of Pragmatics* 7: 49–62.

ERICKSON, F. (1976) Gate-keeping encounters: a social selection process. In P. Sanday (ed.), *Anthropology and the public interest*. New York: Academic Press.

ETHERTON, P. (1975) The language of supervisors and operatives in a spinning mill. M.A. dissertation, University of Lancaster Department of Linguistics and Modern English Language: mimeo.

FAERCH, C. and G. KASPER (eds) (1983) *Strategies in interlanguage communication*. London: Longman.

FAIRCLOUGH, N. (1982) Review of Bolinger: Language the loaded weapon. In *Language in society*, Spring 1982.

FOWLER, R., J. HODGE, G. KRESS and T. TREW (1979) *Language and control*. London: Routledge & Kegan Paul.

GARFINKEL, H. (1967) *Studies in ethnomethodology*. Englewood Cliffs, NJ: Prentice-Hall.

GILLING, A. (1982) Value words. Paper given at the British Sociological Association Language Study Group Conference, University of Lancaster, mimeo.

GUMPERZ, J. (1982) *Language and social identity*. Cambridge University Press.

HABERLAND, H. and J. MEY (1976) Editor's Introduction. *Journal of Pragmatics* 1: 1.

HABERMAS, J. (1970) On communicative competence. *Recent Sociology*, Vol. II. London: Macmillan.

HALL, S. *et al.* (1980) *Culture, media, language*. London: Hutchinson.

HARRIS, S. (1980) Language interaction in magistrates' courts. Unpublished Ph.D. dissertation, University of Nottingham.

HMSO (1978) *Application of the race relations policy in the civil service*. London.

JUPP, T., C. ROBERTS and J. COOK-GUMPERZ (1982) Language and disadvantage: the hidden process. In J. Gumperz (ed.), 1982.

KACHRU, B. (ed.) (1982) *The other tongue: English across cultures*. Urbana: University of Illinois Press.

KAPLAN, R., A. D'ANGLEJAN, J. R. COWAN, B. KACHRU and G. R. TUCKER (eds) (1982) *Annual review of applied linguistics*. Rowley: Newbury House.

KRECKEL, M. (1982) Communicative acts and shared knowledge: a conceptual framework and its empirical application. *Semiotica* **40**: 45–88.

LABOV, W. and D. FANSHEL (1977) *Therapeutic discourse: psychotherapy as conversation*. New York: Academic Press.

LEECH, G. N. (1983) *Principles of pragmatics*. London: Longman.

McKNIGHT, A. (1976) Large-group conversation: some problems for discourse analysis. Unpublished M.A. thesis, Department of Linguistics and Modern English Language, University of Lancaster.

MILROY, L. (1980) *Language and social networks*. Oxford: Blackwell.

PATEMAN, T. (1981) Linguistics as a branch of critical theory. *UEA Papers in Linguistics* **14–15**. UEA, Norwich.

PECHEUX, M. (1982) *Language, semantics and ideology*. London: Macmillan.

RICCARDO, S, (1983) Urbanization of rural dialects in Brazil. Unpublished Ph.D. thesis, Department of Linguistics and Modern English Language, University of Lancaster.

ROMAINE, S. (1982) *Sociolinguistic variation in speech communities*. London: Arnold.

RYAN, E. and H. GILES (1982) *Attitudes towards language variation*. London: Arnold.

SAYERS, P. (1983) Topic collaboration and interview skills. M.A. thesis, Department of Linguistics and Modern English Language, University of Lancaster: mimeo.

SCOLLON, R. and S. SCOLLON (1981) Narrative, literacy and face in interethnic communication. *Advances in discourse processes*, vol. 7. Norwood: Ablex.

SCOLLON, R. and S. SCOLLON (1983) Face in interethnic communication. In *Language and communication*. J. Richards and R. Schmidt (eds). London: Longman.

SEXTON, M. (1976) Acceptance, defiance and evasion in a psychiatric meeting. M.A. Course Project, Department of Linguistics and Modern English Language, University of Lancaster: mimeo.

SMITH, D. (1977) *Racial disadvantage in Britain*. Harmondsworth: Penguin Books.

SMITH, L. (ed.) (1983) *Readings in English as an international language*. Oxford: Pergamon.

TANNEN, D. (1981) Indirectness in discourse: ethnicity as conversational style. *Advances in discourse processes*, vol. 4. Norwood: Ablex.

THERBORN, G. (1976) *The ideology of power and the power of ideology*. London: Verso.

THOMAS, J. (1981) The pragmatic path to peace and understanding. Applied Linguistics Project, Department of Linguistics and Modern English Language, University of Lancaster.

THOMAS, J. (1983a) Cross-cultural pragmatic failure. *Applied Linguistics* **4**, 2.

THOMAS, J. (1983b) Cross-cultural discourse as unequal encounter: towards a pragmatic analysis. University of Lancaster: mimeo.

THORP, D. (1981) Cross-cultural communication in an industrial job interview. M.A. thesis, Department of Linguistics and Modern English Language, University of Lancaster.

TREW, T. (1979) What the papers say: linguistics variation and ideological difference. In Fowler *et al.* (1979).

TRUDGILL, P. (1974) *The social differentiation of English in Norwich*. Cambridge University Press.

VAN DIJK, T. (1977) *Text and context*. London: Longman.

WILLIS, P. (1980) Notes on method. In Hall *et al.*

3

Performative Speech Acts in Poetry

REUEL DENNEY

WE see an increased interest in the application to literary studies of the branch of linguistic investigation called discourse analysis. One of the purposes of that study is to go beyond syntactic and semantic interpretations of a text by observing how, at the pragmatic level, it is shaped in, by, and for the circumstances of, its communication. Among other things, this helps the literary critic to identify the particular kind of literary speech act with which we are dealing. Thus, Culler (1975: 162) remarks that 'the specific features of poetry have the function of differentiating it from speech and altering the circuitry of communication within which it is inscribed'. From the point of view of discourse analysis, we should note here, these features include the pervading rhythm and rhyme of the poem as well as other features that 'frame' the composition above the unit-level of the phrase, clause, or sentence.

Such studies of a literary genre as a speech-act occupying a special sub-domain in the domain of communication have direct consequences for the description of a work of literature and its evaluation. For they face up, in the most concrete and specific way, to the need for dealing with the intents, audiences, and effects of works of literature in particular historical and institutional circumstances. And, in fact, they supply methods for dealing with these issues that are not supplied by syntactic and semantic approaches.

As an example of this, consider the old question of how prose fiction might have been conditioned in its development by the spread of printing and the social psychology of widening literacy. Some new answers to this question have recently been proposed as a result of the examination of 18th-century fiction in English in terms of the modes of discourse employed in it. Banfield (1982), in her study of narration and representation in the language of fiction, concentrates on the employment of 'indirect discourse' (*oratio obliqua*) and is especially interested in its effects on the representation of the self. Using ideas derived from discourse analysis applied to conversation, she identified, in a sample of 18th-century fictional texts, sentences which do or do not have imaginable speakers, do or do not have hearers in this or that stance, do or do not have a temporary present correlated with the moment of utterance.

She summarizes this finding by observing that the reflective consciousness of an imputed self is often communicated by the text in what she calls the 'free indirect style'. The technicalities of this can be pursued in her book; the main point is that this type of narrative discourse appeared first in the 18th century, according to Banfield, when the inexpensive printed book developed forms of speech-acts divorced more widely than before from the *viva voce* speech-act. Presumably, the cheap printed book carried to an extreme a divergence of that kind which was only latent in the manuscript and the small-circulation printed book. Thus an aspect of authorial language, with consequences for the social as well as fictional definition of the self, is shown to be directly related to technical, institutional, and marketing circumstances. As a result it contributes to our understanding, at the fine-grain level, of how notions of the self are mediated in the language of literature.

Despite such developments, there does not appear to be much that has been said about the application of discourse analysis to verse, as in the lyric poem. It is true that Jakobsen (1979) has written about a lyric poem of Baudelaire's (*Spleen*) in terms of the way in which supra-sentential elements such as rhythm, rhyme, and repetitive variation of imagery affect the reader. His central strategy is to search out orderly pattern and contrast in the relation of the stanzas to each other. To do this, he investigates the distribution of certain images and semantic and grammatical items over the whole stanza-to-stanza progression.

From a syntactical point of view, these items are functional *within* the sentences. But from the point of view of discourse analysis these items, when taken together, constitute a supra-sentential frame of sorts, a frame that gives the poem a tenor above and beyond the sentence-enclosed units as such. Moreover, this overall patterning has a certain deictic effect, pointing both the conscious and the unconscious responses of the reader to the basic nature of the text: the fact, already more strongly indicated by metre, rhyme, and manifest brevity, that this is a lyric poem, not a law brief, or a prescription, or a prose fable, or something else.

This suggests that it might be worthwhile to review in brief the major markers of the lyric poem as a certain pattern of speech-acts and, in doing so, to follow the suggestions of Candlin (1977) on speech-act analysis in general that an effort should be made to:

(1) identify the significant units and their number;
(2) say something about their respective 'size';
(3) discuss them in relation to the linkages between grammaticality and meaningfulness.

The lyric poem is a form that anticipates and takes into account what happens when its text is rendered in the specifically formalized speech-act known as a recitation. In that recitation we often find these supra-sentential elements:

(1) bracketing silences before and after the poem (these are also found in other forms such as the prayer, or announcement);
(2) a volume of speech above conversational level;
(3) a slower-than-conversational speed;
(4) certain shifts in basic pitch in order to establish contrast with conversational pitch;
(5) a shift towards formal standards of pronunciation and enunciation.

Such bracketing moves, as we see, are not limited to lyric poems. But others are. As the first few lines are read (or recited from memory), we become aware that the utterance establishes and exploits traits that are specific to poems:

(1) rhythm, formal, or informal;
(2) rhyme and assonance;
(3) end-stopping and enjambement;
(4) lexical and semantic divergence from the language of everyday speech.

It is these specific features that differentiate the poem from ordinary speech and, in Culler's words, 'alter the circuitry of communication in which it is inscribed'. They help in the first place to identify it as a certain kind of fictional or mimetic utterance, and in the second place to reinforce the pleasure of this recognition.

These features are 'selected into' the writing and the printing of the composition when:

(1) bracketing silences are sometimes represented by page space before and after the text;
(2) the units of rhythm are indicated in the use of poetic (as contrasted with a prose typographical line);
(3) rhyme and assonance provided at line-ends;
(4) end-stopping and enjambement (with concurrent controls on intonation) are built in by line-arrangement, rhythm, and assonance placement, the conventions of punctuation.

Such is the beginning of an inventory of features that one might wish to attend to in a poem under critical consideration. And here it is important to remember that Candlin's final point is a point of culmination. We identify, enumerate, and quantify features we are interested in – and we then must discuss them in relation to the linkages between grammaticality and meaningfulness. In other words, we must feed back into our whole view of the poem what we have learned in the process of analysis of it.

Observe now that the foregoing discussion focuses on the ways by which the poetic composition frames itself as such by an appropriate choice of overall discourse pattern. But this is not the only approach to a poem by way of discourse analysis. It is also noticeable that poems draw, phrase by phrase and clause by clause, on the common stock of speech-acts in their attempts to represent, construct, or express something. The particular speech-acts selected, especially at crucial points of movement, help to determine the meaning and quality of the poem.

Suppose then that we take the type of speech-act labelled as 'performative' by Austin (1952) and observe its operation in some lyric poems.

SPEECH-ACT ANALYSIS IN POETRY

Austin, in his well-known, three-fold division of speech-acts, named them the locutionary, the illocutionary, and the perlocutionary. The triad has been criticized, revised, redefined, augmented, and otherwise put through the meta-critical wringer. Yet there is still interest and instruction in his idea that an utterance is locutionary in virtue of what the speaker says, illocutionary in achieving what it says while it says it, and perlocutionary in aiming to bring about an effect. Locutionary: 'The ship sails.' Illocutionary: 'I christen this ship *Alabama.*' Perlocutionary: 'Let Sunday be a day of rest for pagan as well as Christian.' The last two are 'performatives'.

It is true, of course, that an effect such as the perlocutionary can be obtained without using perlocutionary idiom. The Indian linguist Bhartrari observed long ago that when the King in winter remarked, 'The door is open', he meant 'Close the door!' For all that, it might be of interest to explore poetry a bit in Austin's terms.

Many of our oldest poetic texts, especially when they are of a religious nature, open with, and even continue with, a perlocutionary speech-act. This is the case for example with the phrase in the Vedic *Hymn to The Sun*: (Lanman, 1959):

> Let the warmth of the sun bring divine blessings . . .

The illocutionary is much less frequent in early poetry, before Sappho; but there is a powerful first-person illocutionary in the dramatic poetry of the *Agamemnon* (Murray, 1947):

> O gods, I pray for riddance from these troubles . . .

With the phrase 'I pray', Aeschylus sets an illocutionary frame in place in the first line of *Agamemnon*, at the opening of the speech of the watchman on the tower waiting the return from Troy of Agamemnon, the master of the house. This illocutionary clause not only reinforces the verbal action by its partial redundancy, but also has the effect of letting us sense that the watchman is objectifying himself in the self-descriptiveness of 'I pray'. It does not detract from this effect to notice that its origin is ritual-formula.

Consider now the illocutionary thrust at the beginning of a famous English poem by John Milton (Bush, 1965):

> Yet once more, o ye Laurels, and once more
> Ye Myrtles brown, with Ivy never-sear
> I come to pluck your berries harsh and crude
> And with forc'd fingers rude,
> Shatter your leaves before the mellowing year.

In rhetorical terms we call these opening lines from Milton's *Lycidas* an *invocation*. In historical and biographical terms supplied partly from the publication for which it was written – a 1638 collection in memory of Edward King – we know that the poet is here speaking pretty much in his own person as he makes himself ready to write an elegy for a collection honouring his late friend, Edward King, drowned in the Irish Sea. Moreover, we can say a good deal about the way he goes about this by making reference to conventional rhetorical and poetic analysis.

Coming at the beginning of *Lycidas*, the sentence employs personification (talking to the inanimate trees) and allegory (making laurel and myrtle stand for poetry) in the course of conveying the central meaning: that the poet intends to exploit his poetic gifts before they are ripened by age and experience. Analysis of the rhetoric shows this is all reinforced by doubling (*once more . . . once more*; *harsh and crude*), and a suspended sentence structure which concludes with a final line-and-clause which is metrically long and impressive, ending with a final sonority of the 'r' that plays through the whole like a key note.

Such rhetorical analysis does not exhaust the effects of this section of the poem. We need to add to it a consideration of the discursive elements that frame and reinforce the semantic content by acting at a supra-sentential level. The main thing to notice is that the poet has employed here a performative speech-act – the *illocutionary* utterance 'I come . . .'. This does what it says, as well as saying what is done.

The particular form of this speech-act also includes a combination of warning, ('I come to pluck') along with apology ('fingers rude') and, in general, a tone of propitiation. This combination of situational actions along with utterance is not fully brought to our attention by conventional semantic and rhetorical analysis. Finally, the lines also have a *perlocutionary* implication: they have the effect of bringing about the action on the laurels and myrtles that they are telling about.

My suggestion is, of course, that this analysis of the invocation gives us a somewhat more secure sense of the opening lines of *Lycidas* than we have if we use rhetorical, historical, and contextual approaches alone. That is, we are able to say a bit more about it – as for example, that despite the conventional rhetorical apparatus of the invocation, it rises to a certain immediate vitality by its use of performative utterances, a type of utterance which is vivid and immediately commanding of attention.

It can be said that it is in the *nature* of invocations to be performative. Yes, but they have not been named so; and I think that this naming can be useful to the literary critic because it tends to bring to the surface some questions about poems in general and, perhaps, lyrics in particular that might otherwise be neglected.

In proceeding in that direction, however, it must be noticed that we are making a move from a special case to general instances. The special case is *Lycidas*. It was chosen partly because both historical, external, and textual-internal evidences signal to us that it is the poet who is speaking, in this lyrical utterance, in his own person. This gives to the illocutionary and perlocutionary phrases a force that makes them particularly useful for analysis as historical as well as lyrical acts. But – and this is the main point here – many lyrics speak in terms of an 'I' which is not immediately the 'I' of the author. In the following remarks the main emphasis is on lyrical utterance in which, while the 'I' of the author himself is not necessarily involved, there is an effective use of the illocutionary and perlocutionary forms.

The perlocutionary in two modern poems

One of the most famous modern lyrics, Rilke's *Torso of an Archaic Apollo* (McIntyre, 1941) referring to a statue in the Louvre, concludes with this sentence:

. . . Du must deine leben ältern.
. . . You must change your life.

This sentence in the imperative mode is an example of the type of speech-act called perlocutionary.

On reading this quotation from Rilke, certain questions arise: Who is saying this? Rilke? If not, who? To whom is it being said? Rilke himself? The reader? Some other potential viewer of the statue? All three? Whom?

The poem itself suggests that the sentence represents, in Rilke's language, the 'message' that Rilke intuits in the statue. Assuming that this is correct, he is taking up the privilege and responsibility of speaking for the work of art, as well as, no doubt, for himself.

To whom is this being said? If the foregoing interpretation is correct, the sentence is addressed to all readers and, quite possibly, by implication, all potential viewers of the statue – and certainly to Rilke himself.

It is essential at this point to notice two things.

First, the uncertainty about the speaker and listener generated by this poem is not a flaw in conception, but a structured ambiguity which is found widespread in modern poetry. Such ambiguities have been 'explained' as attempts to represent or deal with a 'disassociation of sensibility' or as a response to the uncertainties of identification in the modern world and as any number of such things. This chapter is not concerned directly with such suggestions or their worth. However, the built-in ambiguity, or hermeticism of the self, in this poem and in the one that is to be considered next, pivots heavily on the use of the first-person perlocutionary. This leads to the hypothesis.

Second, that the loading of this ambiguity on the first-person perlocutionary is the consequence of, and an integral part of, newly re-thought views of what a poem can and should do. The three most common terms for labelling the *telos* of a poem today are that it can choose to be, mainly, either expressive, mimetic (representational), or constructive. All elements are present in most poems, but in most poems one of them dominates. The expressive poem forms an intuition, subordinating mimesis or construct to that end. The mimetic provides a fictional representation, subordinating the other two to that end. The constructive aims to make a world or the experience of it, subordinating to that aim both the representation of the world and the personal expression of an experience in it.

Assume that the mimetic mode happens to be the central model – which it, in cultural fact, is – from which the other two are deviations, then the 'breaking out' of the mimetic mode, into either the mainly expressive or the mainly constructive mode, is powerfully assisted – even propelled – by the use of the first person perlocutionary. Thus, we shall see that in the next poem to be considered, as in Rilke's, the perlocutionary utterance of command or warning or such-like in a lyric poem makes it necessary for the reader to know who is speaking to whom on what terms – while at the same time it actually confuses that matter. It threatens to be a breaking out of the mimetic frame of the make-believe into the pragmatic frame of the poet's relation to the reader because it can be interpreted on the one hand as a direct address from the writer to the reader and, on the other hand, as the address of one fictional agent to another in a fictive situation. If it cannot be located fully within the make-believe by the reader, it can only be interpreted as either (1) a constructive ploy – creating a world in which the reader has to take a place assigned by the poet, or (2) an expressive ploy – offering a personal and private intuition of the poet's while denying the right of the reader to ask for much else. Let us see in more detail how this works.

Consider a second example (Ashbery, 1977):

> This poem is concerned with language on a very plain level.
> Look at it talking to you. You look out a window
> Or pretend to fidget. You have it but you don't have it.
> You miss it. It misses you. You miss each other.

This first stanza from Ashbery's *Paradoxes and Oxymorons* prominently uses a speech-act of the perlocutionary type: 'Look at it talking to you'. This deliberately and somewhat archly plays on a cross-over between seeing print and hearing words; but let us stick to the speech-act aspect. Who is saying this? Ashbery? If not, who? To whom is it being said? The reader? Some imagined listener? Whom?

Richman (1982) notes that the poem itself, as it continues, establishes itself as an 'autonomous identity' and it 'becomes a wilful, animate creature and finally becomes the reader'. The final lines are:

> . . .and the poem
> Has set me softly down beside you.
> This poem is you.

This strongly suggests that 'Look at it talking to you' is addressed directly to the reader and not to Ashbery, and probably not to any imagined listener.

Moreover, neither the perlocutionary speech act, nor the poem in which it occurs, contains, as Rilke's does, a firm and vivid reference to something outside itself.

Let us now examine these writers a bit more generally. Thorlby (1983) writes:

> What Rilke's poetry gives us is a remarkable version of life that is not personally oriented. We read him, as we read prophecy, for a revelation beyond the limits of man-centered experience. . . . In a word, towards hints of an unutterable reality. . . . But at the same time, to speak 'in a word' of what is unutterable is to give it utterance. . . . This paradox in the character of words fascinated Rilke. . . . Words have for him more than merely communicative or referential significance. . . . His words do not represent anyone's experience, even his own – they create it.

This quality, which is very evident in Rilke's later poems, is also present in the

Apollo. It is the desire to construct a reality – or alternative reality – rather than to represent one. Thus, although the poem does offer a mimesis of the experience of the Apollo figure, its main aim is to construct a world that the reader is expected in some sense to submit to and occupy. Rilke's poem subordinates expression and mimesis to construction. Now turning again to Ashbery, we can see that the down-playing of mimesis is to be found in him also – to an extreme degree.

The main critical interest of Ashbery's perlocutionary lies in what it asks the listener-reader to do: to pay attention to the poem. It is even more interesting that this attention is requested not for what the poem says about some subject other than itself – for it apparently says nothing on such a subject – but for the poem itself, and nothing more.

Perhaps the poem's very disclaimers about having a conventional subject are a reference to some sort of solipsism or narcissism? A state of mind which denies in some sense that it shares a world of reference with a listener? Or perhaps the poem's subject is an extreme idealist view or an extreme phenomenalist view? Or perhaps it is a self-dialogue in which no subject has to be mentioned because all subjects are referentially possible and implicit as the domain of that dialogue? Vendler (Richman, 1982) finds that, despite their retreat from reference on the surface, Ashbery's poems are really about love, time, or age – and she places his method in the romantic tradition of self-making by the poet. Richman sees Vendler as *willing* the poetry's connection with human life: for him, it does not, as Vendler claims, 'make us feel more and more a part of a human collectivity'. In fact, the opposite.

Contrasting such a use of the perlocutionary with that of Rilke, we notice that Ashbery's anti-mimetic impulse is as noticeable as Rilke's, but operates in a different direction. It does not, as in Rilke, force mimesis to subordinate itself to construction; it forces mimesis to subordinate itself to expression: the expression of the poet and the poem and pretty much nothing else. Taking the two poets together, their use of perlocutionary speech-acts in crucial places is an integral linguistic part of their turning away from conventional mimetic aims. While their work *in general* is not pervaded by the perlocutionary – the work of few poets is – their uses of this speech-act in the cited poems open a way to the understanding of the whole aesthetic of each of the poets.

MIMESIS AND THE PERFORMATIVE

In conclusion, these results suggest two themes that might be worth more consideration. The first is the frequency with which spells, prayers, and other ritual utterances employ performatives, especially of the perlocutionary sort. The second is the importance of performatives in framing the relation of reader to writer, and each of these both to the fictive agents within the poem and the world outside it that the poem refers to.

Apropos the first theme, in remarks at the East-West Center in 1982, Allan Grapard, a student of Japanese religions, analysed a Japanese Buddhist cult that arose out of efforts to 'pacify the angry spirit' of a great lord who fell during inter-clan struggles to control the Imperial family in the 14th century. Some of the rites of pacification and conciliation, he noted, were embodied in devotional poems. Many of these had the form of propitiatory spells, a form which he saw as closely analogous to the 'performative' (in the anthropological sense) verse-spells observed by Malinowski in the practices of Melanesians. Those spells were employed to persuade the spirits in charge of gardens to guarantee a good crop.

Grapard, following Malinowski's usage, referred to such spell poems as 'performative' utterances, in the obvious sense that they not only make statements but make them in a manner and context in which the utterance is regarded as bringing about the action which is the topic of the statement – that is, the supernatural encouragement of the gardens. Grapard then observed that some Japanese lyric poetry, detached from the ritual and the cult, retained some of the form and import of performative types of utterance.

Thus the performative spell of Malinowski and Grapard can be considered to be a type of the perlocutionary. 'Let the Spirit of the garden bring good yams', for example. By this utterance the speaker, from his point of view at least, helps himself to achieve a good garden for the year. From a scientific point of view, that faith may be unfounded. Yet it is also true, as Malinowski observes, that the propitiation can have the effect of focusing the speaker's effort on quite practical horticultural practices, thus helping to bring about the called-for effect.

Verse-spells that are performative in quality stand in some contrast to verses that are mainly mimetic in quality. Of course, both are performative and both are mimetic. But the spell aims to have an effect on the future and takes the stance that the world will not take shape unless the word is spoken. The poetic verse for its own sake may have a performative tone, but this is in turn contained within its emphasis on the evocation of a past or just past human state of affairs – on its mimetic quality. In this sort of poem, Nature speaks, and the result is the poem. In the performative, Word creates World. In the mimetic, World emanates Word. In fact, in Greek usage, mimesis was first a performance – by a priest – of a myth; it only later became generalized into its meaning as a certain kind of imitation or fictional replication.

There are plain survivals of performative types of utterance, in religious rather than magical form, in the Christian devotional poetry of the West. It attained great heights in Latin church texts and it assumed vernacular form of the highest quality in the devotional poetry of Spain and England, for example. In the British line, consider the lyricism of George Herbert (1961), which is unsurpassed in its use of simple language as a vehicle of faith. The prayer is a speech-act of the most universal and at the same time the most particular circumstantiality, and it is understandable that its verbal organization as a secular lyric should, in good hands, show the same rich powers.

Much modern poetry reminds us how strong the pressure is for the modern literary work to engage in religious or crypto-religious moves and, along with that, to use discursive strategies in such a way that the poem strives to rise above the status of being mere 'language as gesture' to the status of action on self and world – 'construction' as much as 'mimesis'.

References

ASHBERY, JOHN (1977) Paradoxes and oxymorons. In *Houseboat days*. New York: Viking Press.

AUSTIN, J. L. (1952) *How to do things with words*. London: Oxford University Press.

BANFIELD, ANNE (1982) *Unspeakable sentences: narration and representation in the language of fiction*. Boston: Routledge and Kegan Paul.

BUSH, DOUGLAS (ed.) (1965) *John Milton. Complete poetical works*. Boston: Houghton Mifflin.

CANDLIN, CHRISTOPHER N. (1977) Preface. In *Introduction to discourse analysis*, edited by M. Coulthard. London and New York: Longman.

CULLER, JONATHAN (1975) *Structuralist poetics*. New York: Cornell University Press.

HERBERT, GEORGE (1961) *Poems*. New York and London: Oxford University Press.

JAKOBSEN, ROMAN (1979) On verse, its masters and explorers. In *Selected writings*, vol. V. The Hague: Mouton.

LANMAN, C. R. (1959) *Sanskrit reader: text and vocabulary and notes*. Cambridge, Mass.: Harvard University Press.

McINTYRE, C. F. (trans.) (1941) Torso von Archaische Apollo. In *Rainer M. Rilke. Selected poems*, bilingual ed. Berkeley: University of California Press.

MURRAY, GILBERT (trans.) (1947) Agamemnon. *Opera Aeschylus*, New York and London: Oxford University Press.

RICHMAN, ROBERT (1982) Our most important living poet. *Commentary* **74**(1), 62.

TATARKIEWICZ, W. (1976) Mimesis. *The dictionary of the history of ideas*. New York: Scribner.

THORLBY, ANTHONY (1983) Poetry that creates experience. *Times Higher Education Supplement* **570**, 16.

PART II

Discourse Expectations and Cross-cultural Communication

INTRODUCTION

THIS section incorporates an empirical study of selected East-West interactions and two text-oriented studies.

The chapter by Tarone and Yule is a report of a small, data-based study investigating the nature of spoken English used when non-native speakers interact with other non-native speakers. The East was represented by native speakers of Chinese, Japanese, and Korean; the West was represented by native speakers of Spanish from different South American countries. The focus of the study was specific communication strategies, not sociocultural factors involved in communication. The situations were designed to elicit transactional rather than interactional communication. Speakers were provided with a predetermined amount of information to convey to their listener who required that information while both were aware that an informa-tion gap existed.

The spoken data elicited under these conditions contained several communication strategies: 'Repetition'' 'explication'' and 'overelaboration' were common. Tarone and Yule claim that these are 'new' strategies in that they 'have not been mentioned in previous studies on communication strategies – possibly because these previous studies have focused on another sort of interaction altogether. 'Topic avoidance' and 'message abandonment' were relatively infrequent. 'Literal translation' was rare and the strategies of 'language switch' and 'appeal to authority' were not found at all. Since many of these strategies have been found in studies of non-native speakers talking to native speakers of English, Tarone and Yule postulate that the non-native to non-native communication situation inhibits the use of such strategies.

Xu Guo-zhang's chapter uses material from China's English-language news-paper – material which was written originally in English, not translated into English from Chinese – and takes the position that this material is a form of discourse between China and the rest of the world. He offers three examples from the *China Daily* and examines misunderstandings that could occur when these are read by native English speakers. He compares this material to a passage by Bertrand Russell and describes possible misunderstandings which fluent, English-speaking Chinese might experience when reading Russell. He makes the point that 'all cross-cultural discourse in English involves some form of translation – of names, of institutions, values, and their interrelations; and when two cultures with widely different value-systems communicate, one is made acutely aware of difficulties of the task, and sometimes not without a sense of helplessness'.

Xu suggests that even in the examples he has used, ones written originally in English, a form of translation is necessary. He cautions, however, that 'improvements' on the text (e.g. change peasants to farmers) to assist in communication across cultures must be done with care; otherwise, the philosophy and/or intention of the writer will be lost.

In Chapter 6 Clyne contrasts the different underlying assumptions held in English-speaking and German-speaking countries regarding written academic discourse structure. Reporting on research in progress contrasting papers written in English by English-educated and German-educated linguists and sociologists, Clyne points to the disadvantage of German-educated scholars whose papers are evaluated by English-educated scholars. His hypothesis is that this disadvantage exists because of the culturally based difference in expectations of written academic structure between English-educated and German-educated people.

In order to study these culturally based differences in written discourse structure, Clyne establishes the following broad parameters: degree of linearity, extent of adherence to formal (prescriptive) discourse rules, the inclusion or exclusion of material in a text (the English notion of 'relevance'), and the flexibility of discourse tempo. He relates these to the comparative importance of form and content in 'Anglo-Saxon' and German cultures and to the role of the educational systems in propagating rules.

Clyne is no doubt aware of the need to tighten the definitions of his parameters and to establish more objective criteria for determining degrees of such things as digression, linearity, circularity, etc.

It should be clear that Clyne is not being critical of either pattern but is claiming that the use of English as an international academic language will probably increase, and that it is important to be aware that different discourse expectations can lead to the development of 'national' stereotypes concerning coherence, relevance, longwindedness, and meaningfulness.

The significance of these studies is substantial. The Tarone and Yule study must be followed up to see how the non-native to non-native communication situations inhibit the use of some communication strategies while encouraging others. It is obvious from the Xu study that the use of a single linguistic medium (in this case English) used around the world does not, of itself, solve the communication problems across cultures. Clyne's study reinforces Xu's position by pointing out that assumptions and expectations which underlie communication must be taken into account if genuine understanding is to take place.

4
Communication Strategies in East–West Interactions

ELAINE TARONE AND GEORGE YULE

THE use of English as an international language for communication is probably more common today than ever before.[1] It must now be a regular occurrence that East–West interaction, as between Japanese and Mexican businessmen for example, takes place in neither Japanese nor Spanish, but in English. This international use of English should make us even more cognizant of the factors involved in the way non-native speakers (NNS) of English develop communicative skills in a language which, for many, has been learned at school or college. In this chapter we would like to present the preliminary results of an investigation of one set of such factors, namely the use of communication strategies by these learners of English as a second language (ESL).

It has been suggested that, to understand the communicative use of a language, we must focus our investigations on aspects of a learner's *communicative competence*. Canale and Swain (1980) have proposed a helpful analysis of the components of communicative competence:

(1) grammatical competence – the knowledge of what is grammatically correct in a language;
(2) sociolinguistic competence – the knowledge of what is socially acceptable in a language;
(3) strategic competence – the knowledge of how to use communication strategies to communicate intended meaning.

Although they are not to be considered discrete, these three components (it is argued) can be mastered with differing degrees of proficiency at any one point in time. That is, a learner in a traditional foreign language classroom may be quite proficient in terms of grammatical competence, being able to achieve high scores on standard language tests (e.g. TOEFL), while at the same time remaining relatively ignorant of speech-act conventions in the target language, or relatively unable to use the language with ease or appropriateness in social interaction.

Mastery of sociolinguistic skills in a language entails mastery of pragmatics and speech-act conventions, norms of stylistic appropriateness, and the uses of language to establish and maintain social relations. Mastery of strategic skills in

49

a language entails the ability to transmit information to a hearer and correctly interpret information received, and includes the mastery of communication strategies, used to deal with problems which may arise in the transmission of this information.

Quite a bit of research has been done on the sociolinguistic competence of ESL learners, covering their mastery of politeness norms (Walters, 1979), of speech-acts (Rintell, 1979), and of register (Schmidt, 1981; Gillette, 1982). Much of the work reported in this volume relates to the sociolinguistic and sociocultural factors involved in producing and understanding English text, both spoken and written.

Research on the strategic competence of ESL learners is quite recent. Two broad areas may be investigated:

(1) the overall skill of a speaker in successfully transmitting information to a hearer;
(2) the use of communication strategies by a speaker when problems are encountered in the process of attempting to transmit information.

To our knowledge, very little research has been done on the learner's overall skills in strategic competence. Paribakht (1982) assessed the success of learners in communicating information by means of a 'simple count of each subject's frequency of successful communication of . . . target items' – subcategorizing these into identification of the concept and identification of the exact word. However, it is not clear what criteria were involved in determining 'success' – and in any case, this was not the primary focus of her study. More systematic research of this sort *has* been done with native speakers of English, assessing their 'transactional speech' – speech where the speaker is primarily concerned with transferring information to a hearer. This research (Yule, 1982; Brown and Yule, 1983) developed a task-based methodology for the objective assessment of the communicative effectiveness of native-speaker adolescents in using the spoken language. In this methodology a series of transactional language tasks (narrative, descriptive and instructional) was devised, in which a speaker had to transfer information to a listener who did not previously possess this information and who required it to complete some specific task. The aim was to situate the speaker in a well-defined position where s/he alone was in possession of the relevant knowledge and where s/he knew that the hearer needed that information in order to complete a task. The problem for the speaker was to determine which aspects of the information s/he possessed were relevant to the task at hand and to control the flow of information to the listener so that the listener was provided with the relevant information and not credited with knowledge which s/he could not reasonably be expected to have. This methodology elicited spontaneous speech from students but at the same time allowed the researcher to determine what the essential content of that speech should be. An objective scoring procedure was developed and applied to speaker performances, so that speakers could be compared with one another with regard to degree of success in communicating the essential information required by the task.

It seems clear that this same research technique could easily be applied in the area of second-language acquisition and use, to systematically assess the communicative effectiveness of a second-language learner in the target language, as well as to elicit the use of communication strategies.

The second area of strategic competence – the use of communication strategies to solve problems encountered in the transmission of information – *has* been investigated by researchers. In fact, this research is summarized and discussed in a recent book, *Strategies in interlanguage communication*, edited by Faerch and Kasper (1983). Faerch and Kasper define communication strategies as 'potentially conscious plans for solving what to an individual presents itself as a problem in reaching a particular communicative goal'. Tarone (1981) sets out the following criteria as characteristic of a communication strategy:

(1) a speaker desires to communicate a meaning X to a listener;
(2) the speaker believes the linguistic or sociolinguistic structure desired to communicate meaning X is unavailable, or is not shared with the listener;
(3) the speaker chooses to:
    (a) avoid – not attempt to communicate meaning X; or
    (b) attempt alternative means to communicate meaning X. The speaker stops trying alternatives when it seems clear to the speaker that there is shared meaning.

Some examples of communication strategies used by second-language learners are provided below. This list of strategies is not intended to be a final categorization of all existent communication strategies; it is simply provided to help clarify the notion of communication strategy.

Avoidance

Topic avoidance – the learner simply tries not to talk about concepts for which the target language item or structure is not known.
Message abandonment – the learner begins to talk about a concept but is unable to continue and stops in mid-utterance.

Paraphrase

Approximation – the learner uses a single target language vocabulary item or structure, which the learner knows is not correct, but which shares enough semantic features in common with the desired item to satisfy the speaker (e.g. *pipe* for *waterpipe*).
Word coinage – the learner makes up a new word in order to communicate a desired concept (e.g. *airball* for *balloon*).
Circumlocution – the learner describes the properties of the object or action instead of using the appropriate target language item or structure (e.g. 'it's oval and shiny', or 'She is, uh, smoking something. . . . That's, uh, Persian, and we use in Turkey, a lot of.')

Borrowing

Literal translation – the learner translates word for word from the native language (e.g. 'He invites him to drink', for 'They toast one another').
Language switch – the learner uses the native language term without bothering to translate (e.g. *balon* for *balloon*, *tirtil* for *caterpillar*).

Appeal for assistance

The learner asks for the correct term (e.g. 'What is this? What called?').

Mime

The learner uses non-verbal tactics in place of a lexical item or action (e.g. clapping one's hands to illustrate applause), or to accompany another communication strategy (e.g. 'It's about this long').

A more detailed typology of communication strategies, providing, for example, a breakdown of types of circumlocution, is available in Paribakht (1982).

Research on communication strategies used by second-language learners has focused primarily on interactions between learners and native speakers of the target language (e.g. Tarone, 1977; Paribakht, 1982).

We know of *no* research in this area of interlanguage studies – either on overall success in communicating information, or on communication strategy use – which examines the interaction between second-language learners who do not share the same native language and who are communicating with each other in the target language – as, for example, in the use of English as a lingua franca or as an international language. Such research is badly needed, we feel, for several reasons.

(1) English is increasingly being used as a lingua franca – in business and politics – by non-native speakers of English. What happens to the transmission of information in such interactions?

(2) This is the most common sort of interaction in the typical ESL classroom where learners have different native languages (NLs) – particularly a class which uses the newer 'communicative approaches' to second-language teaching, where students are given lots of practice using English to talk to each other – but not to talk to native speakers. Do the communication strategies used in such interactions really transfer over to interactions when the non-native speaker (NNS) must use English with a native speaker (NS)? Are they at all similar to communication strategies NS's use with each other?

(3) From the point of view of linguistic theory, it has been argued that pidgin languages developed in the context of the use of a lingua franca by interactants with different NL backgrounds, for the primary purpose of transmitting information (and not for establishment of group membership, social solidarity, etc.). We should know more about how

information is transmitted in such interactions in order to better understand the linguistic structure of the resultant pidgin language.

Because of the absolute lack of research in this area, we decided to undertake a study which might begin to provide some insight into questions such as the following:

(1) What sorts of communication strategies are used by NNS of English from different NL backgrounds in order to describe an object, provide instructions for a series of actions, or narrate a sequence of events?

(2) Do these communication strategies vary depending on the NL and cultural background of the interlocutor?

(3) In what ways does this communication in English by NNS differ from that typically produced by NS of English performing the same tasks?

We were particularly interested in examining interactions between speakers of languages spoken on the Pacific Rim – in particular, between speakers of Spanish and speakers of an Asian language – where English was the language of interaction.

We were, unfortunately, unable to find as many speakers of any one Asian language as of Spanish; consequently, in our study we had three groups of Asian-language speakers: Japanese, Korean and Chinese. Our subjects were 12 Spanish speakers, who interacted with one of the following: 6 Japanese speakers, 5 Korean speakers, and 4 Chinese speakers. In addition, we studied 9 NS of English who performed the same tasks with each other as the NNS of English.

Procedure

Two subjects participated in each session. With the NNS population, one subject was South American and the other was Asian. One subject was given the speaker role and the other was asked to be the listener who would simply pay attention, without interrupting, to what the speaker said. Both subjects were given tasks. The speaker's task was to look at a set of visual stimuli presented on a video screen and to describe, give instructions for, or narrate what was shown. On the screen there appeared, one after the other, four objects to describe, one series of operations to be carried out and one set of events. Thus, for example, the speaker saw a hairbrush on the screen for about 20 seconds and when the screen went blank, was asked to describe what had been shown. After that first description had been completed, the second object to be described was shown on the screen, and so on. The speaker knew s/he was being tape-recorded, and sat face to face with the listener across a table with a low screen. The speaker was allowed as much time as s/he wanted to produce the description. The listener could not see the video screen. To accompany each visual stimulus shown on the screen to the speaker, the listener had a set of still photographs, marked A, B and C. In the description task, for example, the listener had a still photograph of the hairbrush which appeared on the screen, labelled B, plus two other still photographs, (A) and (C), of other types of brushes. The listener's task was to listen to the speaker's description and to identify which of the three photographs best fit the description. The only feedback which the listener could provide the speaker was non-verbal, as the speaker could see the listener's face and upper body; the speaker could not see the still photographs. After the speaker finished all the tasks, the listener and speaker changed places – the listener becoming the speaker on a new round of tasks, and the speaker becoming the listener.[2] With the NS population, the same procedure was followed. Speakers were allowed to use gesture in communicating; however, since speakers were not video-taped, no systematic record of their use of mime was kept.

The aim of this task-based procedure is to provide a speaker with some pre-selected information to convey, a listener who requires that information, and an awareness that an information gap exists. A fuller description of this type of elicitation procedure is presented in Brown and Yule (1983).

The speaker's utterances were tape-recorded and transcribed. An analysis of the transcriptions, involving categorization into communication strategy types, was conducted on both the NNS-NNS interactions, and the NS-NS interactions.

Results

A detailed analysis of the results of this research project is still in progress. However, the more salient characteristics of the communication strategies used in this sort of NNS-NNS interaction are already evident, and will be reported here, together with examples taken from the data. Further analysis will refine and further substantiate the observations we report here.

1. Occurrence of already-documented communication strategies

Several of the categories of communication strategy previously discussed in the literature may be observed in the East-West interactions in this study. For example, the two categories of circumlocution and approximation occurred with particular frequency in these interactions.

Circumlocution, in which the speaker describes the properties of the target object or action (i.e. the colour, size, shape, function, etc.), occurred in NNS accounts such as these:

> (J5) The colour is, uh, dark, and uh . . . the size is just, uh, uh, as a hand . . . . it is made of uh, la, leather.
> (K5) OK this is oval shape one side has a hair and the backside has string in middle in middle part so you can put your fing- – your hands.
> (S1) It is made by rubber – but it is cutted on front – that you can have your fingers out – if you wear that

Approximation, in which the speaker uses a term which shares a number of semantic features with the target lexical item or structure, occurred in this sort of NNS account:

(K2) It's a kind of the mitten.
(K3) And right side he is uh draw a shape. OK? A circle round, triangle here.
(S8) Maybe is something like a rope.
(J6) And the shape is like a octopus (laugh) but it has just three legs. Not eight legs. Head, and, three legs. Like octopus. (laugh)

Note that K2 and K3 above approximate by using a superordinate term ('mitten', 'shape') and then indicate that the target item is related to that term by hyponymy. S8 uses a type of approximation which might be termed *analogy* (see Paribakht, 1982), offering the term 'rope' as an analogy to the target 'electrical cord'. And J6 uses the analogy type of approximation as well, likening a Christmas tree stand to an octopus, and then, by means of circumlocution, indicating which properties of the two objects in the analogy differ.

Other types of communication strategy which occurred in these NNS–NNS interactions include avoidance, message abandonment, mime, and literal translation.

Outright topic avoidance was attempted by a few subjects who, when they saw the object on the video, said they had no name for the object, and made no further attempt to talk about it:

(C2) I don't know what this name.
(C2) I don't know what's this. (laugh)

Message abandonment, in which the speaker starts out using communication strategies but then gives up and stops talking, also occurred in these interactions:

(S3) crush or to – oh I don't know the $\begin{Bmatrix} \text{word?} \\ \text{verb} \end{Bmatrix}$ – I think that's all.
(C4) I saw I saw the TV the first you – eh – eh – lack(?) put together and you – do the next – step – I can't (unintelligible) it I'm sorry.

However, it should be noted that both topic avoidance and message abandonment occurred relatively infrequently in our data; the overwhelming majority of NNS attempted some means of communicating information via communication strategies, even when this attempt seemed to involve great effort.

The communication strategy of mime seemed to be used fairly frequently in these interactions by most NNS. As pointed out earlier, because we did not videotape the NNS-NNS interactions, we have no systematic record of speakers' use of this communication strategy. However, the following two examples will serve to document that this strategy did occur. There were, in fact, two types of mime; in one case, mime took the place of a desired structure or item, as in:

(S6) the oval is the big one and the other part is what, take to (demonstrates holding the handle of a brush)

More frequently, mime accompanied a speaker's use of other communication strategies, as below where the speaker uses circumlocution and mime simultaneously:

(J5) And the shape is, the big, down part is just like, this and uh, this size, and the upper side is just like this.

So far, it seems that the only NNS group which did not use mime to communicate information in these interactions is the Chinese-speaking group; however, as this group was smaller than the others we have examined, we cannot determine whether the omission of mime by this group was significant in any sense.

It is somewhat surprising at first to notice that the strategy of literal translation was used by some NNS in this study – surprising because the listener in each dyad could not be known to speak the native language of the speaker. The success of literal translation as a communication strategy depends to a great extent on the speaker's assumption that either (a) the hearer knows the speaker's native language, or (b) the speaker's native language and the target language are similar enough in structure that a literal translation from the NL might in fact be a cognate in the TL. The fact that all the instances of literal translation we have been able to document thus far were produced by Spanish speakers would seem to favour the second possibility – that the Spanish speaker uses literal translation in hopes of hitting a cognate in English. The use of this strategy would suggest that the speaker believes that English and Spanish are so closely related that many cognates exist. The fact that one never knows whether a communication strategy will be successful until it is tried, and the fact that many words in English and Spanish *are* cognates, make the literal translation strategy a more fruitful one than one might at first suppose. Examples of the use of this strategy include:

(S5)   In each, in each *extreme* (Sp. *extremo = Eng. end*), in each uh . . . is an English
       word, *extreme*? (laugh) has something for connecting, on the equipment.
(S5)   Take it and . . . put, uh, from the side (4-second pause) *inferious. Inferi*, mm, from
       the *inferior* side (Sp. *inferior = Eng. bottom*)
(S4)   and *in this moment* go into the class a – a girl (Sp. *en este momento = Eng. at this
       moment*)
(S6)   It's like a knife, in one of the *extremes*, together, with a little brush
(S2)   what happened with my *explication* and my drawing? (Sp. *explicación = Eng.
       explanation*)

Two communication strategies which did *not* occur in the NNS-NNS interactions were language switch and appeal to authority. Language switch, which is related to the strategy of literal translation described above, relies solely on the assumption that the hearer knows the speaker's native language. It is used when the NL term or structure appears in the TL discourse with no change in pronunciation and word form. The speakers in our study did not attempt to use this strategy at all with one another. Only one use of the NL by a speaker was noted, and this was an utterance produced at low volume in which the speaker was apparently talking to himself, possibly trying to use association with the NL term to retrieve the TL term from his memory:

(S8)   how do you say in English that word? We say in Spanish bujia. Y'espero . . .

The other communication strategy which did not occur in these interactions was appeal to authority. This is not surprising, as, in NNS-NNS interactions the listener cannot be assumed to have either the information or the language to respond to such an appeal. This is one major difference between previous studies which examined NNS-NS interactions, and our study. A NS listener can reasonably be appealed to for assistance; a NNS listener who speaks a different NL from the speaker cannot.

2. Newly-observed aspects of communication strategy use

Certain aspects of communication strategy use are clearly in evidence in these NNS-NNS interactions which have not been mentioned in previous studies on communication strategies – possibly because these previous studies have focused on another sort of interaction altogether. We have observed three new types of communication strategy in use in these interactions, all of which seem to us to serve the same general function of providing the listener with several opportunities to identify the object or entity involved: repetition, explication, and over-explicitness. We have also observed that speakers in these NNS-NNS interactions seem to be particularly careful to avoid the use of culturally bound information in their communication strategies – that is, information which their listener would be unlikely to know.

Little attention has been focused, in the study of communication strategies, on the frequent repetitions which characterize NNS English spoken production. One type of repetition occurs when the NNS appears to stall, trying to find a word or phrase to convey the message. An extended example of this type of repetition is illustrated below:

> (C1) and he, just want to . . . ah, want to . . . to to . . . he wan, he go to the, she go to the blackboard and uh, want to . . . ah . . . wash, wash the . . . the picture off . . .

This type of repetition occurs in varying amounts, throughout many of the NNS data. This phenomenon, however, may not be of primary interest in the study of how NNS set about communicating their intended messages. It is certainly of interest as a clue to points in the discourse where the speaker is having some difficulty finding an appropriate TL expression to convey the intended meaning, but it may be an extremely general *production* strategy in spoken discourse which manifests itself in all spontaneous spoken production, including NS production. The difference between NNS and NS accounts appears to be in the amount of repetition of this type. Within the set of NNS accounts there is also variation in the amount of repeated words and phrases. This type of repetition, with its accompanying pausing and incomplete structures, certainly contributes to the general impression of lack of fluency in NNS speech. Since we do not wish to include lack of fluency (like wrong tense forms, inappropriate prepositions, etc.) as part of any communication strategy, we shall simply note this type of repetition and attempt to keep it distinct from another type which does seem part of an attempt to convey the intended message effectively. It is not always easy to tell whether the use of repetition is serving the function of a production strategy (that is, as a means of 'buying time' to allow the speaker to formulate a plan for the next segment of discourse), or that of a communication strategy, in providing the listener with another chance to hear and process the information. In the example below, the repetition of a part of a story could serve either function:

> (S8) and the teacher all the time is writing on the blackboard. She is writing on the
>   blackboard, she is, eh, she is, she is, looking, looking, she is looking at the
>   blackboard because she is writing.

In this case, there is less disfluency, and (by the end) the addition of information to the original message. The same speaker, S8, actually repeated his entire
narrative (which was already quite lengthy) *twice* from beginning to end. Since
his listener had not (non-verbally) indicated any confusion about the point of
the original narrative, the purpose of this repetition seemed to be less to make
the message clear to the listener than to allow the speaker to formulate the
narrative in a more fluent manner. As used for this purpose, the repetition of
the narrative would be a production strategy rather than a communication
strategy.

On the other hand, some repetitions do seem to be produced when the
listener non-verbally indicates that the message as first formulated has not
been clear. The speaker, in response, repeats the message as originally stated.
In the first example below, K3 repeats the term 'Scotch tape' six times:

> (K3) This is a, *Scotch tape. Tape.* Something, uh (unintell.) tear, uh, uh, tear, eh, at the
>   time, eh, we need uh *Scotch tape*. Eh, goes together, eh, together. To, together,
>   OK? And uh some, sometimes, we, uh, purchase, purchase. Box . . . oh . . . this is
>   uh *Scotch tape. Scotch tape*? And uh . . . oh, this is uh . . . some *Scotch tape, Scotch
>   tape*, put in a box. OK? Little box.

Throughout this monologue, the listener's face looked puzzled, and the
speaker continued trying repetition in response. In the next example, J4
identified a Christmas tree stand as a 'pole stander', and repeated this phrase or
some variation of it throughout her discourse. Her listener also maintained a
puzzled facial expression, and responded negatively twice to J4's comprehension checks:

> (J4) This I guess this is for a, *pole stander*. When you put the *pole* at, uh, *pole* at *stand* . . .
>   youuu . . . mm . . . they have a round material and you put, through and screw the
>   . . . uh . . . (laugh) screw. Screw. From three sides. And this one has three, legs.
>   And the shape is round . . . (laugh) Do you need more? Well, you can *put the poles
>   in* the round thing. And, from, three sides . . . OK, first of all, you *put the poles, in
>   it*? There is no pole, in, in, the picture, and, when you pu-*put a pole in* . . . you,
>   screw, from three sides? and let the *pole stand* . . . this is a, basic of a, *stand, as pole*
>   . . . so you don't need to dig, the ground to *stand the pole*. (laugh) Not enough
>   (laugh)

A less extended type of repetition, which seems to share similarities with the
approximative strategy, occurs when the speaker repeats the term, not exactly,
but in paraphrase. Given the elicitation situation in which our data were
produced, one might expect that each NNS would attempt to make sure that
the NNS listener had every opportunity to understand the conveyed message.
This general motive may be behind the frequent use of the 'paraphrase', or
'double-barrelled' type of repetition which occurs in our data. Let us consider
some examples:

> (S1) she looks the her clock, her watch
> (S3) put her bag, her suitcase

(S4)   two piece of sheet, two paper
(S8)   she pick up the, all the, he raise all the papers
(S10) the lecturer, the teacher
(C4)   his schoolmate, eh classmate
(K5)   her purse, her bag
(J4)   in the student's purse, bag
(S1)   the classroom is, eh, empty – no one else is in there

Examples such as these may be indicative of a communication strategy used by the NNS when using English to convey a message to another NNS. In each case, the speaker is giving an alternative identifying term, not necessarily a synonym, to reinforce the first term used. The pattern does not necessarily illustrate a 'general term – specific term' sequence, but seems more a result of providing two chances for the listener to identify, roughly, the entity or action involved.

Possibly deriving from the same NNS-listener effect is a strategy which could be tentatively characterized as 'explication'. It is not a repetition of an expression or of an alternative identifying expression, but rather a spelling-out of what is meant by the expression used. An example from one of the narratives may clarify this strategy:

(C2)   second picture is, uh, st, triangle – striangle has three sides.
(C?)   draw, a picture, about, uh, the word, uh, circle – circle is, uh, round.

It seems as if this speaker has attempted to make certain that the relevant graphic features of 'triangle' and 'circle' are known to the listener. In a similar way, in the following extract the speaker has decided to explicate what aspect of the identified object should be known:

(S8)   in the arm of the chair – the arm of the chair is when the, when you use for to write

This type of strategy is also noticeable in the description tasks when a speaker first uses a term and then decides to 'explicate' what that English term means:

(S1)   it is like a mitten . . . the glove is a with fing- with fingers and the mitten is without fingers so it is – a mitten

The appearance of such 'explications' may be a reflection of the communication situation in which the listener is not a NS and so the NNS speaker has to gauge how much the listener knows of the language being used as the communicative medium. It is, of course, a strategy which has drawbacks in interpersonal terms, since the listener may not take kindly to having English words (which he may know) explained to him/her by another NNS. Despite this risk, however, the strategy will clearly be a useful device if the speaker wishes to use some technical term which the listener cannot be expected to know. From a pedagogical point of view, it is a strategy which should be encouraged while providing the NNS with the means to use the strategy, suitable hedged, to inform the listener without the implication of ignorance on the listener's part.

The communication strategy of over-explicitness which appeared in the NNS-NNS interactions will be illustrated here by reference to performance on the narration task; however, this strategy also occurred in the other task types.

The term 'over-explicitness' is used to refer to the greater use of detail in the NNS accounts than in the NS accounts.

There is a typical pattern to the NS organization of narrative accounts which divides the event sequence into sets of actions involving each individual character. For example, the teacher is introduced, performs a set of actions, then the first student is introduced, performs a set of actions, and so on. Thus, the basic narrative structure found in NS accounts of one of the stories takes the following form:

> A teacher comes into the classroom, lays a magazine on the desk, starts writing on the blackboard.
> A student comes in, picks up the magazine, pages through the magazine, lays it down, and leaves the room.
> Another student comes in, picks up the magazine, pages through, puts it in the first student's bag.
> The first student comes back, puts the bag on the floor.
> The teacher turns round, starts looking for the magazine.

There are, of course, additional details found in each NS account, but there appears to be a general 'filtering out' of the mass of detail presented visually in order to produce the main events listed above. While a similar 'filtering' process is in evidence in the NNS accounts, there are several ways in which the conveyed narratives exhibit a much more explicit recounting of the events (and their interpretation) than is found in the typical NS version. If the NS versions can be viewed as evidence of the normal amount of explicitness required in producing an oral narrative in English, under the task conditions, then we can point to some critical aspects of over-explicitness in the NNS accounts. It may be, of course, that this 'over-explicitness' is evidence of a general communication strategy which involves an attempt to make sure that everything observed is presented to the listener. This strategy may be occasioned, in part, by uncertainty on the speaker's behalf, regarding what are and what are not crucial elements in a narrative account.

It is, however, more probable that this strategy is prompted by the fact that the listener is not a native speaker of English and may require much more help in understanding what happened. That is, each NNS may decide that another NNS listener will not be able to construct an interpretation from the message unless every story-element is spelled out. At the present stage of our research, this is an untested hypothesis, but it may provide a tentative explanation for some of the linguistic phenomena we shall describe.

Some of the differences in explicitness are relatively straightforward. The most 'detailed' NS account of the first student's arrival is as follows:

> (E1) a student walks in and sits down in the front row

Some typical NNS accounts of this part of the story are as follows:

> (K4) another woman, her hair is blonde, come into the classroom and sit in the front row at the center
> (S1) a girl, a blondie girl, arrived to the classroom, and sit in front of th, in one of the chairs of the classroom but just in front of the desk, of the teacher's desk

There are two aspects of these NNS extracts worth noting. First, there is the obvious inclusion of additional descriptive detail ('blonde hair') and the more precise location of the student's seat. Second, there is a certain amount of information ('into the classroom') included which has to be treated as redundant, in the sense that the classroom setting is established at the beginning of every narrative.

Other examples of additional locational detail can be illustrated, as in the following (characteristically brief) NS extract compared with the next two NNS extracts:

(E7)   a third woman comes in

(K2)   the other, the other woman student came in the classroom and sit next to a woman's, the woman's chair

(S10) in this moment came another, another girl, another woman, and she sit down beside the desk where the other girl left the magazine

Other examples of redundancy are also to be found in the frequent repetition in NNS accounts that the teacher 'is writing on the blackboard' and 'finish to write on the blackboard', when it has already been established at the beginning of the account that the teacher is indeed using the blackboard.

The general feature of repetition in NNS accounts has been commented on already. One manifestation of this general strategy may be discerned in the difference between NS and NNS organization of introductory and subsequent reference to characters in the story. In NS accounts, a typical structure takes the following form:

(E5) one student comes in
  ∅   sees the article on the desk
  ∅   picks it up
  ∅   takes her seat
 and ∅   proceeds to page through it

In this type of structure, a number of actions are predicated of the one character, explicitly identified once, and a conjunction is only used to connect the final predication to the preceding set. This is not a typical structure found in NNS accounts. It is much more common to find each predication joined to the next by a conjunction ('and' or 'and then') and for a pronoun (and occasionally a repetition of the full nominal expression) to be used, rather than ellipsis. The typical discourse structure of NNS accounts takes the following form:

(J6)		a	student	came into the classroom	
	and		she	couldn't settle down	
	because		she	watch her watch	
	or		she	opens	magazine
	but		she	never read it	
	and		she	closes	magazine
	and		she	went somewhere	
(S8)		the	student	take	one magazine
	and		she	began to see, to turn the page	
	and		she	put	one magazine
				in his chair	
	and		she	go out of the classroom	

While this latter type of structure may prove advantageous in terms of explicitly marking out each 'chunk' of information as separate from the preceding 'chunk', it certainly loses some of the naturalness of English oral narrative. The strategy used by the NNS to structure the set of events in their accounts is possibly a further example of the general strategic device of 'over-explicitness', in which the frequent use of conjunctions and pronouns builds in more redundancy in the message than is typically found in the NS accounts.

This general conclusion receives some support from the pattern of distribution of full nominal versus pronominal realizations of reference to the 'magazine' which is at the centre of one of the stories. It might have been expected, on the basis of frequent pronominal reference to the characters, already illustrated, that the NNS would use pronominals ('it', 'that') when talking about the magazine, after the initial introduction. In the NS accounts the magazine is referred to more frequently via pronominals than via full nominal expressions. However, there is an overwhelming preference for repeating the full nominal in all NNS accounts relating to the magazine. As illustration, the following three extracts are from a NS, a native Japanese speaker and a native Spanish speaker respectively:

(E7)   picks up the magazine, looks at it for a while and then puts it back in the bag
(J6)   she began to open the magazine again and soon she close magazine
(S10) to her was kind of interesting the magazine and she took the magazine and become
       to see the magazine

The different ratios of full form to reduced form realizations of reference to the 'magazine' in Narrative One in our data are summarized in the following figures:

	NS	NNS (Asian)	NNS (South American)
Full form	18	49	54
Reduced form	33	12	6

Finally, we may observe additional evidence of the sensitivity of these NNS to the sort of interaction they are involved in by noting their use of culturally bound information in their communication strategies. The role of such information in communication strategy use seems to be much more restricted in these NNS-NNS interactions than in, say, Paribakht's study (where Persian-speaking subjects seem to have made free use of transliterated L1 idioms and proverbs in their interactions). The speakers in our study did not seem to make much use of references to their native cultures in their use of communication strategies; most of the information they included did not seem to require that the listener be familiar with the speaker's culture. A possible exception to this generalization might be the attempt by two Korean speakers to compare a Christmas tree stand to a 'burner' (an object possibly more familiar in Korean culture than in others):

(K1)   there are some steel object like banner(?) –
(K2)   in that video, video picture, uh, someone combined a [banə]

Only Korean speakers referred to this object as a 'burner', and the strategy (confounded as it was by pronunciation problems) did not seem to have been particularly effective as far as the listener was concerned.

The more common tendency of these speakers, as noted above, seems to have been to avoid such 'culturally loaded' references – as when S8 attempts and then abandons an analogy of set screws to sardine can keys, apparently because he decided halfway through that his listener could not be expected to know what a sardine can key was:

(S8)   we have three key, three, three objects that, li like a key, when you open a sardines? Mm, no, no no, no, no. Forget that (laugh) we are going to confuse that.

Thus, the speakers in their attempts to use communication strategies did seem to take the identity of the listener into consideration and to operate with definite hypotheses about the sorts of culturally based information the listener could be expected to have at his/her disposal.

One type of culturally based information which many of the speakers *did* use, was information which people who live in Minnesota can be expected to have – as, for example, when speakers S1, S5, S8, J4, J5, J6, K4 and K5 all identified a paint scraper as a snow scraper. This strategy seemed in fact to be quite effective.

Another sort of culturally based information which some speakers used was information which members of an international sub-culture – specifically, horse-riding culture – might be expected to have. Thus, for example, in describing a crop, speakers who obviously had correctly recognized its function, said:

(J2)   you can use this stick for the horse
(S7)   it's a (unintelligible) using for jocking . . . eh, when they, ride a horse? For to hit the horse?

The inclusion of this sort of information in communicating with NNS was not always successful from the point of view of the listener, who might or might not be familiar with horse riding. However, speakers seemed willing to try to include *this* sort of culturally based information in their communication strategies, perhaps on the twin assumptions that one never knows whether a communication strategy will be successful until it is tried, and that their listeners *might* have been familiar with horse-riding culture, which is more or less international.

All these uses and non-uses of culturally based information by the speakers in these NNS-NNS interactions seem to show that the speakers were making fairly sophisticated and sensitive decisions about the sorts of information which their listeners might reasonably be expected to have at their disposal in decoding communication strategies, and were using this information to produce strategies which were most transparent to their listeners.

To summarize our research to date, then, we have found that a number of the communication strategies already noted in the literature also occurred in these NNS–NNS interactions using English: circumlocution, approximation, avoidance, message abandonment, mime and literal translation. Two strategies did *not* occur: language switch and appeal to authority; their absence seems to us to be due to the type of interaction involved.

Three communication strategies not previously noted in the literature were observed in this study: repetition, explication and over-explicitness. We also observed that NNS seemed to be careful not to use culturally based information which their NNS listeners could not be expected to know, but *were* willing to use culturally based information which their listeners were likely to be familiar with.

Future research in this area could, it seems to us, profitably address itself to the following questions, among others:

> What are the overall skills of NNS in strategic competence? Will the methodology for objectively measuring NS skills in this area be useful in studying NNS skills?
>
> To what extent do speakers from different cultural and linguistic backgrounds use communication strategies differentially?
>
> How successful are these communication strategies in transmitting intended information to listeners from other NL backgrounds?
>
> What are the linguistic consequences of using a particular communication strategy?

Notes

1. We are grateful to the Center for Research in Human Learning at the University of Minnesota for use of its human subject protocol procedure. Our thanks also go to the international students who volunteered their time to help us in this study; to their ESL teachers who made it possible for them to do so, especially Sheryl Holt; and to Pam Couch, Susan Gillette and Lois Malcolm, who assisted in the production of the video tapes used in this study.
2. As yet, we have not examined our data to determine whether there may be any 'listener-effects' noticeable in the performance of those subjects who took the listener-role prior to speaking. Previous research has shown that there can be some role-related effect in terms of specificity of information transferred, but no effect in terms of communication strategies has yet been discerned (cf. Anderson *et al.*, 1982).

References

ANDERSON, A., G. BROWN and G. YULE (1982) Hearers make better speakers: hearer-effects on speaker performance in oral communication tasks. *Work in Progress No. 14*, Linguistics Department, Edinburgh University.

BROWN, G. and G. YULE (1983) *Teaching the spoken language: principles and practice*. Cambridge and New York: Cambridge University Press.

CANALE, M. and M. SWAIN (1980) Theoretical bases of communicative approaches to second language teaching and testing. *Applied Linguistics* **1**: 1–47.

FAERCH, C. and G. KASPER (eds) (1983) *Strategies in interlanguage communication*. New York: Longman.

FRASER, B., E. RINTELL and J. WALTERS (1980) An approach to conducting research on the acquisition of pragmatic competence in a second language. In *Discourse analysis in second language acquisition*, edited by D. Larsen-Freeman. Rowley, Mass.: Newbury House.

GILLETTE, S. (1982) Lecture discourse of a foreign TA. *ESL Working Papers of the University of Minnesota No. 2*, Linguistics Dept., University of Minnesota.

PARIBAKHT, T. (1982) The relationship between the use of communication strategies and aspects of target language proficiency: a study of Persian ESL students. Ph.D. dissertation, University of Toronto.

RINTELL, E. (1979) Getting your speech act together: the pragmatic ability of second language learners. *Working Papers in Bilingualism* **17**: 97–106.

SCHMIDT, M. (1981) Needs assessment in English for special purposes. In *English for academic and technical purposes*, edited by L. Selinker *et al*. Rowley, Mass.: Newbury House.

TARONE, E. (1977) Conscious communication strategies in interlanguage. In *On TESOL '77*, edited by H. D. Brown *et al*. Washington, DC: TESOL.

TARONE, E. (1981) Some thoughts on the notion of communication strategy. *TESOL Quarterly* **15** (reprinted in Faerch and Kasper, 1983: 61–74).

WALTERS, J. (1979) Strategies for requesting in Spanish and English. *Language Learning* **29**: 277–293.

YULE, G. (1982) The objective assessment of aspects of spoken English. *World Language English* **1**: 193–199.

5

Code and Transmission in Cross-cultural Discourse: a Study of Some Samples from Chinese and English

XU GUO-ZHANG

CHINA hands out about seventy pages of news bulletin in English per day and has been publishing an English-language daily (*China Daily*) since 1981. The writing of news reports on China carried in these publications is in most cases done initially in English; it is not a matter of translation from Chinese to English, as is commonly supposed. In this chapter we will consider this body of work as a form of discourse between China and the world outside: each day China, as a party to the discourse, explains its plans and evaluations through English. Now this English, while perfectly grammatical, uses many words which are English in lexical form but Chinese in cultural content – perhaps inevitably so, since the Chinese culture of the 1980s possesses a set of values and concepts peculiar to China and hardly thought of by users of English in the rest of the world. This chapter proposes to look at three sample passages, all from the *China Daily*, and discuss about a dozen words (mostly nouns denoting institutions or institutionalized ideas) to see if a distinct code exists in the English thus sampled, and if so what problems of transmission are involved.

Passage 1: Letter to *China Daily* Editor (25 November 1982)

Editor:
Two significant performances took place recently in Beijing: 'Twelfth Night', a Shakespearean comedy by a London theatre group, and a performance commemorating Tan Fuying, a famous Peking Opera actor who died five years ago. These performances provided a good chance for people here to appreciate and study the traditional theatres of Britain and China.

I hope *China Daily* will report on the theatre regularly. I am especially eager to know the reactions of foreigners to our traditional theatre.

It would be appreciated if *China Daily* were to run an exchange of views, knowledge and feelings between Chinese audiences and foreigners on recent performances. This would help us improve our drama, and help foreigners understand Chinese culture more deeply.

Beijing   Gao Xingsheng

I hope it will be admitted that this letter makes quite smooth reading and that the writer is entirely used to English. Yet Gao Xingsheng, being Chinese, has no choice but to abide by his Chinese cultural code, and I think there are at least three words, or rather the use of them, which tell the tale.

Traditional: Gao put both Shakespeare and Tan Fuying under traditional theatre, and this is noteworthy. Now Peking Opera with its poetry and symbolism is in many ways comparable to Elizabethan drama, but I doubt if a user of English in its first-language code would agree to call Shakespeare traditional. I suppose Shakespeare would be regarded as viable as he ever was, with each notable production trying to find something fresh in him, and in this sense he is neither traditional nor old-fashioned. Gao, however, looks at *traditional* or *modern* chronologically, and this is entirely in keeping with the Chinese cultural code, which has 1919 – the year of that great literary and political movement which pushed China into the Modern Age – as the dividing line, so that an art form (such as Peking Opera) born before that time may well be called traditional. In other words, *traditional* in L1 (English as a primary language) is generally an aesthetic concept, whereas in L2 (English as a secondary language, China) it is frequently a chronological concept. This is of course only another way of saying that Gao's use of *traditional* is L2 restrained.

Foreigner: this word crops up (in plural form) three times in this short letter, presenting a sociolinguistic point which should be interesting. The Chinese are terribly aware of their cultural identity in contacts with things foreign; and foreigners, whatever their origin or creed, are bracketed into a single conceptual category, as if representing one uniform culture from which something interesting but different could always be expected. In this particular context foreigners are asked to exchange their views on recent theatrical performances with Chinese audiences: not someone who speaks English, loves Shakespeare, or is interested in comparative drama, but just foreigners, zero modification. This I would regard as a use peculiar to L2.

There is yet another aspect regarding the use of *foreigner* which I would like to go into, but this can best be done in conjunction with the next word.

Knowledge: Gao asks foreigners to share their knowledge of the theatre with Chinese audiences, and vice versa because he thinks that 'This would help us improve our drama'. Now one might think it a little too generous to assume useful knowledge on the part of all foreign theatre-goers, but this is to miss the whole point: just as foreigners are thought of as one category, so knowledge is an assumed attribute of an idealized category. Altogether it is a broad conceptual entity that reflects a willingness to know the other side on the part of the Chinese intelligentsia.

Passage 2: Discussion of role of intellectuals in the country's modernization plan by a worker and a peasant

> The important role of Chinese intellectuals in the country's modernization drive should be fully appreciated, said delegates [to the conference].
>
> Ma Liuhai, a model worker from Datong coal mines, said: 'We workers have practical experience, but intellectuals have theoretical knowledge. Workers, peasants and intellectuals must work in concert for [the plan's] fulfillment.
>
> Wang Jiming, a peasant from Sichuan, said that agricultural science is of utmost importance in rural areas today. We need science not only in seed breeding, soil improvement and the use of chemical fertilizer but also in the processing of farm produce.
>
> (From *China Daily*, 3 December 1983)

That the role of intellectuals in a large national undertaking should be the concern of a worker and a peasant as representatives to a conference (among hundreds of others) must fall outside the purview of this chapter, but the linguistic disposition of *workers*, *peasants* and *intellectuals* in that order (second paragraph) should be of interest. In the Chinese culture of today workers and peasants enjoy the image of real wealth-producers, with workers as the prime producers ranking first, peasants next, and intellectuals (whose role is only beginning to be recognized) last. This may also be seen in the way the speeches were arranged: the worker first, the peasant after him, and the intellectuals were being appreciated as it were *in absentia*. These linguistic nuances are likely to be lost on those not yet initiated into the Chinese cultural code.

The ideology-laden statement 'We workers have practical experience, but intellectuals have theoretical knowledge' actually contains two binary oppositions: practical vs. theoretical, and experience vs. knowledge. These can be looked at separately.

Practical vs. theoretical: Until quite recently, workers (and peasants) were thought to be doers of practical work; college graduates (intellectuals) had book knowledge which was suspect because it was untested by practical work. Such knowledge was by definition theoretical, however much practical work there was along with the teaching of such knowledge. The new point about his statement is that theoretical knowledge can itself be useful; in fact the speaker, himself (a worker), feels a need for it.

Experience vs. knowledge: The philosophy is, experience itself is as a rule something amorphous; it won't be knowledge except after it has been systematized. Yet there was a time when knowledge from education was identified as book knowledge and thought worthless; today knowledge has been given a more equitable place. A theoretical opposition, however, remains.

Sciences: Science is a word which is always spoken of with unreserved respect in China today, vaguely understood to be a do-all, cure-all formula, cherished by government leaders and working people alike, and so Wang Jiming, a peasant from Sichuan, said 'We need science in rural areas.' Often it means technical efficiency using some factory-produced chemical or school-taught method; it is a catchword brought in by the modernization drive, and it enjoys acceptance by faith.

Intellectuals: Edmund Wilson, I remember, once theorized on the difference between *intellectual* in American English and *intellectual* in Russian. Today in China (and apparently also in the Soviet Union) *intellectual* is a class (or semi-class) distinction rather than an educational or literary distinction, as it is in America.

Peasants: Why *peasants* instead of *farmers*? The distinction is deliberate. *Farmer* is thought to be a bourgeois concept: after all he can be a rich owner of some large farm. The word *peasant* has been carefully preserved by China's users of English, who see in him the image of one who labours on the land and whose fruits of labour are the nation's food. Four-fifths of China's huge population are peasants and it would be unimaginable to call them farmers.

Finally, why 'We workers'? Could that particular worker (Ma Liuhai) be using a domineering tone, as I imagine it would seem to an L1 user of English? In reality this has to do with a basic concept of the ideology: workers (that is, industrial workers) form the leading class of the state and their views on state affairs are held important. It would be wrong to imagine that Ma Liuhai was posing for 'making a statement'; no, he was just using an everyday expression in a political discussion.

However, whatever rationale I might offer for the above-discussed words, we have one working man here talking of practical experience and theoretical knowledge and intellectuals and all that, and another talking of agricultural science and the processing of farm produce, and I know both individuals must sound terribly insincere to the Western ear. Can there have been something wrong in the English used by our L2 newswriter, since neither the worker nor the peasant could have been quoted in English? The answer is, in the Chinese used by China's working people today, thanks to decades of mass education (largely orally conducted), many words which used to be of the academic register have switched to the colloquial register, so that although both working men were using a large number of what in English must appear to be academic words, they were in their Chinese context talking quite naturally, each using a common-core vocabulary, not too colloquial, but certainly not academic. This forms a very striking feature of the English in many China-based English-language journals; it is not a very welcome feature to the L1 readers, but there is no getting away from it with the L2 writer. In other words here we face a very serious problem of transmission.

I must now use a third passage about which I must confess I had considerable hesitation. This is because the passage has so many L2 words that my comments are likely to be little better than a glossary which may not be sociolinguistically interesting. But my second thoughts were more favourable: why not use that obscure passage after all, since it more than anything else will serve to bring out the L2 code in its stark outline?

Passage 3: A policy statement on China's united front

China's united front has expanded on an unprecedented scale, comprising not only all socialist labourers but also patriots who support socialism, and those who support the unification of the motherland – the broadest united front of patriots.

(From *China Daily*, 25 November 1982)

Certain glosses may be made right at the start to make the statement easier to understand.

United front – political coalition;
has expanded – has been broadened to take in more parties to the front;
socialist – dedicated to socialism;
those who support socialism – those who are willing to live in a socialist society without necessarily being dedicated to its fulfilment;
those who support the unification of the motherland – all people who support the policy of having Taiwan united to the motherland.

Translated into plainer language this means: China's united front has been broadened to include all people in Taiwan willing to return to the embrace of the motherland.

However, there still remain two words which need explanation.

Labourer: One who lives by his own labour, not on the labour of other people, hence one practising a great virtue in a socialist society, and for this reason enjoying great respect. The idea of a labourer as an unskilled working man is not found in L2 English.

Patriot: In L2 English the idea of love for one's country (to the point of giving one's life for it) is not necessarily predominant; it is rather the greatest common denominator of three kinds of people:

(1) those who live in China and are dedicated to socialism;
(2) those who live in China and support socialism;
(3) those who live outside the country but support the policy of Taiwan being united to the motherland.

All three display their love for China (in different ways it is true) and are patriots.

I believe I have provided a fair number of examples to show that there is a point in saying that such a thing as L2 English exists in an English-language publication in China. I hope I haven't been over-generalizing: I am only saying that this may be a worthwhile research point. I will now try to look at the problem from the opposite angle. Instead of investigating how L2 English may appear to a L1 reader, and what semantic nuances are likely to escape him, I will make a study of a passage from Bertrand Russell (1947: 509), an authentic L1 piece of English, to see what difficulties it presents for the L2 reader in China.

The modern world was born

During the 15th century, various other causes were added to the decline of the Papacy to produce a very rapid change, both political and cultural. Gunpowder strengthened central government at the expense of feudal nobility. In France and England, Louis XI and Edward IV allied themselves with the rich middle class, who helped them to quell aristocratic anarchy. Italy, until the last years of the century, was fairly free from Northern armies, and advanced rapidly both in wealth and culture. The new culture was essentially pagan, admiring Greece and Rome, and despising the Middle Ages. Architecture and literary style were adapted to ancient models. When Constantinople, the last survival of antiquity, was captured by the Turks, Greek refugees were welcomed by the humanists. Vasco da Gama and Columbus enlarged the world, and Copernicus enlarged the heavens. . . . In this moment of joyful liberation the modern world was born.

A History of Western Philosophy, London: Allen & Unwin, 1947

Assuming the role of a reader not yet fully initiated into L1, I will now ask the following questions of the Russell passage:

Why was the decline of the Papacy such an important happening? (Compare: why was the expansion of China's united front front-page news?)

How could gunpowder have strengthened central government? And what was feudal nobility? People or institution? This is maddeningly vague! (Compare: socialist labourer.)

The kings of France and England *allied themselves with the rich middle class* – but what was the middle class? Why are they rich? (Compare: what are the intellectuals? Why are they assumed to have theoretical knowledge?)

The new culture was essentially pagan – but why should *pagan* make for what was new? And what was *pagan* in the first place? (Compare: why should being *socialist* be held in such high esteem? And what is it to be socialist?)

Architecture and literary style were adapted to ancient models – but why should the modern man use ancient models for buildings and writings? He should have looked forward. (Compare: how can the Chinese have bracketed Shakespeare as traditional?)

In what ways can Copernicus have enlarged the heavens? (Compare: why is science so very important to a Chinese peasant?)

Finally, how could the modern world have been born as early as the 15th century? I would have thought the modern age came much later. (Compare: how strange that the Chinese should still cherish the word *peasant*!)

I am afraid that some, if not all, of my comparisons may seem irrelevant, but I think it only fair to allow for the difficulties that an L2 reader might experience with a piece of L1 English (however well written and however authoritative), and equally fair to allow for the difficulties that an L1 reader might run into in a piece of L2 English based on an entirely different pattern of culture. An L1 reader has every right to dislike L2 English, but I plead for the adaptability and understanding a modern man needs.

It is also fair to admit that there is room for improvement in L2 English. Thus *foreigners* may be replaced by, say, *overseas viewers*, or *colleagues from abroad*, and the letter to the editor might read a bit more smoothly, but some of the intellectual urge will be gone, and in the end elegance could be achieved at the expense of intent. With the discussion on the role of intellectuals, I don't think there is much to change: the two working men are certainly not using working-class language used as an L1, but I doubt if either speech can be rewritten into L1 working-class language without making a travesty of the whole discussion. As to the policy statement, that can perhaps be drastically reworded as 'China's united front policy has now been redefined to include Taiwan', and that, in fact, is the way most foreign newsmen choose to report of China. However, with a new wording the whole philosophy of the united front will be lost.

I think all cross-cultural discourse in English involves some form of translation – of names, of institutions, values, and their inter-relations; and when two cultures with widely different value-systems communicate, one is made acutely aware of difficulties of the task, and sometimes not without a sense of helplessness. It is a form of translation even though, as I said earlier, this writing was initially done in English and so there is always the question of translatability or lack of it.

So English, in spite of its currency and eminent adaptability as an international language, will necessarily have to leave many problems of cross-cultural discourse to its users from different cultures. Admittedly, an international language ought to have a communicable, cross-cultural load to bear, and a discussion of problems involved in its transmission should be worthwhile in itself. Here I have raised a problem without more than a few clues to a solution.

Bibliography

BASKIN, WADE (trans.) (1966) *Ferdinand De Saussure: course in general linguistics*. New York: McGraw-Hill.

BASSNETT-MCGUIRE, SUSAN (1980) Untranslatability. In *Translation studies*. New York: Methuen.

EMPSON, WILLIAM (1930). *Seven types of ambiguity*. London: Chatto and Windus.

HUDSON, R. A. (1980) Language, culture and thought. In *Sociolinguistics*. New York: Cambridge University Press.

WHORF, BENJAMIN LEE (1956) Science and linguistics. In *Language, thought and reality: selected writings of Benjamin Lee Whorf*, edited by J. B. Carroll. Cambridge, Mass.: Technology Press.

WITTEGENSTEIN, LUDWIG (1958) *Philosophical investigations*. Oxford: Blackwell.

XU, GUO-ZHANG (1980) Culturally-loaded words and English language teaching. In *Quarterly Journal of Guanzhou Institute of Foreign Languages*, December.

6

Discourse Structures and Discourse Expectations: Implications for Anglo-German Academic Communication in English[1]

MICHAEL CLYNE

EFFICIENT communication and mutual respect between academics are essential for scientific exchange. To an increasing extent, German-speaking scholars in most disciplines are expected to present conference papers and journal articles in English, the academic lingua franca. The decline of German as an international language in the West since World War II, the rise of international journals published wholly or largely in English, the development of international research centres across the Atlantic, and the alternation of conference venues are all symptomatic of this reality. In Eastern Europe, German still functions more as an international language, and contact with Anglo-American scholarship is not always so extensive.

Most graduates in the Federal Republic of Germany (FRG) will have taken at least nine years of English at school,[2] and tourism, pop culture, and the media, as well as the reading of specialized literature, provide further input of English. While this facilitates their fluency and command of English grammar and phonology, the graduates can and do encounter problems at the discourse level when they have to write English. To begin with, the expectations of acceptable discourse structures may be different in English- and German-speaking countries. These expectations will be the starting-point for this chapter, in which I will also outline a recently commenced project that attempts to examine the nature of cultural differences in discourse structures and expectations. It is hoped that the parameters proposed for this study may have some general validity for English as an international language.

ESSAY WRITING NORMS[3]

The expectations of good discourse are transmitted through the education system. This is particularly so in Britain and Australia, where the essay is the

73

main medium of examination in upper secondary school as well as in tertiary institutions, and a great deal of emphasis is placed *throughout the curriculum* on the techniques of essay writing. In the US, the stress on essay writing seems to come somewhat later, i.e. 1st year college. In continental Europe, oracy tends to be stressed, and knowledge is largely tested orally. Essay writing is primarily a language exercise.

A comparison between English- and German-language school essay norms derived from manuals and educational articles[4] reveals the following expectations of discourse in English that are not present in German:

(1) In English the aim of the essay should be deduced strictly from the wording of the topic or question, which needs to be defined at the beginning. In German, the question is usually more general, and can even be adjusted (as Standop, 1965, points out for the tertiary level). Its definition is generally taken as read.

(2) In English, *relevance* is advocated as the primary virtue to be aimed at in the construction of an essay.

(3) The end of one paragraph must lead on to the beginning of the next. By introducing facts or ideas that do not contribute to linear progression, the unity of the discourse is broken. Each paragraph should begin with a topic sentence. In German, a logical progression is also required from introduction to conclusion, but there appear to be few explicit limitations on inclusion of material.

(4) Repetition is deemed undesirable in English, whereas in German, where digressions are tolerated more, a logical development may entail more recapitulation (thereby increasing the length of the text).

Of course, boundaries may be vague and norms are not necessarily followed to the letter.

EXAMINATIONS

If Australia is at all typical of English-speaking countries, adherence to particular discourse patterns in such countries is an essential requirement of the essays which form all or most of the examinations in practically every subject. This was revealed in a study of four years of examiners' reports for the Higher School Certificate (external high school graduation) examination in the state of Victoria. Examiners generally argued for linearity in structure and 'relevance' (i.e. narrow limits to the area dictated by the wording of the question). A few representative examples:

'Clearly many candidates had either a general knowledge of the topic . . . or a thorough specific knowledge. . . . But just having such information is not what is required by most HSC essays . . . those who write controlled relevant essays will always be appropriately advantaged.' (18th-century history) (VUSEB, 1978)

'Lack of relevance remains the main cause of failure' (Politics).

A Biology report found that 'Rather than answer in structural terms, many resorted to circular arguments' (VUSEB, 1972).

'Plenty of essay-writing practice', so advised the History examiners, 'will train students to marshal their ideas in an orderly fashion.'

An analysis of examiners' handwritten comments on 400 History papers, sometimes with recourse to the actual papers, showed the same pattern. Failed essays and those on the borderline frequently received comments on the organization (incoherent; confused and irrelevant; very jumbled; irrelevant; disoriented; disorganized; rambling) rather than on the content of the essays.

SCHOOL ASSIGNMENTS

A comparison of one set of upper secondary school assignments each in three subjects, from different Australian and FRG schools, together with marks and teachers' comments, yielded the following results:

(i) The best marks were given in Australia to essays with the highest degree of linearity, and low marks were awarded to those with digressive or more circular discourse patterns, regardless of the content. The prerequisites for something to be judged acceptable, logical or coherent are thus influenced by a particular discourse pattern.

(ii) The German assignments were accepted even in note or point form (i.e. incomplete sentences). There was a striking freedom of format. The emphasis in both pupils' work and teachers' corrections was on content learning and the reiteration of knowledge rather than on discussion and analysis. The teachers' changes were minimal and involved primarily content deficiencies, lexical and grammatical errors, and register. A large amount of repetition was tolerated. 'Relevance' was mentioned only where a pupil failed to refer to the most important issues.

This does not necessarily mean that linearity is not regarded as a virtue in Germany, but it is not nearly as important there as in Australia, where it is a key objective of years of drill in essay-writing techniques. I will attempt to summarize the problem in terms of four indices of cultural differences.

FORMAL RULES

The relative importance of the formal rules of communication in Anglo-Celtic cultures as opposed to those of the German-speaking countries can be seen in the conduct of formal meetings. Trade unions, school parents' association meetings and even hobby clubs in English-speaking countries tend to adhere to rules based on the Westminster parliamentary conventions. This is borne out by a comparison – by questionnaire and observation – between meeting routines in twenty general Australian and twenty comparable (social, cultural, religious, sporting, welfare) organizations in each of four ethnic groups (Dutch, German, Greek, Italian) (Clyne and Manton, 1979). 'General Australian' meeting rules often have an alienating effect on immigrants, even those with a good knowledge of English. The need for adherence to strict formal rules is common to verbal communication (as in meetings) and written communication (as in essays and academic discourse). In German-speaking countries, on the other hand, any suggestion that knowledge may be less acceptable because of the way in which it is presented would border on sacrilege.

LINEARITY VS. DIGRESSIVENESS

In his study of the essays of foreign students in the US, Kaplan (1972) contrasted Anglo-Saxon linearity ➝ with a number of other culturally based structures:

(1) Parallel constructions, with the first idea completed in the second part:

(2) Circularity, with the topic looked at from different tangents.

(3) Freedom to digress and introduce 'extraneous' material.

(4) Similar to (3) but with different lengths, parenthetical amplifications, and an abrupt stop.

(Kaplan, 1972: 257)

While Kaplan links his discourse types with genetic language types (Semitic, Oriental, Romance, Russian respectively), German discourse structures, I would argue, tend towards (3) and (4),[5] and those of French probably towards Anglo-Saxon ones. The cultural rather than genetic-linguistic foundations of discourse structure differences is demonstrated in our study of meeting routines. Such rules for meetings in English-speaking countries as only one motion being allowed before the chair at a time, which represent linearity in discourse, are not generally followed in German-Australian organizations (Clyne and Manton, 1979).

In Germany, digressions in discourse have been institutionalized in the form of lengthy *Exkurse* which form part of academic books and dissertations. It should be noted, however, that with the strong interest in philosophy in German-speaking countries, and the recent influence of Marxism on the social sciences and humanities, even in the Federal Republic, dialectics play an important role in argumentation. (This was so even in a set of secondary school essays analysed.) Dialectic argumentation renders linear structures more difficult, and some writers develop spiral-type structures to reflect the structure of the argument.

INCLUSION AND EXCLUSION OF MATERIAL

As I have already mentioned, the topic of written discourse is often narrowly defined in English-speaking countries, and the degree of tolerance as to what can be included is not very great. Of course, this question is relative, and there is a point at which something may be dismissed in German, too, as being outside the area under discussion. However, in the evaluation of the essays analysed, German teachers would comment on the exclusion of essential material but not on the inclusion of 'extraneous' material. Just as Anglo-Saxon rules outlaw structural digressions, they also disallow content digressions (designated as 'irrelevance'). To continue our analogy with meeting routines, the chairman's prerogative of ruling out of order something that is not relevant is rarely exercised in German or German-Australian meetings (a reflection of both the chairman's role and the discourse rules).

The majority of German-Australian organizations studied (Clyne and Manton, 1979) do not allow business to be hurried up by moving 'that the motion now be put'. This may be an indication of *cultural differences in discourse tempo*, for in academic texts, too, German-educated scholars will not infrequently write at length on a sub-topic that is of subsidiary importance to the main argument (cf. in other contexts, Grimes, 1976; Elzinga, 1978; Barkowski *et al.*, 1976).

LITERACY VS. ORACY

Some societies are more verbal, others more literate in orientation. This division, too, is propagated by the requirements of the education system. In Australia, some of the most capable upper secondary and university students, who write well, are reluctant to express their thoughts orally. This could be attributed to 'egalitarian' principles ('don't show off your knowledge') and to the emphasis on essay writing. American students are trained far more in oral expression, while their German counterparts have tended to demonstrate their general knowledge and expertise in public exhibitions of eloquence (see below). However, there are indications that this has changed in the generation following the post-1968 student movement (see e.g. Greiner, 1982).

'ACADEMIC REGISTER' IN ENGLISH AND GERMAN

When the English-speaking student reaches the university, s/he is usually equipped with formal rules for the production of written discourse (including linearity and 'relevance') to which s/he will not only need to adhere, but which s/he will expect others to follow. Students from other cultural or educational systems must urgently learn to present material this way – something that their fellows have had most of their schooling to do – or risk failure.

The value of a piece of academic writing may not be appreciated unless it follows the rules. Academics may judge the work of their peers by these criteria. And yet, academics correcting the English of their non-native-speaker colleagues will often be unaware of problems with discourse rules and simply make lexical and syntactic changes. On the other hand, 'errors' in discourse rules will sometimes be written off as illogicalities or bad style, just as non-adherence to Anglo-Saxon meeting rules is seen as an indication of totalitarian behaviour.

It should not be assumed that German discourse pays no attention to form. The student entering a German university does not know or follow most of the Anglo-Saxon essay rules. S/he is, however, in the process of acquiring an academic register of the kind described in various papers in Bungarten (1981). Apart from *Fachsprache*, the technical terms of the discipline concerned, the German academic register is marked by:

(a) Agentless passives, and impersonal and reflexive constructions (Polenz, 1981; Panther, 1981),[6]

    e.g. A's allgemeiner Begriff *empfiehlt sich*
         (A's general concept *recommends itself*)

(b) Hedged performatives using modals *kann*, *muß* and *darf* and passive infinitives (Panther, 1981),

      e.g. Wir *können* allgemeine Übereinstimmung *voraussagen*
           (We *can predict* general agreement)
           Ein Kreis von Entscheidungen ist *zuskennzeichnen* als Aggression.
           (A group of decisions is *to be characterized* as aggression)

'Empty' discourse markers, such as

    Es fragt sich, ob . . .
    (literally 'It asks itself if . . .')

are prevalent.

(c) Many nominalizations and compound nouns (Polenz, 1963).
(d) Syntactic complexity – although Beneš's (1981) sample of 100 sentences from each of ten disciplines bears this out only for sociology and linguistics (and not for chemistry, zoology, medicine, technology, history, mathematics, and logic).

German syntactic constructions not shared with English – participial clauses and left-branching embedding – contribute greatly to the variation between the 'learned' and 'ordinary' registers, e.g.

    die *als fast paradoxes Bewußtseinsphänomen zu bewertende* Tatsache
    ('the   as (an) almost paradoxical consciousness phenomenon to be evaluated fact').

(Participial clause – A more 'ordinary' alternative would be the formation of a relative clause)

DEPENDENT CLAUSE 1	DEPENDENT CLAUSE 2
. . . daß diese Veröffentlichung,	die erst jetzt, wo die
('that this publication	which only now when the

DEPENDENT CLAUSE 3	VERB OF DEPENDENT CLAUSE 3
Ergebnisse schon ohnehin bekannt sind,	erschienen ist . . .
results already anyhow known are	appeared has')

(Left-branching embedding – A more 'ordinary' alternative would be to let clause 3 follow clause 2. This would avoid the clustering of verbs at the end.)

The above constructions force the flow of one's thoughts to be interrupted, something that contradicts the principle of linearity.

The kind of patterns I am referring to are exemplified not only in the total structure of Fritz Schütze's *Sprache soziologisch gesehen* (1975) but also in many individual sentences in it. Here is one instance:

Die intellektuellen Impulse der Kaderelite als Avantgarde des Proletariats oder umgekehrt die als fast paradoxes Bewußtseinsphänomen zu bewertende Tatsache, daß aus den materiellen Bedingungen der bürgerlichen Lebensweise hervorgangene Gesellschaftsmitglieder sich einer dieser bürgerlichen Lebensweise und ihren Interessen zuwiderlaufenden gesellschaftspolitischen Tätigkeit zuwenden, und die erhoffte, das materielle Lebensmilieu der Unterschichten transzendierende Bewußtseinslage der revolutionären Massen in Wohlstandsgesellschaften, die ja kein materielles Massenelend mehr kennen und deshalb auch eine revolutionäre Bewußtseinslage nicht rein materiellökonomisch erzwingen – diese Bewußtseinsphänomene lassen sich ja nicht mit der materialistischen Widerspiegelungstheorie erklären.

(The intellectual impulses of the cadre élite as an avantgarde of the proletariat or, expressed conversely, the fact – which in itself is an almost paradoxical phenomenon of consciousness – that members of society emerging from material conditions of bourgeois living, turn to a socio-political activity which runs counter to this bourgeois living and its interests – and the level of consciousness that was hoped for, transcending the material milieu of the lower classes, of the revolutionary masses in wealthy societies which no longer know mass poverty and can therefore not enforce a revolutionary conscience level on purely material, economic grounds – these phenomena of conscience simply cannot be explained in terms of a materialist reflection theory.)

This sentence contains four participial clauses, each of which encapsulates one set of ideas in a compact surface structure NP compartment used as part of a dialectic argument. The first facilitates the contrast between 'intellectual impulses' and the 'almost paradoxical phenomenon' he discusses. The second and third provide an antithesis between members of society from bourgeois environments and their sociopolitical activities. The fourth – 'transcending the material milieu of the lower classes' – gives the synthesis. Schütze constructs one relative clause, which represents a digression from the main argument of the paragraph (to the 'wealthy societies'). At this point he neglects to add the verb to complete the previous clause, depriving it of its intended meaning. In order to return to the main argument, he has to form a new summarizing, partly reiterative, main clause.

While Anglo-Saxon academics may miss linearity and 'relevance' in German discourse, and characterize German academic register as heavy, longwinded or even incoherent, German academics may seek in vain for lexical and syntactic markers of a general academic register in the publications of most English-speaking scholars. Such a register conveys the image of being learned and saying something scientifically significant. It is in this academic register that students and staff 'perform' (or 'have performed') in German university seminars as they digress from the central theme to a related one in which they have special expertise. As I have mentioned, there appear to be changes towards a less articulate, less exhibitionist type of behaviour. Both English and German academic texts not only present information about the topic; they also transmit a message about the writer. The English-speaking scholar wishes, above all, to show that his/her argument is well thought out; the German-speaking counterpart presents his/her credentials as a *Wissenschaftler*.

In connection with the preliminary study of essay routines, a spot check was made of reviews of two German books on sociolinguistics. Only reviewers from English-speaking countries commented on the discourse structures (Clyne, 1981). If English- and German-educated scholars apply different criteria to judge the acceptability of academic writings, and cultural differences make them susceptible to such judgements, international academic exchange and co-operation may suffer.

Bungarten (1981) shows that, apart from its primary cognitive and communication functions, academic register signals group solidarity. That being the case, a German academic might present a paper in a particular register to express solidarity with the international audience and find them switching off *because* of that register. Internationalization has, however, led to some alleviation of differences, with the natural and behavioural sciences on the continent adapting more to Anglo-Saxon structures, and 'Anglo-Saxon' scholars in literary theory and some social sciences adopting academic 'in-group' registers of the German type. The latter applies especially to certain theoretically oriented schools. The role of immigrant scholars in the US in this development needs to be examined.

RESEARCH PROJECT

I have embarked on a more ambitious project. I am attempting to study:

(1) the nature of 'English' and 'German' patterns on what can be included and what should be excluded from an academic text;
(2) the extent to which the organization of academic discourse written by German- and English-educated scholars varies; and
(3) whether non-linear discourse is, in fact, perceived as harder to follow, even by people who produce it themselves and/or do not have a cultural distaste for it.

The first step is to collect and analyse data – comparable conference papers and articles, in English and German – by English- and German-educated scholars in two disciplines, linguistics, and sociology. Both English and German discourse by the German-educated are required in order to establish to what extent the non-observance of English discourse rules is due to interference from L1 discourse routines, and to what extent they are markers of the writer's interlanguage. Questionnaires and interviews will be used to test authors' perceptions of their discourse, and any possible modifications according to audience. Of particular interest are scholars who are conscious of cultural differences in discourse models and (re)structure their material differently according to audience.

The following seem to have emerged as possible differences relating to linearity:

   (i) German-educated scholars are less likely than their English-educated counterparts to lead the reader through the text in an introductory section.

  (ii) They are also less likely to develop the first section from the title.

 (iii) While the paragraphs of English speakers tend to begin with topic sentences, those of German speakers rather commence with bridge sentences.

 (iv) Some German educated linguists list their examples at the end of a section rather than integrating them in the text.

MODELS

Of course, an essential for this kind of research is the development of a model for analysis and description. Ehlich (1982) points out that students of 'textual sciences' do not enjoy the advantages of coming into a field with existing tools, methods and parameters. The methods I am seeking would need to distinguish hierarchical and spatial relations for *broad* aspects of discourse organization. Unlike most existing models, this would have to build on propositions rather than discourse markers, and deal with semantic and pragmatic constraints on linearization. Perception and expectations, as well as production, would have to be accounted for. Perhaps Van Dijk (1977) could be used as a basis for extension.

Since linearity and digressiveness have played a significant role in this discussion, studies of linearization – such as Levelt (1981), Linde and Labov (1975), Ullmer-Ehlich (1979), Klein (1979), and Senft (1982) – could provide useful input. It should be noted, however, that these studies were conducted from a monolingual/monocultural perspective. In his general paper, Levelt (1981) gives three criteria for linearization:

   (i) maximization of connectivity;

  (ii) returns to choice items made in first-in, last-out fashion;

 (iii) minimization of the load of memorizing return addreses.

On the basis of descriptions of machines by Kaiserslautern factory workers, Senft (1982: 384) challenges the 'maximum connectivity' criterion. The workers frequently digressed. What is not clear is whether class, educational or cultural factors influence the application of Levelt's criterion. Other psycholinguists such as Kintsch and Rumelhart could add perspectives such as memory, attention and consciousness to the discussion.

FURTHER QUESTIONS

There are innumerable questions to be answered in this field. What aspects of sociocultural history explain which differences in discourse organization? How much do nations using pluricentric languages (e.g. the US, Britain, Canada, Australia) deviate? Have different political organization and international realignment affected differences in discourse structures (e.g. in East and West Germany)? And there are many more.

If the assumptions on which I am working are correct, then ESP and foreign language courses would need to place more emphasis on the higher levels of discourse. In an international network employing English, all the participants must be given the opportunity to have their contributions judged on their merit. So it is up to academics from English and non-English educational backgrounds to learn to understand and respect one another's discourse patterns.

Notes

1. This research is supported by an ARGS Grant. I thank Gisela Tiemann-Kaplan for research assistance.
2. Six years in Austria and Switzerland.
3. This topic is dealt with more comprehensively in Clyne (1980).
4. Anderson (1971), Britain; Chessell (1976), Australia; Edwards (1975), Australia; Brunnen and Dorstal (n.d.), FRG; Eder (1976), Austria; Hoppe (1976), FRG; Killinger (1969–75), Austria.
5. Peter Ellinger has suggested to me that Modern Israeli discourse structures are also of these types.
6. In his contrastive study of English and German fine arts texts, Lodge (1982) pinpoints relations between different grammatical choices (e.g. German: reflexives, English: passives) and the way in which the authors view their objects of study.

References

ANDERSON, W. E. K. (1971) *The written word: some uses of English*. Oxford: Oxford University Press.

BARKOWSKI, H., U. HARNISCH, and S. KRUMM (1976) Sprachhandlungstheorie und Gastarbeiterdeutsch. *Linguistische Berichte* 45: 42–56.

BENEŠ, E. (1981) Die formale Struktur der wissenschaftlichen Fachsprache in syntaktischer Hinsicht. In Bungarten (1981), pp. 185–212.

BRUNNEN, E. and T. DORSTAL (n.d.) *Der deutsche Aufsatz*. 2 vols. Wünsiedel.

BUNGARTEN, T. (ed.) (1981) *Wissenschaftssprache*. München: Fink.

CHESSELL, P. (1976) *Essay writing: a guide*. Melbourne.

CLYNE, M. G. (1980) Writing, testing and culture. *The Secondary Teacher* 11: 13–16.

CLYNE, M. G. (1981) Culture and discourse structure. *Journal of Pragmatics* **5**: 61–66.

CLYNE, M. G. and S. I. MANTON (1979) Routines for conducting meetings in Australia: an inter-ethnic study. *Ethnic Studies* **3**(1): 25–34.

EDER, A. (1976) Texttheoretisches zum Aufsatzunterricht. *Wiener Linguistische Gazette* **12**: 25–56.

EDWARDS, H. (1975) *Writing better essays: study manual*. Geelong.

EHLICH, K. (1982) Tekst over Tekst. *Openbare Redes. Tilburg Studies in Language and Literature* **3**: 7–33. Tilburg.

ELZINGA, R. H. (1978) Temporal organization of conversation. *Sociolinguistics newsletter* **9**(2): 29–31.

GREINER, U. (1982) Gezielte Flucht. *Die Zeit*, 17 December. **50**: 17–18.

GRIMES, J. E. (1976) *The thread of discourse*. The Hague: Mouton.

HOPPE, O. (1976) Thesen zur Aufsatzbeurteilung. *Linguistische Berichte* **45**: 70–76.

KAPLAN, R. B. (1972) Cultural thought patterns in inter-cultural education. In *Readings on English as a Second Language*, edited by K. Croft, pp. 245–262. Cambridge, Mass.: Winthrop.

KILLINGER, R. (1969–75) *Sprachübungen für allgemein-bildende höhere Schulen* (3 vols). Vienna.

KLEIN, W. (1979) Wegauskünfte. *Zeitschrift für Literaturwissenschaft und Linguistik* **9**: 9–57.

LEVELT, W. J. M. (1981) The speakers linearization problem. *Philosophical Transactions of the Royal Society of London. B*. London.

LINDE, C. and W. F. LABOV (1975) Spatial networks as a site for the study of language and thought. *Language* **51**: 929–939.

LODGE, K. (1982) Transitivity, transformation and text in art-historical German. *Journal of Pragmatics* **6**, 159–184.

PANTHER, K. U. (1981) Einige typische indirekte sprachliche Handlungen im wissenschaftlichen Diskurs. In Bungarten (1981), pp. 231–260.

POLENZ, P. v. (1963) *Funktionsverben im heutigen Deutsch*. Düsseldorf.

POLENZ, P. v. (1981) Uber die Jargonisierung von Wisenschaftssprache und wider die Deagentivierung. In Bungarten (1981), pp. 85–110.

SCHÜTZE, F. (1975) *Sprache soziologisch gesehen*, vol. 1. München.

SENFT, G. (1982) *Sprachliche Varietät und Variation im Sprachverhalten Kaiserslauterner Metallarbeiter*. Bern.

STANDOP, E. (1965) *Die Form der wissenschaftlichen Arbeit*, 4th edn. Dortmund.

ULLMER-EHRICH, V. (1979) Wohnraumbeschreibungen. *Zeitschrift für Literaturwissenschaft und Linguistik* **9**: 58–83.

VAN DIJK, T. (1977) *Text und Context*. London: Longman.

VUSEB (1972–74–76–78) *Reports of examiners: Higher school certificate examinations*. Melbourne.

PART III

Text, Context and Culture

INTRODUCTION

THE three chapters in this section provide a logical next step from the first two sections: the relationship of text, context, and culture. The texts are primarily from three Asian cultures and clearly demonstrate that the discourse strategies are deeply embedded in cultural matrices. Y. Kachru illustrates how cultural patterns are realized in the syntactic structures and rhetorical conventions of cross-cultural texts. She identifies points of potential misinterpretations of such texts by speakers of other varieties of English. In her view, readers of such texts ideally need three types of competence: linguistic, cultural, and textual. The text, then, has to be interpreted and explained to students within the appropriate context of situation.

The chapter on *aizuchi* by LoCastro is a contrastive study in conventional outlines of back-channelling in two cultures – Japanese and American. Even the restricted data of her study confirms her hypothesis that native speakers of Japanese use *aizuchi* more frequently and in greater varieties than Americans use back-channelling when speaking English. She shows that bilingual Japanese tend to make less use of the formal equivalent of this strategy in English than in their native language, Japanese. What is the importance of *aizuchi*? This strategy is an exponent of group harmony and the Japanese value system. In language teaching and learning, awareness about the conventions of back-channelling is an essential part of communicative competence.

The chapter by Dissanayake and Nichter focuses on a previously unexplored aspect of Sri Lanka English texts. The broad issues it raises are more or less the same as raised by Y. Kachru and LoCastro. Using examples from Punyakante Wijenaike, a well-known contemporary Sri Lankan writer, the authors show how metaphor, referential frameworks, and tacit literary conventions of Sri Lanka are incorporated into Wijenaike's English fiction.

These three chapters will no doubt be of interest to a large audience since they raise questions which directly relate to curriculum designers, teacher trainers, and textbook writers.

7

Cross-cultural Texts, Discourse Strategies and Discourse Interpretation

YAMUNA KACHRU

A SIGNIFICANT part of recent research in discourse analysis has been concerned with the problem of understanding the relationship between language and cognition by attempting to answer the questions of whether and how culture influences thought patterns (e.g. Scribner, 1979; Tannen, 1980). There are several positions one might take with respect to these questions, as is evident from the controversy surrounding the Whorfian hypothesis. As a linguist searching for universals and an applied linguist interested in translation, I assume that there are no differences in underlying cognitive processes among various populations; the differences are in conventionalization of appropriate rhetorical forms in different languages and cultures.[1] This does not mean that I am denying the real observable differences in habitual ways of producing and interpreting discourse in different cultures. In fact, this chapter examines selected aspects of these habitual ways of producing discourse in Indian English and discusses the problems in interpretation these discourse strategies may create for speakers of other varieties of English.

I am using 'cross-cultural texts' to refer to a body of texts bilinguals (or multilinguals) produce in a transplanted language in a speech community that does not share the native cultural contexts of the transplanted language. The texts written in Persian by the Indians in medieval times, and in English by the indigenous peoples of Africa, Asia, and other parts of the world in their own, un-English socio-cultural contexts, are good examples of such cross-cultural texts. These texts have a number of properties not shared by texts produced by monolinguals in monolingual speech communities (B. Kachru, 1982; Taiwo, 1976, and other works dealing with world varieties of English). This will become clearer as we proceed with the discussion of Indian English texts in this chapter.

I am using 'interpretation' to refer to something that is different from mere decoding of a text. Interpretation involves, in addition to decoding, the imposition of one's own knowledge, experience, beliefs, and expectations on what one reads.[2] In this chapter I am interested in identifying those factors which have a bearing on interpreting Indian English texts.

For convenience of exposition, the chapter is organized as follows. First, a selected range of differences between the syntactic structures of English and those of major Indic languages are very briefly discussed. The focus is on factors such as clausalization and subjecthood (Bernardo, 1980). This is followed by a brief description of the rhetorical conventions in major Indic languages. A number of examples from Indian writings in English are then presented to demonstrate how syntactic structures and rhetorical conventions of Indic languages are reflected in Indian English texts. Several of the same characteristics are shown to occur in the English translations of Indic language texts by native speakers of English. Finally, the factors that enter into interpreting Indian English texts are clearly identified.

'CLAUSE' AND 'SUBJECT' IN HINDI

According to Bernardo (1980), discourse largely involves the expression of conceptual material such as one's knowledge, beliefs, on-going perceptions, memories of past experiences, etc. When the conceptual material is activated or brought to consciousness, it is in unified chunks with names such as 'our vacation', 'my sister's wedding', 'the nuclear freeze movement', etc. There are two sorts of elements in these chunks: (1) individuals and (2) states, processes, actions, experiences, etc. In encoding these chunks into language, the writer has to sub-chunk a large piece into smaller units so that the relationships between these two types of element are clearly expressed. This process of sub-chunking is not automatic: different participants describe the same event in different ways, and the same person may describe the same event in different ways at different times. The process of sub-chunking is directly involved in encoding events in clauses and also in the choice of subjects for the clauses. A 'minichunk', i.e. a sub-chunk conceived as a single state, process or action, is usually expressed as a clause in English. One of the component individuals in the minichunk is selected as the subject of the clause. This is the individual that has a higher degree of prior activation in the consciousness of the writer and a human or causal role in the event.[3] Other things being equal, the subject is also the theme or topic of the sentence and occurs as the left-most constituent of the sentence in English (Halliday, 1967–68).

Although the process of sub-chunking is universal, the conventions of clausal encoding and subject selection differ from language to language (Sridhar, 1980). For instance, unlike English, the major Indic languages prefer to express a series of temporally sequential events in one clause.[4] Consider the following examples from Hindi.[5]

(1)

jaldii se	ghar	aakar	haath-mūh	dho	kar	parhne	*baiṭh jaao*
quickly	home	having come	hand face	having washed	to	read	sit down

Come home and *wash* yourself quickly and (then) *sit down* to study.

(2) vah   tumhaare   kahne   par   bhii   dillii   pahŭcte   hii   sumit
    he   your   saying on   even   Delhi   arriving   as soon as Sumit
    se   mil   kar   sab   baatē   tay karne ko   taiyaar   nahīī   *hai*
    with   having   met   all   matters deciding for   ready   not   is

Although you *asked* him/(her) to, (s)he *is* not ready to meet Sumit and settle everything as soon as (s)he *arrives* in Delhi.

In the Hindi examples above, we have just as many clauses underlyingly as in the English translation equivalents. On the surface, however, English requires at least three clauses in each as compared to only one clause in Hindi (the finite verbs that are obligatory constituents of the English and Hindi clauses are italicized.[6]

As regards subjecthood, unlike English, Indic languages have a low subject number (Keenan, 1976; Y. Kachru *et al.*, 1976; Y. Kachru, 1983; Pandhari-pande, 1981, 1983; Sridhar, 1976). They allow for sentences with no grammatical subjects or marginal grammatical subjects as in the following.

(3) baahar   thaṇḍ   hai
    outside   cold   iṣ

It is cold outside.

(4) dhuup   mē garmii   nahīī   hai
    sun   in heat   not   is

There is no warmth in the sun(light).

(5) mez   par   kitaab   hai
    table   on   book   is

There is a book on the table.

(6) kaar   mē   koii   aadmii   hai
    car   in   some   man   is

There is a man in the car.

Also, there is a subjecthood hierarchy in Indic languages which works as follows. Sentences that express a volitional act require an agent-subject, whereas a major class of sentences that express non-volitional processes and states have as subjects a noun with dative or some other case marking. Only the active agent subjects – whether unmarked or marked with an agentive marking – have all the behavioural properties of a grammatical subject (Keenan, 1976). The dative, instrumental, and genitive marked subjects have fewer subject properties, and the locative marked subject has no subject properties (Pandharipande, 1981; Verma, 1976). A comparison of the following Hindi sentences with their English translation equivalents will clarify the notion of case marked subjects.

(7) ramesh   kavitaa   likh   rahaa   hai[7]
    Ramesh   poem   write   ing   is

Ramesh is writing a poem.

(8) ushaa   ko   buxaar   thaa
    Usha   dat.   fever   was
    (f)   (m)   (m)

Usha had a fever

(9) ramesh   ko   bhuukh   lag   rahii   hai
    Ramesh   dat.   hunger   feel   ing   is
    (m)   (f)   (f)

Ramesh is feeling hungry.

(10) mujhko   sab   baatē   yaad   haī
     me dat.   all   matters   memory   are

I remember everything.

(11) meraa   iraadaa   hai   ki   ek axbaar   nikaalūū
     my   intention   is   that   a newspaper   bring out

I intend to publish a newspaper.

(12) uske   sir   mē   dard   hai
     his/   head   in   ache   is
     her

(S)He has a headache.

Notice that, in English, the sentences in (7)–(12) all have an unmarked subject. In contrast, in Hindi, only sentence (7) has an unmarked active subject. Sentences (8)–(10) have dative subjects, sentence (11) has a genitive subject and in sentence (12) we have a possessive phrase with a locative postposition, 'in his/her head'. Sentences (8), (10), (11), and (12) express non-volitional states while sentence (9) concerns a process and sentence (7) an action.

The clausalization and subjecthood facts discussed here have important consequences for discourse coherence. Also involved in discourse coherence are the tense-aspect-mood systems and anaphoric processes in Hindi, which have been described elsewhere (Y. Kachru, 1983). The role of these grammatical features in discourse structure is discussed in the section on Indian English texts in some detail.[8]

DISCOURSE IN INDIC LANGUAGES

The limited research heretofore in the area of contrastive discourse analysis (e.g. Kaplan, 1980; Y. Kachru, 1983; Pandharipande, 1983) links the strategies of expository discourse structure in different languages to popular conventions of logic in their respective cultures. For instance, an ideal English expository paragraph is often described as having a straight linear progression, from the topic sentence in the beginning to the last sentence of the conclusion, a preferred structure said to be derived from a Platonic-Aristotelian model (Kaplan, 1966; see also Clyne, this volume). As opposed to this, Hindi and Marathi have been shown to have a spiral-like and a circular structure respectively (Y. Kachru, 1983; Pandharipande, 1983).[9] The paragraph structures in Indic languages have been linked to the tradition of oral narratives in these languages (Y. Kachru, 1983; Pandharipande, 1983). Furthermore, it has been demonstrated that the patterns that occur in Hindi also occur in the English written by Hindi speakers, no matter how high their competence in English (Y. Kachru, 1983). That the Indic patterns of discourse structure also appear in English writings by speakers of other Indic languages is clear from the examples in the next section.

DISCOURSAL AND STYLISTIC CONVENTIONS IN IE TEXTS

The following paragraph from an Indian English expository text exemplifies the deviations from native varieties of English that are observable in the South Asian variety of English.

1. Sanskrit, the classical language of India, has had a history	1
of four thousand years in this country, its earliest literature, the
hymns of the *Rigveda*, being also the oldest and most extensive remains
of Indo-European literature. The antiquity of Sanskrit is well known
but its continuity is not less remarkable. In the same accents in which the	5
Vedic seer uttered, his mantra is even now intoned; and in the same
cadence and diction in which Kalidasa and Bana composed, a Sanskritist
today writes his verse or prose. The Vedic dialects, the freedom of
the popular epic style, the rules for the spoken word in Panini's
grammar, the diction of early drama, all point to a period when Sanskrit	10
was a living, spoken tongue. When out of its dialects a literary norm
got standardised and the early primary Prakrits were coming into increasing literary use, Sanskrit still continued to hold its authoritative
position; for, as observed by the latest writer on the language,
'though it appears paradoxical at first sight, the Sanskrit language only	15
reached its full development as a language of culture and administration
at a time when it had ceased to be a mother tongue.' Buddhism and Jainism
which started with using the popular languages, could not by-pass
Sanskrit to which they had eventually to come. Sanskrit consolidated
itself as a pan-Indian language by reason of the common culture and thought	20
it embodied; the mother of most of the mother-tongues of the country,
it was and is still the strongest bond of the country's unity (Raghavan,
1957: 201).

Note the use of the adversative 'but' and the phrasal negative 'not less remarkable' so close together in the second sentence; the use of *utter* as a 'deletable transitive' verb in the third sentence (line 6); and the adverb preposing, more appropriate in affective styles of writing, similar to inversions, in the two clauses of the third sentence (lines 5 and 6) and the fifth sentence (line 11). All these are deviant from the native norms. According to Green (1982), the use of inversions in expository prose by native speakers of English is unlikely if not totally unattested. In fact, the whole tone of the paragraph is oratorical rather than expository. The factors that are responsible for this tone have largely to do with the structure of clauses and the combining of clauses into sentences. Note that what seem to be inversions according to the native norms of English may not be inversions in Indian English; the order of the prepositional phrase and the rest of the clause in lines 5, 6, and 11 would be unmarked in most Indic languges. Additionally, an affective style, not appropriate in expository prose according to native norms of English, is not unusual in Indic language scholarly texts, especially in the genre of literary criticism.

The greater toleration of digression that characterizes Indic language texts can be seen in the following example of Indian English expository prose.

2. Among Indian languages Kannada is next only to Sanskrit and Tamil   1
in its antiquity **and** its claims for attention, however, are not based
only on its antiquity. Writers who can be called great from a comparative
point of view have written in Kannada, **and** one of the most striking
features of Kannada literature is its ability to assimilate influences.   5
Even the earliest extant evidence of the literary uses of the language,
the inscriptions from the 5th century A.D. onwards, show the influences
of Sanskrit language and literature on Kannada. In its openness to influences Kannada contrasts with its sister language, Tamil. Unlike Tamil,
Kannada has no 'indigenous' epics, **and** the first extant book in the   10
language *Kavirájámárga*, a book on poetics written by Sri Vijaya, a court
poet of the Rashtrakuta king Nrpatumga, of the 9th century A.D., refers
to some Kannada versions of the *Ramayana* which are now lost. Many
of the extant Kannada versions of the Hindu epics, the *Ramayana* and
the *Mahabharata* are not mere translations from Sanskrit. The authors   15
of these epics borrow the frame work from Sanskrit **and** the feel of
their versions differs from that of the Sanskrit epics on the one hand
and from that of the versions of the same epics in other Indian languages.
Another interesting feature of Kannada literature is the writers' attitudes   20
to Sanskrit. Sri Vijaya is one of the many who attack indiscriminate
borrowings from Sanskrit, and the best among the Kannada writers have
always been aware of the dangers of an over-Sanskritization of the
language. In fact, a Kannada writer's use of Sanskrit can be used
as a measure of his greatness as a creative artist. Some of the best
writers in Kannada have successfully exploited the 'bilingualism' of   25
their language. The Kannada and the Sanskrit words in a passage often
balance one another and are sometimes used to suggest different levels
of experience. Some of the vacanas of the sayings of the Virasaiva
mystics of the 12th century provide some of the most fascinating examples
of the exploitation of this bilingualism of Kannada (Krishnamurthi,   30
1967: vii).

There are several features of this paragraph that warrant attention. First, notice the internal structure of the first sentence and the sentence 'The authors of these epics . . . other Indian languages' (lines 15–18). In the first sentence it is difficult to see why the co-ordinator **and** is needed to link the two clauses. In the other sentence, clearly an adversative rather than a co-ordinating conjunction is required. In fact the four instances of **and** in the text above are all, according to the norms of native speakers of English, misplaced. Also, the expectation of 'on the other hand' to balance the expression 'on the one hand' in the text (in lines 15–18) is not satisfied. Another striking attribute of this paragraph is the lack of a straight linear progression of thought. The first sentence does not make a clear topic statement. In fact, it only implies that the greatness of Kannada lies partly in its antiquity and partly in other characteristics. These other characteristics, again merely implied in later sentences, are its openness to outside (i.e. Sanskritic) influences; the originality of its writers; and the exploitation of the 'bilingualism' of Kannada, introduced into Kannada by Sanskrit, for creative purposes. In a sense the topic 'greatness of Kannada literature' is to be inferred; it is not explicitly stated at the beginning.

I have already discussed the preferred process of clausalization in Indic languages. Since English does not normally accommodate complexity in single clauses of the type that Indic languages allow for, Indian writers of English have to find a way of expressing what they perceive to be related events in single sentences. The co-ordinator **and** provides one such device for expressing relatedness. Note that this is not a simple case of transfer of an Indic language phonological, syntactic, or lexical feature; this is an example of a complex phenomenon. **And** is the least marked conjunction in English; hence the choice of **and** for marking relations which are not otherwise expressible in English is understandable. This, however, does not mean that there is no effect of language contact discernible here. In part, the reason for choosing **and** to express an adversative or concessive relationship may be that co-ordinating and concessive structures in Kannada employ clitics on the verb which are phonologically identical.[10] Note that the first and the fourth instances of **and** could be replaced by a concessive structure, which would also bring out the contrast in the clauses being conjoined.[11]

What this discussion brings out is the fact that the grammar of Indian English is different in some respects from the grammar of the native varieties of English. However, it is by now well recognized that just as the native varieties differ from each other, the 'interference' varieties (Quirk *et al.*, 1972) likewise differ from the native varieties.

As regards paragraph structure, the above passage again violates the norms of native English expository writing. It has the loose structure of an oral narrative where a great deal is left to inferences the audience is expected to be able to draw. The paragraph does not lack coherence; only the linguistic expression of the thoughts is 'deviant'.

The greater toleration of digression is not confined only to the writings by scholars of Indic languages. Consider the following paragraph from a well-known Indian literary critic and Professor of English.

3. Several such 'Indian' themes have emerged to form recurrent   1
patterns in Indo-Anglian fiction, and the patterns are more easily
discernible today than they were even ten years ago. The novels
laid in the nineteen-thirties and 'forties invariably touch upon
the national movement for political independence. This is inevitable   5
because the long years of struggle and sacrifice have shaped and coloured
every experience of modern India. A great national experience must
surely help in maturing the novel form, because an experience shared
by the people at large becomes the matrix of a society and the novel
flourishes best in a society that is integrated. The struggle for   10
independence became one such unifying force in the two decades preceding
the actual achievement of political freedom, and no novelist living
in or dealing with this period could avoid writing about it. This
is not a situation unique to Indo-Anglian fiction, because novels in
other Indian languages also testify to their intense concern with the   15
national movement. But the phenomenon assumes greater significance
in English because this is one of the few pan-Indian experiences of
our time and English remains the only pan-Indian language of modern
India. [   ] Northrop Frye has noted the 'alliance of time and the western
man' as the defining characteristic of the novel as distinct from   20
other genres of literature. The very genre is western, and it is perhaps

a sign of maturity that Indo-Anglian fiction reflects this characteristic
orientation of modern thought. E. M. Forster sees the portrayal
of 'life by time' as the special role which the novel has added to
literature's more ancient preoccupation with portraying 'life by   25
values.' The concern of the Indo-Anglian novel today is the 'ultra-
historical' modern man whose individuality and personal life are
shaped by factors of history (Mukherjee, 1971: 26).

Note the break in the tight structure of the paragraph marked by [   ] in line
19. The topic of 'Indian themes' suddenly gives way to the topics 'the novel as a
western literary genre' and 'the novel as concerned with modern man'. Again,
the topics fit together in the structure of the longer section even though their
occurrence makes the paragraph quoted above 'deviant'.

Translations into English of Indic language texts exhibit similar deviations
from norms of grammatical cohesion and discourse coherence generally
followed by native-speaking writers of English. Consider the following from a
translation of a Hindi short story by a native speaker of English.

4. Suddenly the doorbell rang. I *had* just *been thinking* that   1
I'd saved some time from the office, and was wondering what to do if
she wasn't free . . . Still buttoning my shirt, I opened the door and
was taken by surprise – she was standing right in front of me. Eyeing
her from head to toe, I couldn't figure out which aspect of my surprise   5
to express first – her unexpected arrival or that outfit of hers.
      'I just *couldn't believe* it was you!' I stammered. 'What gave
you the courage to come at this hour?'
      She *had seated* herself casually on the sofa, after throwing her
books on my table . . . (Roadarmel, 1972: 176–177).   10

The past tense in the first sentences of the narrator's quoted speech (line 7)
as well as the past perfect in the last sentence of the text (line 9) are
unexpected. One has to presuppose that the seating took place before the
speech was over to make any sense of this use of the past perfect in line 9. Also,
one has to presuppose something similar to 'when I opened the door and saw
you . . .' to account for the use of the past tense in the first sentence of the
direct quote in line 7.

In the original Hindi version of the above text, the entire narrative portion is
written in the past perfect in order to make it clear that the protagonist is
'reliving' a past experience. The excerpt quoted here is part of a long beginning
paragraph of the original; the paragraph structure in English reflects the
translator's organization. The tense sequence in the Hindi story is different.
For instance, the first sentence of the direct quote has no tense marker in the
Hindi version; the tense marker can be dropped in negative sentences in Hindi,
as it is recoverable from the linguistic context. In the original text in Hindi, this
absence of the tense marker in the direct quote creates an interesting ambiguity
between present versus past, as both are possible in direct quotes, e.g. 'I
cannot imagine . . .' vs. 'I could not imagine . . .'. In the English text cited
above, however, the translator is forced to choose a tense in the first sentence
of the direct quote because a tense-less finite clause in the indicative mood is
ungrammatical in English; and he elects to use the past tense. In the last
narrative sentence of the passage the translator decides to keep the same tense

(past perfect) as in the Hindi original to maintain the 'flavour' of the original. Note, however, the consequences of these choices. The translation gives the impression that the sentences with simple past represent the 'main line' events of the story, whereas the ones with past perfect or past perfect progressive indicate the 'background' events (Aristar and Dry, 1982). This, however, is not true of the original. The entire excerpt quoted here represents 'background' events. Also, it's worth noting that unlike in English, the past perfect is not just a 'backgrounding' tense in Hindi.[12] If the translator had attempted to preserve the tense sequence of the original to the extent that it was possible, the English text would have been incomprehensible. The tension between the need to produce a reasonably transparent English text on the one hand and the attempt to maintain the backgrounding function of the passage under discussion on the other hand has resulted in the specific choice of tense forms in example 4. The tense forms in the above translation are thus indicators of a process of accommodation on the part of the translator.

In addition to structural and rhetorical conventions, Indian English texts display characteristic conventions of use of familiar English structures and lexicon which are likely to be missed completely by readers not familiar with these conventions. Consider the following paragraphs.

5. When they got to the jeep, they saw a sikh peasant talking to the boy they had left behind. He was obviously waiting for them. When the man saw what the boys had brought, he spat on the ground: 'Sardarji, why did you have to take the life of this poor creature? Is anyone going to eat it?' He spoke to Sher Singh as Sher Singh was the only one carrying a gun.

'Oi Sardara, what do you know about these things? Be on your way,' answered the boy holding one end of the crane's wings. . . . He [Sher Singh] put his arm around the peasant's shoulder and took him aside: 'Come along. Lambardar Sahib, you have become angry for no reason . . .

'I am your slave,' said the peasant, touching Sher Singh's knee. 'The slave of your slaves. You must come to my humble home for some water or something.'

'That is very kind of you; we will another day. Do see my license. And this is for your children.'

'No, no, Sardar Sahib,' protested the headman, 'Do not shame me. I am not short of money. By the Guru's blessing I have plenty to eat and drink. I only need your kindness. If you step into the hut of Jhimma Singh I will ask nothing more. Your slave is named Jhimma Singh.'

. . . 'We will ask you when the shooting season opens,' answered Madan.

'Now you are making fun of me, I was only doing my duty as a headman. Sardar Buta Singh is the king of this district, who dare tell his son when he can or can not shoot? Isn't that so Babujii . . . Babujii . . . What is our name?' (Singh, 1959: 9–11)

Notice the patterns of address in the passages quoted above. The peasant addresses Sher Singh respectfully, but Sher Singh's companion uses the vulgar style of address, 'Oi Sardara' which is reserved for one's inferiors or intimate equals. As it becomes clear that the peasant is the headman of the village and has the authority to question the boys with regard to their possession of fire arms and out-of-season shooting, Sher Singh makes a friendly gesture and addresses him with his official title and the honorific 'sahib'. This and the information that Sher Singh is the son of the District Magistrate, Buta Singh, provides the clue for the headman to switch to an extremely formal style. The passages relating to the declaration 'I am your slave', the reference to 'humble home', the offer of 'some water or something', the manner in which the headman's name is revealed, and the final question 'What is our name?' are all direct translations of the extremely formal style employed by Hindi-Urdu and Panjabi speakers in selected contexts. The word 'slave' has nothing to do with one's status; even a noble would apply the term to himself in his interactions with an equal or superior. Offering food and drink is an integral part of Indian hospitality. And expressions such as 'What is your name?' and 'my name is . . .' do not exist in the formal style. Even in normal speech, people prefer to say something like '(they) call me . . .' instead of 'My name is . . .'. Without the cultural context, the sentence 'What is our name' as a genuine question addressed to an adult is semantically anomalous in native varieties of English. It is not the case that the first-person forms are never used for an addressee in native varieties of English. They are used when addressing children and in certain social contexts for polite suggestions. But all such contexts have one thing in common: the speaker controls the situation. This is not true of Indian English. The domain of such use in Indic languages is much wider, and this is reflected in Indian English texts such as the one quoted above.

The following stanzas from Ramanujan's poem *Prayers to Lord Murugan* present similar problems of interpretation.

> **6**. Twelve etched arrowheads
>   for eyes and six unforeseen
>   faces, and you were not embarrassed.
>   Unlike other gods
>   you found work
>   for every face
>   and made
>   eyes at only one
>   woman. And your arms
>   are like faces with proper
>   names. (Ramanujan, 1971: 57–58)

This is a strange prayer. As observed by Parthasarathy (1982), the tone throughout is bantering and the poem is full of verbal paradoxes. That is, however, not unique in the Indian context. Indian devotional poetry is full of instances of 'the ambivalent, invective-like invocations or prayers to a god' (Ramanujan, 1973: 192 fn 23). One such instance is provided by the Kannada devotional poet Basavanna (1106–67/68).

> **7**. he's really the whore who takes every last bit
>   of her night's wages,
>   and will take no words
>   for payment,
>   he, my lord of the meeting rivers. (Ramanujan, 1973: 81)

The 'lord of the meeting rivers' is a form of Shiva, Basavanna's chosen personal god, *Kūḍalsaṅgàma* is a holy place in North Karnatake where two rivers meet and Basavanna addresses Shiva as *Kūḍalsaṅgàmadeva* 'Lord of the meeting rivers'. Devotion to a personal god in Indian tradition is of several forms, one of which is the devotion of an intimate friend (Sakhyabhāva). Intimate friends use a vulgar style, full of insults and curses, to show their solidarity. Examples of this are available in several texts, including the following two from Roadarmel (1972).

8. Kedar had been speaking on the other end of the phone: 'Worthless wretch! Jackass! I hear you've become a real big shot along with your Minister Sahab. Phone a dozen times and your secretary says the Sahab's doing this or doing that. If I'd not reached you this time, I wouldn't have spoken to you the rest of my life, you bastard.'

The two creases on Nath's forehead had deepened into troughs. 'Yess . . . yes . . .' he stammered, 'I didn't recognize you.'

'Of course, of course, you grandson of a governor, why would you recognize even your own father now?' came the response.

The voice was very familiar but he couldn't quite place it. The operator must be listening. Suppressing his irritation, he said, 'Look, I'm hanging up the phone, you . . .'

Lest the connection actually be cut off, the speaker on the other end identified himself. 'Hey, what are you doing? Don't you recognize the venerable Kedarji?'

'Oh, it's you, Kedarji! Well, when did you arrive?' How he produced that sentence, only he knew. Internally he had been rocked by an explosion that made him want to wave the receiver and start dancing – Hey, you bastard Kedarey! Where are you, old pal? When did you get in? Come over right away . . . (Roadarmel, 1972: 82–83).

9. For example, at a meal, one would urge the other on with full courtly gestures. He would speak very slowly in Hindi – 'You bastard, if you have to do things your way, then glut yourself with this cattle fodder.' With equal solemnity the other would reply, 'Thank you, you son of a bitch. First give me something to drink, though, you sister __' There was great pleasure in having their own language, unintelligible to those around. Nevertheless the words were spoken in such a way that even someone knowing the language could not have understood.

Ever since childhood, there was almost no abusive term they had not tried on each other, repressing their laughter as they softened the cursing with English words such as 'sorry . . . sure . . . thank you.' Back in seventh class, the two once arrived in class dressed as Ram and Lakshman and carrying real bows and arrows. Ever since, they had kept practising the art of keeping a straight face during their devilry. Recalling all this, they both rocked with laughter (Roadarmel, 1972: 85–86).

The texts represent the habitual speech patterns of two intimate friends. Saint poets of Indic languages have adopted this social behaviour pattern with great effect, and a whole genre of *nindaastuti* 'praise through defamation' exists in almost all Indic languges.

CONCLUSION

The discussion so far makes it clear that a number factors are involved in producing discourse in Indian English. One major factor is the habitual ways of encoding conceptual material in language. English is a second language in India. Linguistic competence in English is acquired by the Indians within the socio-cultural and intellectual contexts of India and not in the Anglo-European, Judeo-Christian socio-cultural and intellectual milieu of the native varieties of English. It is clear that the discourse strategies developed along with the acquisition of Indic languages are discernible in Indian English discourse as well (B. Kachru, 1982, 1983; Y. Kachru, 1983). A second related factor that needs to be recognized is that Indian English discourse expresses the experiences, beliefs, and knowledge gained in the Indian context, or at least, against the background of the Indian context in the case of the expatriate

Indian writers. This makes the adoption of Indic discourse strategies even more appropriate for Indian English discourse (B. Kachru, 1983; Mukherjee, 1971). A similar situation obtains in other non-native varieties, too (e.g. for Nigerian culture in the Nigerian English novel, see Taiwo, 1976).

Having identified the factors that are responsible for the characteristic discourse structures of Indian English, let us look at the factors that enter into their interpretation. In this chapter I have discussed two sets of relevant factors. One set is related to the grammatical structure and discourse patterns of Indic languages and their influence on Indian English. These include grammatical deviation, non-native lexicalization, and non-native style features. Obviously a reader of Indian English literary texts needs to be informed of these characteristics of Indian English. Otherwise texts such as the ones cited in this chapter will be evaluated as poor examples of writing and hence not worth taking seriously. The second set of factors is related to the socio-cultural and intellectual traditions of India. Just as *learners* of English all over the world have to familiarize themselves with the socio-cultural traditions and intellectual heritage of the native varieties, *readers* of Indian English have to develop the necessary textual competence (Beaugrande, 1980) for this variety. This would involve three types of knowledge: (a) knowledge of the linguistic characteristics of Indian English; (b) familiarity with the beliefs, expectations, experiences, and knowledge of the world of the Indian people; and (c) knowledge of the text types in Indic literatures. The examples quoted and analysed in this paper make it clear that all three types of knowledge listed above are required for an adequate interpretation of these texts.

It is obvious that unless such textual competence as discussed above is developed, works such as those created by Raja Rao, Ramanujan, Parthasarathy, Narayana, Markandaya, Anand, and others will remain to a large extent uninterpretable to users of other varieties of English. In fact, a reader lacking textual competence in world varieties of English will only react to texts created in them with puzzlement, bewilderment, shock, or even resentment, depending upon the nature of the text.

I have confined my discussion of cross-cultural texts and interpretation to the written mode. Note, however, that the same factors are relevant for cross-cultural conversational interaction, too. For the latter, of course, certain phonological features and conventions of conversational interaction such as pause, turn-taking and tempo will be relevant as well. Only the factors common to both modes of interaction have been discussed in this chapter. Also, I have discussed the question of interpretation from the point of view of the optimum level of competence required for interpreting literary texts. This does not mean that I am overlooking the fact that different levels of interpretation exist, or that texts create their own context. Note, however, that in spite of the context-creating capacity of texts, in cross-cultural situations, extensive cultural notes are still felt to be essential for an adequate level of interpretation.

Even this brief discussion raises several important theoretical and empirical questions. Theoretically it raises questions about the place of pragmatics in linguistic descriptions, especially in descriptions of a bilingual's (or multilingual's) linguistic repertoire. Empirically it raises two sets of questions. One set has to do with research on cross-cultural texts, whether oral or written, and the other with the teaching of textual competence, which subsumes communicative competence, in cross-cultural contexts. Such research – and the incorporation of the research findings into activities leading to an awareness of sociocultural factors in communicative acts – is essential for achieving adequate levels of cross-cultural communication.

Notes

1. The same position has been taken by others working in this area, e.g. Tannen (1980).
2. This is nothing new. The active participation of the reader/hearer in interpreting discourse is well established in psychological and psycholinguistic literature.
3. This discussion of clausalization and subjecthood is based on Bernardo (1980).
4. This is an oversimplification. In fact the relationship may be of temporal sequence, simultaneity, manner of performing an action, or cause-effect.
5. For convenience, all the examples of syntax in Indic languages cited in this paper are from Hindi, one of India's official languages and the most widely known and understood language in India.
6. I am not claiming here that there are no versions of possible translation equivalents in English which would have only one finite verb. I am only claiming here that participialization of this kind is much less common or frequent in English as compared to Indic languages. This is clear from the grammatical descriptions of phenomena such as relativization, too.
7. The (m) and the (f) in the glosses indicate the masculine and the feminine gender, respectively. Note that the subject does not always control verbal agreement in Hindi.
8. In addition to the sentence-level grammatical facts discussed here, it would be useful to consider discourse-level phenomena such as staging, foregrounding, and backgrounding as well. Unfortunately, not much research is available on these topics in Indic languages as yet. Moreover, the limitation on space makes it difficult to discuss all relevant facts in detail. Nevertheless, the sentence-level phenomena discussed here are of considerable value in understanding the structure of Indian English texts.
9. Sanskrit and Ancient Greek also have similar structures. For Sanskrit, see the sources referred to in Y. Kachru (1983). The Greek facts were pointed out to me by Ladislav Zgusta.
10. I am grateful to S. N. Sridhar for this information. Note that the concessive in Kannada has one other element, too, in addition to the clitic, which keeps the two structures distinct.
11. The two sentences would then read as follows:
    Although Kannada, among Indian languages, is next only to Sanskrit and Tamil in its antiquity, its claims for attention are not based only on its antiquity.
    Although the authors of these epics borrow the framework from Sanskrit, the feel of their versions differs from that of the Sanskrit epics on the one hand and from that of the versions of the same epics in other Indian languages.
12. See Hackman (1976) for a description of the Hindi tense-aspect system.

References

ARISTAR, A. and H. DRY (1982) The origin of background tenses in English. *CLS* **18**: 1–13.
BEAUGRANDE, R. DE (1980) *Text, discourse and process.* Norwood: Ablex.
BERNARDO, R. (1980) Subjecthood and consciousness. In *The pear stories: cognitive, cultural, and linguistic aspects of narrative production*, vol. III: *Advances in discourse processes*, edited by W. L. Chafe. Norwood: Ablex.
GREEN, G. M. (1982) Colloquial and literary uses of inversions. In *Spoken and written language: exploring orality and literacy*, vol. IX: *Advances in discourse processes*, edited by D. Tannen. Norwood: Ablex.

HACKMAN, J. (1976) An integrated analysis of the Hindi tense and aspect system. Ph.D. dissertation, University of Illinois.

HALLIDAY, M. A. K. (1967–68) Notes on transitivity and theme in English. *Journal of Linguistics* **3**: 37–81, 199–244; and **4**: 179–216.

KACHRU, B. (1982) Meaning in deviation: toward understanding non-native English texts. In *The other tongue: English across cultures*, edited by B. Kachru. Urbana: University of Illinois Press. (Paperback edition: Oxford: Pergamon Press, 1983.)

KACHRU, B. (1983) The bilinguals' creativity: discoursal and stylistic strategies in contact literatures in English. Paper presented at the conference on English as an international language; East-West Center. A revised version in this volume.

KACHRU, Y. (1983) Linguistics and written discourse in particular languages. Contrastive studies English and Hindi. *Annual Review of Applied Linguistics*, 50–77.

KACHRU, Y., B. KACHRU and T. K. BHATIA (1976) The notion subject: a note on Hindi–Urdu, Kashmiri and Punjabi. In *The notion of subject in South Asian languages*, edited by M. K. Verma. Madison: Department of South Asian languages and literatures.

KAPLAN, R. B. (1980) Cultural thought patterns in inter-cultural education. In *Readings on English as a second language for teachers and teacher trainees*, edited by K. Croft. pp. 245–262. Cambridge, Mass.: Winthrop. An earlier version in *Language Learning* (1966) **16**: 1–20.

KEENAN, E. L. (1976) Towards a universal definition of subject. In *Subject and topic*, edited by C. N. Li. New York: Academic Press.

KRISHNAMURTHI, M. G. (ed.) (1967) *Modern Kannada Fiction; a critical anthology*. Madison: Department of Indian Studies.

MUKHERJEE, M. (1971) *The twice born fiction: themes and techniques of the Indian novel in English*. Delhi: Arnold–Heinemann.

PANDHARIPANDE, R. (1981) Syntax and semantics of the passive construction in selected South Asian languages. Unpublished Ph.D. dissertation, University of Illinois.

PANDHARIPANDE, R. (1983) Linguistics and written discourse in particular languages. Contrastive studies in English and Marathi. *Annual Review of Applied Linguistics*, 118–136.

PARTHASARATHY, R. (1982) Whoring after English gods. In *Writers in East–West encounter*, edited by G. Amirthanayagam. London: Macmillan.

QUIRK, R., S. GREENBAUM, G. LEECH and J. SVARTVIK (1972) *A grammar of contemporary English*. New York: Seminar Press.

RAGHAVAN, V. (1968) Sanskrit literature. In *Contemporary Indian literature: a symposium, 1957*. Delhi: Sahitya Akademi.

RAMANUJAN, A. K. (1971) *Relations*. London: Oxford University Press.

RAMANUJAN, A. K. (1973) *Speaking of Siva*. Baltimore: Penguin.

ROADARMEL, G. C. (trans.) (1972) *Modern Hindi short stories*. Berkeley: University of California Press.

SCRIBNER, S. (1979) Modes of thinking and ways of speaking: culture and logic reconsidered. In *New directions in discourse processing*, vol. II: *Advances in discourse processes*, edited by R. O. Freedle. Norwood: Ablex.

SINGH, K. (1959) *I shall not hear the nightingale*. London: John Calder.

SRIDHAR, S. N. (1976) Dative subjects. *Chicago Linguistic Society Papers* **12**: 582–593.

SRIDHAR, S. N. (1980) Cognitive determinants of linguistic structures: a cross-linguistic study of sentence production. Ph.D. dissertation, University of Illinois.

TAIWO, O. (1976) *Culture and the Nigerian novel*. New York: St Martin's Press.

TANNEN, D. (1980) A comparative analysis of oral narrative strategies: Athenian Greek and American English. In *The pear stories: cognitive, cultural, and linguistic aspects of narrative production*, vol. III: *Advances in discourse processes*, edited by W. L. Chafe. Norwood: Ablex.

VERMA, M. K. (ed.) (1976) *The notion of subject in south Asian languages*. Madison: Department of South Asian languages and literatures.

8

Aizuchi: A Japanese Conversational Routine

VIRGINIA LoCASTRO

THE idea for this chapter began to germinate about three years ago when I first arrived in Japan. Being totally illiterate and unable to understand any of the language, one does a lot of observing, especially on trains in Tokyo. One notices that Japanese punctuate their flow of discourse by stressing certain syllables or words and moving their heads forward with a definite, clear nod. The listener would do something similar with his/her head, making almost a 'tic' type of movement, and making sounds ('heh', 'humm', and 'ne') and/or using fixed expressions, such as *so desu ne*, *soo . . . nee*, and *naruhodo*. It seemed that this behaviour, verbal and non-verbal, occurred most frequently in relaxed situations, when one person was telling a story or going on for several utterances before relinquishing his/her turn to the listener.

In addition, I was also curious about conversational interactions among Japanese; this was due to experiences I had had and stories I had heard about Japanese not being very good at communication. Non-verbal behaviour and use of what I was told was *aizuchi* led me to conclude that communication was certainly occurring, at least as much as between and among people of any language, and that use of *aizuchi* represented one variable in the conversational routines typical of Japanese-speaking people. I shall, therefore, use this term as a cover term for this form of verbal and non-verbal behaviour.

Other observations led me further along this line of thinking. English-speaking foreigners living in Japan seem to begin to use more 'hum's and 'ee's and head movements, even when speaking their own language with others. The foreigners who do this have a lot of contact with Japanese people and have varying degrees of proficiency in the language. Without actually counting the number of *aizuchi* used or head nods, I believe there is a difference; that is, the frequency of *aizuchi* increases as the foreigner becomes more 'japanized'.

Another observation is the problem of phone calls. It is almost a cliché that unless one carries on a phone conversation in Japanese with what seems to be frequent use of *hai* and *so desu ne*, the other party will come to a halt and will check to see that the first party is still there by saying '*moshi-moshi*'. This, of course, can happen even with English phone conversations; it is nevertheless particularly noticeable when one overhears only one side of a phone conversation in Japanese.

Finally, when discussing the topic of *aizuchi* with various Japanese speakers of English, I found they are frequently very aware of the use of *aizuchi*. Some commented they feel the weakness in their English language ability is their inability to use proper English *aizuchi* and to carry on small talk. Then they will say that to speak 'good' Japanese, one must use *aizuchi* such as *so desu ne*. To do otherwise is to be impolite to one's conversational partner. It also seems one would be judged as being too assertive not using *aizuchi*, as one might be perceived as not showing enough deference to the speaker.

As a result of these observations, a study of *aizuchi* seemed to be a fruitful area of inquiry in the field of discourse analysis. My own Japanese is at a point where I have to begin to use *aizuchi* in my speech, and I had noticed myself using more 'he's, 'hum's and head nods when speaking English. Also I began to ask what effect the improper use of such sounds and forms could have on one's communicative ability in a foreign language. How important are they? Is the problem similar to the folklore notion that good pronunciation rather than grammatical correctness by a non-native speaker of a language is more salient to native speakers of that language?

These are the same questions language teachers ask when contemplating helping students learn other sociolinguistic variables inherent in the communicative competence of a particular language. Should we teach body language and gestures appropriate to specific situations in the target language and how do we do this? Should we teach *aizuchi* and how do we do it? When do *aizuchi* occur: at the ends of sense groupings, or of clauses; at the beginnings of utterances, or at the ends? Is their use idiosyncratic? Do women use them more frequently than men? Is one apt to find them in certain situations or forms of spoken discourse? (As this chapter is only concerned with spoken discourse, it is to be assumed by the reader that the word 'discourse' refers only to *spoken* discourse.)

Final confirmation that the subject was of interest came in January when an article appeared in *The Japan Times* (29 January 1983) concerning the IBM-Hitachi-Mitsubishi computer case. A defendant in the case, Mr Ishida of Mitsubishi, claimed that he had not agreed with the FBI undercover agents when they told him there was no choice but to steal the information/documents Mr Ishida was seeking. His defence counsellor stated that Mr Ishida's use of 'yeah' and 'uh huh' was not to show agreement, but rather simply to indicate he was listening or attending to what they were saying.

The article cited Theodore F. Welch of Northwestern University's Center for the Study of US-Japan Relations. According to Welch, Japanese use 'yeah' and 'uh huh', whether they are speaking in English or Japanese, to 'keep the conversation going smoothly'. It is considered polite by Japanese in conversation to constantly let the speaker know one is listening.

Thus, the use of such *aizuchi* as 'yeah' and 'uh huh' could be a crucial variable in the IBM-Hitachi-Mitsubishi case. If it is believed that Mr Ishida did in fact know the materials he received were stolen and, moreover, that he had in effect agreed to have them stolen for him, then the penalty is apt to be greater.

This example, then, seemed to support my general hypothesis that the use of *aizuchi* differs in American English and Japanese. The differences in this conversational routine between Japanese and American English have led to a possibly major misunderstanding.

This chapter will examine some of the possible differences in the use of *aizuchi* between Japanese and American English, although my remarks can be taken only as tentative, based on (1) some reported research done in the field of conversational analysis, (2) some audio recordings, and (3) some personal observations. As a pilot study, it is a point of departure for further research.

First, the generally accepted categorization of *aizuchi* and secondly, the functions ascribed to this form of behaviour by researchers, is of interest. After reviewing some of the literature on the subject, a preliminary analysis of some authentic language samples, both in English and in Japanese, will be carried out to see if there is agreement with the ideas derived from previously reported studies, as well as to see if there are differences in the use of *aizuchi* between Japanese and American English speakers. A discussion of possible reasons for the differences will conclude this chapter.

The first study to discuss the role of short messages such as 'uh huh' and 'yes' in conversational settings in English is that of Yngve (1970); he describes a situation in which 'the person who has the turn and his partner are simultaneously engaged in speaking and listening'. This is possible due to what he calls the 'back-channel', enabling the listener not only to listen but also to utter short messages in the back-channel at the same time. The terms *aizuchi* and back-channel behaviour will be used interchangeably throughout this chapter.

Although Yngve is mostly concerned with the signals used to indicate turns in conversation, he comments on the importance of back-channel cues for monitoring the quality of communication. The back-channel cues frequently occur simultaneously with the main message, whether they be verbal or non-verbal signals such as nodding the head. They may also be sentence completions such as when the listener provides a word the speaker is searching for.

Yngve further points out that back-channel cues can range from simply indicating interest and attention on the part of the listener to asking short questions to get the speaker to continue ('You've started writing it then, your dissertation?' p. 574). Back-channel cues thus enable the speaker to continue to 'have the floor' (see Goffman, 1981, and Allen and Guy, 1974).

While Yngve seems to accept a wide range of utterances as back-channel signals, Coulthard (1977) points out that there are some disagreements on this matter, related to what constitutes a turn in turn-taking analysis. Most researchers agree that nods and murmurs of assent and agreement do not constitute turns. Duncan (1974) refers to such utterances as sentence completions, requests for clarification and brief restatements as back-channel elements, while Coulthard questions where the boundary of turn-taking should fall.

As far as the types of *aizuchi* are concerned, certainly, 'm-hm', 'yeah', 'right', etc., as well as 'yes, quite', 'surely', 'I see', 'that's true', and the like, occurring singly or in repeated groups, are generally accepted as back-channel cues or *aizuchi*.

Once there is some agreement on what constitutes *aizuchi* it is necessary to examine the functions of these utterances in conversation. Richards (1982) calls back-channel cues examples of 'phatic communion', showing that the listener is interested and values what the conversational partner is saying.

In his 1974 study, Duncan presents research on speaker-auditor interaction during speaking turns. The 'auditor back-channel signal' appears to be a means by which the auditor can participate in the dyadic conversation and can acknowledge understanding or lack of understanding of the speaker's message. In addition, although the speaker may give a turn signal – by means of behavioural cues such as (1) intonation, (2) content, (3) body motion, to give three examples – the auditor may remain silent or communicate in the back-channel, indicating thereby that the speaker should continue.

The study, however, was an attempt to set these ideas in a broader communication context. Analysing a variety of language samples, Duncan explored to what extent auditor back-channel signals along with other variables are rule-governed behaviour. The results reported were not conclusive, but did show some interesting patterns: (1) the auditor would use a back-channel signal just before claiming a speaking turn and (2) two cues from the speaker found to correlate highly with the occurrence of auditor back-channel signals were (a) completion of a grammatical clause and (b) turning of the head of the speaker towards the auditor.

Schegloff's work (1982) adds to Duncan's findings. Focusing on the interactional nature of discourse, Schegloff's thesis is (1) that discourse should be treated as an 'achievement' and (2) that such achievement is an 'interactional one'. He states that from such a point of view a conversation thus becomes possible only if co-operation or collaboration occurs between the participants. His paper examines one 'class of behaviour' – *aizuchi* – that accompanies conversational discourse.

One of Schegloff's primary concerns is that such behaviour (vocalizations) as 'uh huh', 'mmhmm', 'yeah', etc. not be analysed separately from the context of the discourse of which they are integral parts. He is critical of researchers who talk of 'accompaniment signals' or 'back-channel signals', as if *aizuchi* were 'conversational "detritus" . . . lacking of semantic content' (p. 74). Rather, all the 'yeah's, in his opinion, contribute to the substance of the discourse and are analysable *with* discourse.

Schegloff's first observation about the use of *aizuchi* is that they act as 'continuers', that is, they signal to the speaker that the speaker's turn should continue. The listener conveys an understanding that an extended unit of talk is in progress. This, however, does not mean agreement with the speaker or even general understanding of the message. The listener is simply passing the opportunity to take over the 'floor'. Thus, the 'uh huh's are signals of the collaborative nature of discourse, recognizable only through analysis of an extended unit of discourse.

A second observation concerning the functions of *aizuchi* in extended discourse comes from examining 'repairs', which are used by the listener to remedy some problem of hearing or understanding what the speaker just said. There exist various cues to repair problems of understanding. Using 'uh huh' is not a clear semantic means to signal lack of understanding. Rather an 'uh huh' can be seen to be 'passing an opportunity to initiate repair on the immediately preceding talk' (p. 88). In other words, the listener claims there are no problems of hearing or understanding the speaker's previous utterance and that the speaker should continue. The 'uh huh' itself does *not*, however, signal understanding. It means only that no repair behaviour will be initiated.

This is where, according to Schegloff, misunderstanding can arise as the speaker, in the absence of an attempt on the part of the listener to initiate repair behaviour, believes that there is no disagreement and that there is, as a result, understanding and agreement in general. The speaker assumes the listener would signal disagreement if such existed.

The use of 'uh huh', then, as a continuer differs from this usage. Here, 'uh huh' is a *claim* of understanding, but that claim may be incorrect. Schegloff states:

> The status of 'uh huh' as an indication of understanding or agreement is equivocal in a way in which its status as a continuer is not, as participants who have relied on it will have discovered and regretted (p. 88).

Schegloff seems to have opened up a train of thinking that points to critical differences in the way *aizuchi* are used. Viewing the class of behaviour of 'uh huh' as continuers dovetails with the statements of most other researchers. However, his second observation, which underlines the aspect of *aizuchi* as being possibly merely *claims* of understanding and/or agreement, may be fruitful as a direction to pursue.

Hinds (1978) has reported on Japanese conversational routines in particular, his work contributing further to attaining clearer insights into the use of back-channel cues. Overlapping speech, where there is more than one speaker at a time, is not a dominant feature of American English. This is not so for Japanese, where overlapping is common and extended. The listener uses various *aizuchi*, keeping up a constant stream of language so as to reinforce what the speaker is saying, not infrequently completing the speaker's utterance. A good conversation partner tends to empathize with others, being aware enough to jointly create a conversation; this contrasts with American discourse patterns where conversations seem to be displays of 'antagonistic behaviour' (p. 107).

Hinds also notes that the ability to use *aizuchi* and carry on overlapping is not easy to acquire. Foreign speakers of Japanese may over-use back-channel cues and, in particular, at the wrong places, causing the speaker to stop.

There is one more study, done by Hata (1982), which has a direct bearing on the subject of this chapter. Hata did a case study of an Australian woman, Maria, who had been studying Japanese for 2½ years and who was perceived by Japanese as being a successful communicator in the language. Upon analysing tape-recorded conversations of Maria speaking Japanese, Hata found that her grammar and vocabulary are limited, but she uses *aizuchi* frequently. *Aizuchi*, according to Hata, is a symbol of participating in a conversation and, moreover, it is not the quantity or varieties of *aizuchi*, but the timing, that is important.

Hata explains that *aizuchi* in Japanese has two functions; one is to indicate that the speaker should keep talking; the other, that the listener wants to begin to speak.

The conclusion of the case study of Maria is that, with limited vocabulary and grammar, Maria is considered to be a fairly successful communicator in Japanese, as she is able through proper use of *aizuchi* to address one of the basic tenets of conversation, i.e. that it be a co-operative effort. We see also that Hata's explanations of the functions of *aizuchi* in Japanese dovetails with those of Schegloff and Duncan, among others. *Aizuchi* has essentially an interactional function in conversational discourse.

This review of the literature by no means exhausts the field. Yet it seems more appropriate at this point to tie observations drawn from these studies to others, particularly those which have developed as a result of cross-cultural experiences. We need to look for possible connections between back-channel behaviour and culture.

ANALYSIS

One major weakness of many attempts to analyse the use of such classes of behaviour as *aizuchi* is, as Schegloff states, they treat all the 'yeah's and 'uh huh's separately from actual, extended texts of discourse. Examining variables in context, one is able to add a semantic dimension by studying back-channel cues as part of the interactional nature of discourse.

To further amplify the semantic dimension of language, it seems advisable to include social and/or cultural knowledge in one's analysis and not separate such knowledge from linguistic signals. Gumperz (1982) makes a clear case for this approach to the analysis of discourse. Frequently, researchers continue to use sentence-level linguistic analysis and then see extralinguistic socio-cultural variables as forces which determine only how and when the linguistic elements are used. Gumperz is of the opinion that socio-cultural norms determine all levels of linguistic production and interpretation,

> from the abstract cultural logic that underlies all interpretation to the division of speech into episodes; from their categorization in terms of semantically relevant activities and interpretive frames, to the mapping of prosodic contours into syntactic strings and to selection among lexical and grammatical options (p. 186).

In other words, all the variables are interdependent. Taking the transformational generative model of language, we would claim that socio-cultural variables influence deep-structure level choices of such elements as passive verb forms: for example, it may be impolite in certain situations not to take responsibility for breaking something even if no individual had anything to do with the object being broken.

Thus, conversational analysis from Gumperz's sociologist's point of view must take into account what the speaker-listener must know in order to initiate a conversation as well as the inferences that underlie maintaining a smooth, on-going conversation in the target language.

An example of the extent to which even back-channel cues are important indicators of this interdependence and of the underlying co-operative nature of discourse can be seen in studies done at Berkeley, which Gumperz (1982) cites. They examined the occurrence of back-channel cues in ethnically mixed student groups. There appeared to be a direct relationship between back-channel cues and speakers' utterances and interactional 'synchrony' on a non-verbal level. Back-channel cues clustered around points of maximum information in the speaker's message when there was conversational synchrony. This was not so in asynchronous phases.

This experimental evidence supports one's intuitions that this is probably so; conversational synchrony implies co-operation on the part of the participants at the level of automatic behaviour which may have no relationship to understanding or agreement with the semantic content of the speaker's messge.

These results support Schegloff's idea that the auditor's 'uh huh' may not be a signal of understanding or agreement, but rather a signal to 'go on' and/or that all involved are participating willingly in the co-operative, interactional discourse act. *Aizuchi* or back-channel cues communicate conversational co-operation and allow the speaker to monitor for its presence. If back-channel cues do not occur at all, or are out of 'synch' with the expectations of the speaker, then one can apparently conclude that some sort of communication breakdown or misunderstanding is occurring or about to occur. Or the listener is tired, wants to go home, or may not like the speaker as a person; in other words, the listener does not want to co-operate for some reason that may not have anything to do with what the speaker is talking about or saying.

Another explanation for back-channel cues occurring less frequently or at 'unexpected' places or with different prosodic features, for example, is ethnic or cultural differences. Asynchrony and perceived differences in back-channel behaviour in a conversation may result not from lack of co-operativeness, but from different cultural norms associated with *aizuchi*. In the introduction to this chapter it was reported that, on the basis of some personal observations in Japan, Japanese seem to use more *aizuchi* in everyday talk than Americans would in similar kinds of conversations in English. Can some generalizations be made on the basis of a limited sample of authentic language samples about the use of *aizuchi* by Japanese speaking to each other in Japanese and their use by Americans speaking to each other in American English?

Audiotape recordings were made of Japanese speaking to Japanese and Americans speaking to Americans in a variety of situations. As this was merely a pilot study to see if there was any basis for a more elaborate study in the future, no effort was made to control strictly for the variable.

Tapes were made of people in social gatherings of small groups or pairs where the participants knew each other, sometimes intimately, and then of phone conversations, again when the speaker-listener pairs knew each other.

In some cases the participants were aware their conversation was being recorded; in others, not.

Some types of back-channel cues in American English include the following. (The notes in parentheses indicate what function the back-channel cue seemed to have.)

> Right./Yeah. (Agreement/confirmation.)
> Yeah, bamboo forests over there. (Restatement.)
> Oh, yeah? (Surprise.)
> Jewel? (Clarification.)
> I like that . . .
> . . . excellent . . . (Completion.)
> um . . . um . . .
> uh huh . . .
> O.K.
> Oh, I see.

A list of *aizuchi* could include the following which I have learnt from personal communications from native Japanese speakers:

> *haa* (yes, formal)
> *hai* (yes, formal)
> *so desu ka* (Is that so?)
> *naruhodo* (indeed)
> *ee . . . eee . . .* (yes, informal)
> *usoo*
> *uso* (I can't believe it; literally, It must be a lie.)
> *usobakkari* (female)
> *honto* (Is that true? Really?)
> *hontoo*
> *sooka mo ne*
> *soo ka mo nee* (Could be)
> *ka mo ne*
> *ka mo nee*
> *soo yo* (agreement)
> *soo da yo*
> *soo*
> *soo deshoo*
> *soo deshoo tomo* (I think so.)
> *soo yo nee* (female)
> *soo dayo nee* (male)
> *hun*
> *soo*
> *soo soo*
> *sore de?*
> *sore kara?*
> *doo natta?* (What happened?)
> *doo shite?* (Why?)
> *sugoi!*
> *sugoi nee!* (How wonderful, marvellous, terrible, etc.)
> *sugoi wa nee!* (female)

The notes after the various *aizuchi* give some ideas about what they mean and who uses them. As is well known, male and female speech tends to differ in Japanese.

Only two example conversations are given below for the purpose of observing differences in the use of *aizuchi*.

S: They're little tea sets.
V: Yeah.
S: Oh, yeah. You can see that. This guy, Alice and I ran into a shop where this guy actually makes them. They're like a souvenir from Nikko and they sell them all over the city.
V: Uh huh.
S: And we just stumbled into the place and the guy like I don't think he'd had any one that interested in it or any foreigner that spoke Japanese. And he started telling me the whole story.
V: Ummm.
S: And we went into his workshop and we took a whole roll of film of him, doing it . . . and
V: Oh, I see.
S: And I didn't have enough cash and so I got it by, like, genkin kakitome-one.
V: Yeah.
S: And he sent me the whole thing, thanking me for the pictures. And he sent me a return postcard which I really never sent back. And pictures and postcards of Nikko
V: Umm.
S: The workmanship is incredible.
V: Yeah.

And now a conversation in Japanese between three housewives who have small children; they are talking about the children getting sick.

A: *Mukashi no hito iu jya nai?*
B: *Um, so so so.*
    Demo, honto so o yo . . .
C: *Um, um.*
B: *Yochien-no-toki, sugoku itagaru ko ga ite, yappari . . .*
C: *Um.*
B: *Donna Sensei-no-toko ittemo, kekkyoku Seicho-ki de . . .*
C: *Um.*
B: *Hone no nobiru noto, Kinniku toka I toka no ne . . .*
C: *Um.*
B: *Baransu ga torenai toki no . . .*
C: *Um . . .*
B: *Itami ga okorutte.*
C: *Um . . . un . . .*
B: *Sooyo.*
C: *Sono Shoojyoo ga deta toki wa moo osoi-tte iu ne.*
B: *Um . . .*
A: *Moo hantashi de ittei shiyasui . . .*
C: *Um . . .*

There is no question that even in these two examples, taken from five audiotapes as representative, the Japanese sample shows more frequent use of back-channelling. Yet as merely samples of the use of *aizuchi*, this very limited study leaves many variables unaccounted for. The types of discourse (narration, interviews, exchanges where the speaker's turn consists of one utterance, etc.), the degree of intimacy between the participants, the subject, sex, age, socio-economic group, setting and level of education could all influence back-channel behaviour. In addition, audiotapes of conversations are not adequate, as nods, smiles, eye contact, head turns are all forms of non-verbal *aizuchi*. Videotapes are therefore necessary.

One personal observation that can be made upon listening to one of the recordings is that the husband of one American-Japanese couple appeared to use 'um' more frequently than the other two Americans, a man and a woman, whom he was talking with. This could indicate a tendency noted earlier among foreigners in Japan to begin using more back-channel cues even when speaking in English. He could have picked up his wife's habit of using the 'um' found in spoken Japanese discourse.

An interesting comment made by an American man who participated in one of the recordings shows an awareness of back-channel cues in his profession. He is a radio announcer and explained, after the recording when he learned the object of the study, that radio announcers on talk shows in particular are trained not to use a lot of back-channel signals as it is felt to interfere with the clear transmission of the radio programme to the listeners.

Nevertheless, we can see from this limited sample that there seems to be a greater use of and a greater variety of *aizuchi* in Japanese than in American English. Socio-cultural knowledge and awareness of norms of Japanese society would lead us to expect as much.

Firstly, the emphasis on maintaining group harmony and on having smooth relations would probably cause speaker-listeners to use more *aizuchi* to show willingness to co-operate in the conversation and to show support of and attach value to the speaker on the part of the listener. This could be the underlying factor behind the notion that it is impolite in Japanese not to use back-channel cues.

In addition, as it is also considered impolite to interrupt a speaker to ask for clarification or restatement directly, *aizuchi* serves in the continuer function, signalling that the speaker should go on. The listener may allow the speaker to hold the floor for a longer period of time.

In both cases, American culture appears to be rather different. Confrontation is accepted, and asking for clarification if one does not hear or understand is expected. Moreover, concern for maintaining smooth relations with others is not manifested in the same way. Two American individuals are not so apt to place conversational harmony or synchrony over frankness or telling of necessary even though unpleasant facts, whereas Japanese speakers very well may.

Another norm of Japanese behaviour, found in other Oriental cultures as well, is that of telling a higher-status person what the speaker-listener thinks they want to hear, rather than the real facts. A straight, direct answer, particularly in situations where there is a status difference between the people involved, is considered impolite.

Now, Japanese know this and therefore would not have assumed, as in the IBM case mentioned earlier, that use of *aizuchi* such as 'yeah' and 'uh huh' signalled understanding and agreement. For a Japanese, use of *aizuchi*, even in situations where they completely disagree with what the speaker is saying, only means they are attending to what is being said. *Aizuchi* can be a means to defer to the higher-level person, managing the conversation so it goes smoothly, thus avoiding giving bad news or telling the real facts or one's real feelings.

Subordinating telling necessary or useful facts to conversational synchrony seems contrary to one's expectations of human behaviour at first; however, there is ample evidence to the contrary. The fact that Grice (1975), in *Logic and conversation*, outlined categories of what he calls the Co-operative Principle of conversation assumes that such rules or maxims are violated. Grice's maxims are as follows:

(1) Maxim of quantity: be as informative as possible.
(2) Maxim of quality: be as truthful as possible.
(3) Maxim of relation: be as relevant as possible.
(4) Maxim of manner: be brief and orderly, avoiding obscurity and ambiguity.

Grice possibly meant these 'maxims' to be prescriptive rather than descriptive. Moreover, Grice was concerned with maximally effective exchanges of information. They are nevertheless useful in pointing out some components of conversation acts.

Yet it is clear that these rules are violated in conversational interaction, particularly where there may be different cultural norms attached to what constitutes 'good' communication; i.e. notions concerning communication are likely to be culturally bound. Whereas Americans, it is said, may prefer, even demand, direct answers, others from different cultural groups may value the preservation of goodwill. It may be incorrect even to assume that 'all' Americans prefer direct answers in most situations.

Olsen (1981) studied *Masked negatives in intercultural encounters* – 'masked negatives' meaning answers which at first appear to be affirmative but later prove to be negative. It is her opinion that such a phenomenon is in fact general to all human interaction. Cross-cultural situations, however, tend to blur our ability to recognize that, perhaps because the subtle cues indicating the 'real' answer may not be obvious to a person foreign to the culture in question.

Another reason, according to Olsen, is the mistaken notion that transference of information is the most important function of language. It is quite possible the phatic function – that is, the use of language to promote and maintain agreeable social interactions – is by far the most frequent use of language in everyday life. Grice's maxims may be violated or ignored not out of any malicious intent, but simply because a 'general rapport rule' is valued as more important by speakers of certain cultures than of others. Exchanging information may be secondary.

Barnlund reports in his often-cited study 'The public self and private self in Japan and the United States' (1974) that when asked to say 'what I wish I were like in interpersonal relationships', Japanese respondents listed the following:

I try to be as polite as possible.
I don't say all of what I think.
I try to keep the conversation pleasant.
I try to behave smoothly.
I try not to disagree (p. 56).

It thus seems that a general rapport rule would have greater explanatory power in accounting for Japanese interpersonal behaviour. Such a rule would emphasize the use of *aizuchi* to keep a conversation going smoothly. Back-channel signals, as shown above, function as one means to maintain pleasant conversational interaction. They are part of conversational routines for Japanese, whether the language of communication is Japanese or English, for *aizuchi* fulfil the cultural expectations of politeness. To borrow from Brown and Levinson's (1978) notions of positive and negative face, back-channelling is addressing the Japanese need to preserve positive face, i.e. to preserve one's public 'self-image'. The tendency among Americans appears to be to wish to preserve negative face, with the goal being to emphasize long-term benefit for the parties involved.

One last example will serve to conclude this study. Another characteristic of Japanese interactions is to focus on the here-and-now. That the present evening or day or moment be pleasant with feelings of goodwill is of greatest import. The foreigner may mistakenly assume this means communication is occurring, or at the least that all future interactions with the same individuals will be equally pleasant. As any foreigner who has spent time in Japan knows, this may not be so.

So emphasis on the here-and-now of interactions, as well as a tendency to say what one perceives someone seen as a superior wants to hear, results in a realization that conversational routines and conversational interactions serve different functions in Japan. A closer examination of these areas may reveal a wide range of differences, resulting from the socio-cultural background of the people. The real challenge with such findings is when these differences are carried over by the various speakers into their second language, as when English is used with the conversational routines and expectations of the speaker's primary culture.

This study represents merely a beginning, an exploration of possible directions to pursue in an area which appears to be fruitful for gaining insights into conversational routines and the cultural expectations that accompany them. Moreover, focusing on the relationship between culture and back-channel behaviour forces a re-examination, a fresh look at the various stereotypes of American and Japanese behaviour. Observing back-channelling brings recognition of the extent to which the conversational routines of these two cultures are similar and different.

For language teachers and learners, this chapter lends support to intuitions about successful communicators in target language cultures. Appropriate use of back-channel cues or *aizuchi* for the particular cultural context is as much, or even more, a part of what constitutes fluency in that language as grammatical accuracy and an extensive vocabulary.

However, whether this can be taught and how, especially outside the target language community, is a question all language teachers struggle with. The use of notional/functional as well as situational syllabuses to structure language learning has resulted in greater awareness on the part of both learners and teachers of communicative competence. Yet the materials only help the speaker to carry on a conversation; there is a need to train the listener to interact in conversations by means of back-channel cues.

The first step is training in recognizing back-channel cues and then in awareness of their role in conversational discourse. This can be done with audiotapes, or ideally videotapes, of authentic, everyday interactions. Students could be asked to listen to and observe only what the listener says and does. It is important as well, as we saw above in Hata's study, to use *aizuchi* at the appropriate places; timing is important. Once awareness and knowledge of what back-channel cues are and do are achieved, then the instructor could use various drama and role-play techniques to get students to practise their use. In spite of the fact that proficiency in the use of *aizuchi* is not likely to be attained by the average language learner, the learner should, however, at least be exposed to the role of this form of language behaviour.

One final point concerns the issue raised about what happens when non-native speakers of English from various cultures carry over into English conversational interactions the routines and expectations of their primary cultures. This relates to the problem of intelligibility when discussing English as an international language. It seems that intelligibility involves not only pronunciation, syntax and vocabulary, but such factors as conversational routines of which back-channel behaviour is only one variable. As the concept of English as an international language is adopted more widely, it will be necessary for contrastive discourse analysis studies to contribute to its further development.

References

ALLEN, D. E. and R. F. GUY (1974) *Conversational analysis: the sociology of talk.* The Hague: Mouton.

BARNLUND, D. C. (1974) The public self and private self in Japan and the United States. In *Intercultural encounters with Japan*, edited by G. Condon and M. Saito. Tokyo: Simul Press, pp. 27–96.

BROWN, P. and S. LEVINSON (1978) Universals in language usage: politeness phenomena. In *Questions and politeness: strategies in social interaction*, edited by E. Goody. New York: Cambridge University Press, pp. 56–289.

COULTHARD, M. (1977) *An introduction to discourse analysis.* London: Longman.

DUNCAN, S. (1974) On the structure of speaker–auditor interaction during speaker turns. *Language in society* **2**: 161–180.

GOFFMAN, E. (1981) *Forms of talk.* Philadelphia: University of Pennsylvania Press.

GRICE, H. (1975) Logic and conversation. In *Syntax and semantics 3: speech acts*, edited by P. Cole and J. L. Morgan. New York: Academic Press, pp. 41–58.

GUMPERZ, J. J. (1982) *Discourse strategies.* Studies in Interactional Sociolinguistics 1. Cambridge: Cambridge University Press.

HATA, H. (1982) Japanese language education for the purpose of communication. *Gengo* **11**(13): 56–70. (In Japanese.)

HINDS, J. (1978) Conversational structure: an investigation based on Japanese interview discourse. In *Problems in Japanese syntax and semantics*, edited by J. Hinds and I. Howard. Tokyo: Kaitakusha Co., Ltd, pp. 79–121.

Japanese mannerism is key point in IBM case. In *The Japan Times*, 29 January 1983, p. 2.

OLSEN, J. E. WINN-BELL (1981) Masked negatives in intercultural encounters. Unpublished manuscript.

RICHARDS, J. C. (1982) Communicative needs in foreign language. *JALT Journal* **4**: 1–16.

SCHEGLOFF, E. A. (1982) Discourse as an interactional achievement. In *Analyzing discourse: text and talk*, edited by D. Tannen. Washington, DC: Georgetown University Press, pp. 71–93.

YNGVE, V. (1970) On getting a word in edgewise. In *Papers from the Sixth Regional Meeting*, the Chicago Linguistic Society. Chicago: Chicago Linguistic Society, pp. 567–577.

9

Native Sensibility and Literary Discourse

WIMAL DISSANAYAKE AND MIMI NICHTER

As an international language, English has become a potent vehicle of communication for people living in diverse cultures. One result of this cross-cultural use of English is that it has been creatively modified to reflect the sensibilities, inherited cultural patterns and dispositions of its users with varied language backgrounds. This point is well illustrated in this volume, particularly in Chapters 7, 10, 11 and 12. However, the influence of native patterns of discourse on English is an area of study that merits closer attention than it has so far received.

Such study is as complex as it is important, involving a great measure of circumspection in examining the dimensions and layers of verbal communication. The concept of native sensibility is elusive and resists easy formulation. Thus, in the past, linguists have tended to focus on lexical and syntactic levels of native patterns of discourse in English (though there are some exceptions, e.g. see Chishimba, 1983). While these are natural starting-points and ones which lend themselves to easy operationalization, the need remains to move beyond them to a cultural, hermeneutic approach to the sensibilities of non-native users of English.

The object of this chapter is to initiate a discussion along these lines, a discussion based on the metaphors, referential frameworks and patterns of tacit communication in the work of Punyakante Wijenaike (b. 1933), a highly regarded Sri Lankan writer of English fiction.

Other researchers have already noted that the study of metaphor provides insights to cultural thinking (e.g. Beck, 1982; Blake, 1979; Fernandez, 1974); but the perspective which underlies this chapter is that metaphor plays a particularly critical role in cross-cultural understanding because of the nature of its basic mechanism as a form of communication (see e.g. Lakoff and Johnson, 1980).

Metaphor creates a new mode of feeling or sensibility through the juxta-position of two known experiences; thus metaphors have the power to convey new meanings, new similarities, and thereby define new realities. The understanding of a metaphor, as discussed by Tylor (1978: 318) is not of two distinct concepts but rather: 'as a whole conception, which illuminates not only the part of the metaphor itself but more importantly that part of the discourse to which it is relevant'.

Tylor stresses that the meaning and usefulness of metaphor must be discussed situationally in relation to a context of sentences, not simply in the relationship between words. Kachru (1982) has noted that the appropriate functional meaning of non-native literature is to be understood within situational contexts. It is necessary to move from text to context in order to gain appreciation of the horizon of a subject – that which is assumed and not made explicit. While words, expressions or images used by the non-native writer of English may be familiar, individually and superficially, to the native English reader, their deeper significance may not be understood. Their sociocultural meanings may not be obvious to 'outsiders', as has been shown in Chapters 10, 11 and 12 in this volume.

Some metaphors may overlap cultures, which can lead to a mistaken assumption that they have the same meaning. For example the expression 'the girl is spoiled' has cultural overlap. It may be interpreted by a native English speaker from the western world to mean either that the girl is a 'spoilt brat' who has been overindulged by her parents; or that she is a young woman who has lost her virginity. However in a context of Indian English the sentence is more likely to mean merely that the girl's mind has turned to thinking about boys.

Appropriate contextual meaning is seldom explicitly stated, leaving much to the reader. A study of the implications and applications of verbal images is needed for cultural understanding. A native speaker of English may miss the subtleties of indirect, non-native English speech such as the forms of address common in Wijenaike's novels. Examples are *the one in my house* (spoken by a husband of his wife) and *the father of the children* (by a wife of her husband). These expressions are direct translations from Sinhala, and actually convey a great deal of respect.

More general indirect speech may reduce effrontery or arrogance on the part of the speaker. As noted by Chishimba (1983), some cultures hold ambiguity or obscurity to be marks of wisdom because they are associated with knowing how to manipulate language. Chishimba has provided several examples to support his point from African varieties of English.

Investigation of pervasive cultural metaphors yields insights to idioms through which emotion is expressed. In some cultures, direct expression of emotion is not sanctioned. This could lead strangers to believe that in these cultures emotions are not highly differentiated (Leff, 1973). However, an investigation of cultural sensibility may reveal that particular metaphors and images are used within the culture as a highly expressive means of conveying different kinds of emotion – intuitively rather than overtly. Furthermore, a study of the metaphorical frames which support the common sense of a culture (Geertz, 1975) may represent analogical models from which experience is generalized.

An analysis can be made of recurrent referential frameworks and metaphors in Wijenaike's novels *The Waiting Earth* (hereafter *WE*) and *The Rebel* (hereafter R), as an attempt to 'move from the sense of what a person says or does to reference, from what is said to what is talked about' (Ricoeur, 1979). This is an attempt to demonstrate the kind of analysis that will foster foreign readers' familiarity with, and understanding of, pervasive themes in Sri Lankan or other cultures.

Within Sri Lanka, Punyakante Wijenaike (Niven, 1977) is regarded as the foremost writer in English, though her works have not received adequate recognition outside the country. The central theme in her novels is the conflict between tradition and change, and its impact on family relationships. This theme is handled with a remarkable degree of sensitivity and sympathetic understanding. Although she was born and bred in the city the author writes mainly about the problems, hardships and frustrations of rural villagers. She explores the inward life of those individuals, men and women, who are unable to fulfil themselves due to social constraints and their economic condition.

Unlike many writers in the Third World, Wijenaike does not adopt an attitude of cynicism to traditional modes of behaviour and folk beliefs. Rather she seeks to understand and depict how these traditional modes influence and shape the day-to-day lives of their owners. As with all works of creative literature, Wijenaike's novels operate at two levels, the universal and the culture-specific. In an otherwise perceptive article on Wijenaike's novels, Niven (1977) has noted:

> The refusal to express outwardly one's inner emotions, however intense they are, lies at the heart of Mrs. Wijenaike's tragic method. The need to preserve a consistent public face draws the main characters further from each other and from an honest avowal of what they actually feel . . . The universality of Mrs. Wijenaike's insights lies in this ability to separate a character's inner tensions from the outer manner.

By stressing the universality of Wijenaike's characters Niven misses their 'Sri Lankanness', that is, the specific and particular dimension of their behaviour. What Niven perceives as a conscious literary device – the 'refusal to express outwardly one's inner emotions, however intense' – is in fact natural and culturally appropriate behaviour; and to impose an interpretation of tragedy upon the characters' silence is to ignore this dimension. As a result of his insensitivity to the subtleties of cultural communication, Niven pays inadequate attention to the meaning of silence. Yet it is just this kind of behaviour that illustrates the concept of native sensibility.

Clearly the term native sensibility is not one that admits of a near or elegant definition. However, for the purpose of this study the term can be taken to include behaviour such as culturally accepted ways of thinking, reasoning and feeling. Punyakante Wijenaike's novels are particularly illuminating in this respect because much of the implicit meaning and emotional power of the actions, events and happenings recounted in her novels and short stories occurs within a context of native sensibility.

Analysis of the concept of native sensibility begins with a discussion of emotions that are expressed culturally in Wijenaike's novels *vis-à-vis* what can be termed her use of 'food idioms', her 'hot/cold dichotomy' and her characters' use of silence.

REFERENTIAL FRAMEWORK: THE FOOD IDIOM

Through the food idiom, cultural behaviours are presented in a tacit communication mode. While this is expressed in language in the context of the novels, it may be fair to state there is no linguistic creativity involved. Rather the writer is a reporter of this meta-communication process.

In Sri Lankan culture individuals, particularly women, are socialized against the overt expression of emotion. Within the domain of the household, subtle dynamics in the relationship of a woman to her family members find expression metaphorically in terms of how the woman serves food and what she chooses to serve despite limited resources. One image that emerges frequently in Wijenaike's novels is cooking, and by extension, the serving of food as a metaphor for nurturance and growth. In the passage below, for example, the wife's devotion, love, and sacrifice for her husband are subtly depicted through the serving of tea. The husband's tea is thickened with milk (a primary symbol of nurturance) and sugar, a food conveying status.

> She brought him tea the way he liked, but could not afford to drink always, strong and sweet and thick with sugar and milk all stirred together. He saw that her own tea was plain with no milk and she took her sugar the normal frugal way, licking it from the palm of her hand. She would lick a grain or two of the sugar and then drink a hot mouthful of the tea. That way there was a sweetened taste in her mouth when she drank the tea and not more than a few grains of sugar were used (*WE*, p. 13).

As a means of expressing love towards her husband, the wife provides him with the food he relishes. While this behaviour may be common across cultures (take for example the expression 'the way to a man's heart is through his stomach'), what is particular to this culture is the wife's method of offering the food. It demonstrates the importance of this kind of metacommunication in a culture where direct communication often is not overt.

The woman's emotions must be well hidden – and so too must the extra fish be well hidden, the nurturance she offers her husband beneath his daily sustenance of rice – in the following passage:

> When she helped dish out the rice the farmer's wife had prepared for the reapers [she] took care not to fill his plate more than other plates and when he came up for it, she handed it to him indifferently as she did to all the other men and women. Only when he began to eat did he find this difference. Where no one could see, buried underneath the rice she had hidden an extra piece of fish, a good piece of fish with hardly any bone in it (*WF*, p. 15).

In a culture where overt expression of emotion is not allowed, individuals become acutely attuned to subtleties within non-verbal communication. Where emotions may be communicated directly or indirectly, as in western cultures, indirect (non-verbal) expression is only one possible mode selected from a range of expressive choices available to communicate feelings. In South Asia, the codification of non-verbal behaviour is greater than in the west, as individuals search for subtle cues which indicate particular moods or feelings. What may seem to an outsider to be silence, or what appears to be merely a casual glance, may be imbued in effect with cultural meaning.

The serving of food may also become an expression of distress, signalling indirect messages about relationships to family members. In a paper on idioms of distress utilized by Havik Brahmin women in South India, Mark Nichter observes (1981: 382):

> While a Havik woman cannot openly express her feelings towards her husband or in-laws, she can communicate her mood within the culinary sphere by her attentiveness in serving family, guests and visiting kin. Haviks often speak of the quality of a marital relationship by referring to a wife's attentiveness in providing customary drinks and eatables to guests and relatives. The presentation of a particular food or drink involves subtle kitchen politics.

Analysis of *The Waiting Earth* reveals that 'subtle kitchen politics' are manifest in Sri Lanka not only in relation to guests and relatives but within the immediate family. For example in the passage below, the mother dislikes her step-daughter intensely and feels threatened by her presence in the household. The denial of love to this girl is depicted metaphorically:

> Sophie Nona went into the dark little room which served as a kitchen and banged down a tin plate on the tiny table. She filled it reluctantly with the last of the rice scraped up from the bottom of the pot. It was half burnt and it gave her satisfaction to serve burnt rice to her wayward step-daughter. . . . She poured a spoonful of curry over the burnt rice and added a bone left over from the fish. She covered the whole thing with a plantain leaf and went out. She had done her duty (*R*, p. 6).

The intensity of the stepmother's hostile feelings towards the girl is culturally expressed by the offering of sustenance – rice – from the bottom of the pot. This rice is usually not eaten in Sri Lankan homes. The substance of the fish, like the quality of their relationship, is depicted by the absence of anything but bone. In a similar manner, when the wife wants to express her anger towards her husband, it is expressed in the way she serves rice:

> And the next day he brought home three measures of rice and she took it in silence. It was not the wife's concern to ask from where the rice came. But somehow she could not bring herself to look upon it as good rice, even though the grain was polished white and smooth and round like pearls. And when she washed it she did so without her usual care, so that when it was cooked it was full of stones that made Podi Singho (her husband) curse every time he bit on them (*WE*, p. 246).

Under normal conditions the Sri Lankan wife serves her husband and male children rice, fish and vegetables first and takes her meal afterwards, sharing what remains with her daughters. In the passage below, the wife shows her defiance of her husband's actions by her manner of serving food; her fulfilling of a duty while displaying a lack of devotion.

> She pursed her lips proudly. She could be cold and hard too. She sat down and waited until they had finished dishing out their own curries. Then instead of waiting until Podi Singho had finished eating, she took her plate and dished herself a large portion of rice and a good piece of fish. Then she sat down and ate it heartily, sucking loudly at the fishbone. Today she would dare show her anger (*WE*, p. 102).

In *The Quarrel* (hereafter *Q*), a short story in the collection *The Third Woman*, about a wife who leaves her husband, Wijenaike metaphorizes the situation as the cessation of cooking; the warmth of the hearth, like the wife's love for her husband, has gone cold.

When the sun set behind the hills, he got up, yawned, stretched himself and waited for his cup of tea. But the woman did not come with it. He got up and went into the kitchen. She was not there. Nor was the kettle on the fire. For a moment, he stood gaping at the cold dark hearth. Never before had she let the fire down completely. With his mouth still hanging open in wonder, he went out (*Q*, p. 102).

While a South Asian husband usually ventures into the kitchen only to take meals, Wijenaike expresses the extreme anger of this husband towards his wife in the following manner:

He went inside and though it was past noon and he had eaten well an hour or two before, he opened the pots one by one, making a great noise as he did so, and suddenly he took one and dashed it to the floor. It broke into pieces. . . . He took another pot and smashed it too. Then he spat on the ground and went outside (*Q*, p. 103).

These examples and their brief analysis provide opportunity for readers unfamiliar with Sri Lankan culture to glean insights to the appropriate manner of expressing emotions *vis-à-vis* the food idiom. This is not to suggest that readers cannot find meaning through a more superficial study of the relevant passages. However, an understanding of the cultural importance of pervasive referential frameworks and contextual applications lends a deeper appreciation of cultural sensibility and a sharing of richer imagery. Expressive modes are culturally constituted in the sense they initiate particular types of interaction and are associated with culturally pervasive values, norms and generative themes (Nichter, 1981).

Thus a woman's emotions can be understood not only in terms of the form and content of their expression, but also in relation to alternative communication modes which are acceptable within the dictates of her culture, but which she has chosen – for her own good reasons – to reject.

THE CONNOTATIONS OF THE 'HOT/COLD' IDIOM

The following section of the chapter moves into a brief discussion of the *hot/cold idiom* in which tacit communication finds expression overtly in language. At this stage the study moves into a deeper level of examination of native sensibility. The hot/cold dichotomy in South Asian culture is intimately connected to culturally determined patterns of thinking, and finds metaphorical expression in diverse areas such as medicine, food, personality types, etc. Such dichotomies are formative influences on indigenous sensibilities in a manner which an expression via the food idiom is not.

Native speakers of English use many conventional metaphors which are cultural survivors of hot-cold thematics derived from their humoral heritage: *hothead*, *hot under the collar*, and *cool as a cucumber*. In South Asia, however, references to hot/cold are culturally significant and not mere conventional metaphors. They denote psychological as well as physiological states in a culture where the Cartesian division between body and mind is not relevant. To describe someone as 'hot', physically, is also to make reference to a mental condition.

In the story *The Third Woman* (1963) the main character has two wives and describes one of them as 'all hot chili and fire', while the other 'remained cool and sweet as the milk rice she prepared in the morning'. Culturally, *hot chili* and *fire* convey an image of a woman who is passionate and who also lacks self-control – a concept having many cultural shades of meaning. The description of the other wife as *cool as milk rice* refers to a woman who is in control of her duties in the kitchen and also in control of her virtue. To be described as *milk rice*, a pure substance offered to the gods, implies she is virtuous, and it is generally believed that purity is associated with control of self and social space.

SILENCE AS A SPEECH ACT

In this section an analysis of examples from the novels clarifies some uses of silence within their cultural context (see also Tannen and Saville-Troike, 1985). When emotions are expressed through the *food idiom* or the *hot/cold* framework the reader decodes the meaning. When the characters are silent the reader must creatively interpret their behaviour in order to derive meaning.

Within the Sri Lankan context, silence which emerges as meaningful dialogue between characters may be easily overlooked or 'misread' if reference is not made to native sensibility. Moreover, a discussion of silence moves analysis into a more subtle level of native sensibility, because its use as a referential framework provides a good example of how cultural values may underscore the surface meaning of action sequences.

In Wijenaike's novels, reticence emerges as a culturally sanctioned value. A Sri Lankan proverb states that 'a pot full of water makes less noise'. That is, someone who is full of knowledge makes less noise about it than a person who has little or none. This cultural notion is reflected in the passages below.

> He knew there was nothing in her words. Her words always fell too easily and quickly like the small red berries on a lovi tree. Though ripe they were too light in weight to hurt even an ant on the ground (*WE*, p. 134).

> He talked easily too, the words flowing like water from his mouth as if he was sure that they brought nothing but pleasure to his listeners. . . . So this was what learning did to a man (*WE*, p. 134).

The value of silence has other cultural meanings and associations, strikingly portrayed by Wijenaike in her description of husband–wife relationships. What emerges in the passages below is the importance of tacit communication between husband and wife. What is left undescribed, assumed, is that the overt expression of emotion denotes insincerity and a lack of discipline within Sri Lankan culture. This is only implied in the description of how a man may suffer his wife's loss of respect. A man's strength is expressed by his silence; to be talkative is to be weak and easy to manipulate. A man who can control his words is in control of his being; to be unable to control words reflects a state of weakness and hence vulnerability.

In one of Wijenaike's stories a husband has the impulse to speak to his wife of his love, but:

He bit back the words and said nothing. How could he admit without shame that his wife meant so much to him? (*WE*, p. 13).

She was his wife, there was no need to say such things to her. And yet how could he always keep silent? Sweat broke over him. He had been a fool to speak. She would take it for weakness and secretly laugh at him. He never knew what went on inside her for she never spoke much and what she felt she took care not to show on her face. One never knew with women. Even the best of them could not understand a man's kindness (*WE*, p. 11).

A man could, without shame and fear, speak out his mind to another woman, to a mistress whom he could treat as an equal. But to his own wife, how could a man betray his weakness and then continue to live in dignity under the same roof? Would he lose her respect? The moment a man showed too much kindness, a wife would begin to rule him (*WE*, p. 9).

CONCLUSION

This chapter has been an attempt to examine the concept of native sensibility in the creative writing of Punyakante Wijenaike. For this purpose three kinds of metaphor have been studied; the 'food idiom', the 'hot/cold dualism' and the use of silence. Analysis has moved from a relatively simple to more complex levels; and the categories were chosen to indicate the kind of analysis that needs to be done in order to increase readers' understanding of the influence of native sensibility on discourse patterns.

When seeking to identify the peculiarities of discourse patterns of non-native users of English, the standard procedure has been to adopt what can be referred to, for want of a better term, as a *deviational* model. That is, a model that demonstrates how far the language used by a non-native speaker deviates from standard usage in terms of syntax, idiom, vocabulary and so on. These comparisons have no doubt yielded some important results. It can be contended, however, that such an approach is limiting and fails to capture the essence of the *interactional process*, which may be defined as the generation of meaning between two universes of discourse.

These universes are those of standard English usage, and of the cultural discourse from which native sensibility arises. In creative writing much room must be allowed for individual play of imagination and creative freedom in interpretation. Indeed at this point the widely used deviational model can be counter-productive, because it ignores the dynamics of the interactional process.

Creative writers constantly experiment with language. Writers seek to create new and original metaphors, or in linguistic terms, new collocations. When non-native writers of English experiment in this way, they naturally draw on their native sensibilities and inherited forms of culturally sanctioned discourse patterns. By adopting an interactional perspective it is possible to understand these discoursal rules. As Strevens (1980: 68) has noted:

The pragmatics of discourse seem to be prone to display features transferred from the local culture in the same way as pronunciation does. This is perhaps not surprising; the pragmatics of discourse constitute a major part of our rules for regulating both interpersonal relations in general and at the same time the subtle ways in which we express our own requirements and understand what other human beings are doing. Such rules are learned within our particular culture from a very early age – certainly before mastery of language – and over a long period, perhaps one's entire lifetime. Yet they are made explicit only rarely . . . the point at issue is that local forms of English vary in the detail of their discoursal rules; the appropriate set of detailed rules is an essential defining feature.

To understand the complexities of English in non-native contexts, it is necessary to examine the impact of native sensibility as well as the other interactional processes which are central to discourse. It has been suggested in this chapter that this is a difficult task, as discourse patterns are multilayered and need to be uncovered sequentially. The above attempt has been a preliminary effort to delineate the notion of native sensibility; a notion which may be relevant to a variety of academic disciplines, not the least significant of which are language learning and teaching.

References

BECK, BRENDA (1982) Root metaphor patterns: a review of *Metaphors we live by*. *Semiotic Inquiry* **2**(1): 86–97.

BLAKE, C. A. (1979) Rhetoric and intercultural communication. In *Handbook of Intercultural Communication*, edited by M. Asante, E. Newmark and C. A. Blake, Beverly Hills: Sage Publications.

CHISHIMBA, MAURICE M. (1983) African varieties of English: text in context. Ph.D. dissertation, University of Illinois.

FERNANDEZ, J. (1974) The mission of metaphor in expressive culture, *Current Anthropology* **15**: 119–145.

GEERTZ, C. (1975) Common sense as a cultural system, *Antioch Review* **33**: 1.

KACHRU, B. (1982) Meaning in deviation: toward understanding non-native English texts. In *The other tongue: English across cultures*, edited by B. Kachru. Urbana: University of Illinois Press.

LAKOFF, G. and M. JOHNSON (1980) *Metaphors we live by*. Chicago: University of Chicago Press.

LEFF, J. (1973) Culture and the differentiation of emotional states, *British Journal of Psychiatry* **123**: 299–306.

NICHTER, MARK (1981) Idioms of distress: alternatives in the expression of psychosocial distress, a case study from South India. *Culture, Medicine and Psychiatry* **5**: 379–408.

NIVEN, A. (1977) The fiction of Punyakante Wijenaike. *Journal of Commonwealth Literature* **12**(1): 55–65.

RICOEUR, P. (1979) The model of the text: meaningful action considered as a text. In *Interpretive Social Science: a Reader*, edited by P. Rabinow and W. Smith. Berkeley: University of California Press.

STREVENS, P. (1980) *Teaching English as an international language*. Oxford and New York: Pergamon Institute of English.

TANNEN, DEBORAH and MURIEL SAVILLE-TROIKE (1985) *Perspectives on silence*. Northwood: Ablex.

TYLOR, S. (1978) *The said and the unsaid: mind, meaning and culture*. New York: Academic Press.

WIJENAIKE, P. (1963) *The third woman*. Maharagama: Saman Publishers.

WIJENAIKE, P. (1966) *The waiting earth*. Colombo: Colombo Apothecaries' Company.

WIJENAIKE, P. (1979) *The rebel*. Colombo: Lake House Investments Ltd.

PART IV

The Bilinguals' Creativity and Contact Literatures in English

INTRODUCTION

THIS section provides evidence for the use of the term 'literatures in English' as opposed to the generally used term 'English literature'. The three chapters deal with the distinctiveness of the bilinguals' creativity in non-native English literatures. In order to draw attention to such characteristics, the term 'contact literatures' is used. The contact literatures, as B. Kachru suggests, 'reveal a blend of two or more linguistic textures and literary traditions'. These literatures show a range of discourse devices and cultural assumptions distinct from the ones associated with the native varieties of English. The assumptions are different from the Judaic-Christian traditions and Greek and Roman traditions. In a sense, new paradigms of literary, cultural, and stylistic traditions have been introduced into English. Kachru argues that the use of English in contact literatures introduces a new 'meaning system' to the language. It is like redefining the semantic and semiotic potential of English. In this case, then, it is making English *mean* what it does not normally *mean* when used by native speakers.

Gonzalez's chapter provides a different insight for understanding contact literatures. He examines poetry and fiction (short stories) written in English by Filipinos for traces of discourse transfer from the native literary tradition. Gonzalez claims that although in oral Philippine English there is extensive transfer of discourse patterns from the first Philippine language; in the written mode no such transfer occurs. Only in referent, theme, and situation can one speak of distinctively Philippine features. In his view the innovations made by Philippine writers in English are experiments within Western tradition. He sees that lack of an indigenized Philippine literature in English as being the manifestation of literary imperialism. An imperialism, beginning with the Spanish and continued with the Americans, which has almost destroyed the indigenous literary tradition.

The last chapter in this section brings us to a specific writer: Raj Rao, an Indian novelist and philosopher who, as Parthasarathy observes, has through-out been innovative in his attempt not only to nativize but also to Sanskritize the English language. As a result the Indian reality that emerges from his writing is authentic. Rao overcomes the problem of finding words for culturally bound objects by contextualizing them so that their meanings are self-evident. Raja Rao invariably draws upon Kannada and Sanskrit, and in the process uses devices like calquing or loan translation, idiomatic and syntactic equivalencies, and the imitation of native speaker repertoires. By evoking the necessary cultural ambiance, these devices help to reduce the problem of linguistic alienation that has troubled non-native writers. English as a code is now universally shared by both native and non-native speakers. What isn't always shared are the manifestations of a specific culture embedded by the writer in the language. To undersand them, Parthasarathy suggests that the reader, particularly the native speaker, will have to seriously equip himself with knowledge of the writer's socioculture milieu. Wouldn't he be expected to do so if he were to read an English translation of, say, a Sanskrit epic? Parthasarathy's chapter addresses itself to some of these problems which are of interest to the literary critic as well as the language teacher.

10

The Bilingual's Creativity: Discoursal and Stylistic Strategies in Contact Literatures

BRAJ B. KACHRU

THE bilingual's creativity[1] in English on a global scale, and the issues concerning nativization of discourse patterns, discourse strategies and speech acts, are a natural consequence of the unprecedented world-wide uses of English, mainly since the early 1920s. The phenomenon of a language with fast-increasing diaspora varieties – and significantly more non-native users than native speakers[2] – has naturally resulted in the pluricentricity[3] of English. The sociolinguistic import of this pluricentricity is that the non-native users of English can choose to acquire a variety of English which may be distinct from the native varieties. As a result, two types of model of English have developed: native and institutionalized non-native (see Kachru, 1982c). It is with reference to these models that the innovations, creativity and emerging literary traditions in English must be seen.[4] Each model has its own linguistic and literary norms – or a tendency to develop such norms. This is the linguistic reality of English in its world context. Attitudinally, however, the way people react to this situation opens up an entirely different can of worms, not directly related to the discussion in this chapter.[5]

The concept 'pluricentricity' of English is a useful beginning point for this chapter. I will address certain issues which, it seems to me, are related to both Western and non-Western pluricentricity of the English language. I will first raise a theoretical question concerning linguists' common perception of a speech community, particularly their understanding of the linguistic behaviour of the members of a speech community which alternately uses two, three or more languages depending on the situation and function. One might ask: How valid is a theory of grammar which treats monolingualism as the norm for description and analysis of the linguistic interaction of traditional multilingual societies? Yet in linguistic description – save a few exceptions – the dominant paradigms have considered monolingualism as the norm (i.e. judgements based on the ideal speaker–hearer).[6] My second concern – not unrelated to the first point – is with description and methodology: Are the models proposed for

125

discourse and text-analysis of monolinguals' linguistic interaction observationally, descriptively, and explanatorily adequate for the analysis of bilinguals' language use? My third aim is to discuss some underlying processes of nativization and innovations which characterize *literariness*[7] (both formal and contextual) of selected texts manifesting the bilingual's creativity. The examples have been taken primarily from what has earlier been termed 'contact literature'.[8] Finally, I shall refer to the issue of relationship between this creativity and underlying thought patterns of bilinguals.

I believe that the theoretical and methodological tracks followed to date in the study of contact literatures in English fail on several counts.[9] The foremost limitation one detects in a majority of studies is that of using almost identical approaches for the description of the bilingual's and monolingual's creativity. Literary creativity in English has until now been studied within the Western Judeo-Christian heritage and its implications for understanding English literature. True, the English language shows typical characteristics of a 'mixed' language development in its layer after layer of borrowings, adaptations, and various levels of language contact.[10] But even there, the earlier main intrusion has been essentially European and more or less consistent with the Hellenistic and Roman traditions.

However, the prolonged colonial period substantially changed that situation in the linguistic fabric of the English langauge, and extended its use as a medium for ethnic and regional literatures in the non-Western world (e.g. Indian English, West African English; see Kachru, 1980). The extreme results of this extension can be observed in the 'Sanskritization' and 'Kannadaization' of Raja Rao's English,[11] and in the 'Yorubaization' and 'Igboization' of Amos Tutuola and Chinua Achebe. The labels indicate that these authors have exploited two or more linguistic – and cultural – resources which do not fit into the paradigms of what Kaplan (1966) terms 'the Platonic-Aristotelian sequence'[12] and the dominant Anglo-Saxon thought patterns of the native speakers of English. Recognition of this mixing of Western and non-Western resources has implications for our use of terms such as *cohesion* or *coherence*,[13] and even *communicative competence*. We should also be cautious in suggesting typologies of culture-specific speech acts in various varieties of English (see Chishimba, 1983 and Magura, 1984).

In contact literature the bilingual's creativity introduces a nativized thought process (e.g. Sanskritic, Yoruba, Malaysian) which does not conform to the recognized canons of discourse types, text design, stylistic conventions, and traditional thematic range of the English language, as viewed from the major Judeo-Christian traditions of literary and linguistic creativity.

The linguistic realization of the underlying traditions and thought processes for a bilingual may then entail a *transfer* of discoursal patterns from one's other (perhaps more dominant) linguistic code(s) and cultural and literary traditions. That such organization of discourse strategies – conscious or unconscious – arises in different ways in different cultures has been shown in several studies on non-Western languages.[14]

'CONTACT' IN CONTACT LITERATURES

What does the term 'contact literatures' imply? The term refers to the literatures in English written by the users of English as a second language to delineate contexts which generally do not form part of what may be labelled the traditions of English literature (African, Malaysian, Indian and so on). Such literatures, as I have stated elsewhere, are 'a product of multicultural and multilingual speech communities' (Kachru, 1982b: 330). Furthermore:

> The concept of 'contact literature' is an extension of 'contact language'. A language in contact is two-faced; it has its own face, and the face it acquires from the language with which it has contact. The degree of contact varies from lexical borrowing to intensive mixing of units. Contact literatures (for example, non-native English literatures of India, Nigeria or Ghana; the Francophone literatures; or the Indian-Persian literature) have certain formal and thematic characteristics which make the use of the term 'contact' appropriate (Kachru, 1982b: 341).

It has already been shown that contact literatures have both a national identity and a linguistic distinctiveness (e.g., *Indianness*, *Africanness*). The 'linguistic realization' of such identities is achieved in several ways: the text may have both a surface and an underlying identity with the native varieties of English; it may show only partial identity with the native norms; or it may entail a culture-specific (e.g. African, Asian) identity both at the surface and the underlying levels and share nothing with the native variety. Thus contact literatures have several linguistic and cultural faces: they reveal a blend of two or more linguistic textures and literary traditions, and they provide the English language with extended contexts of situation within which such literatures may be interpreted and understood. In such literatures there is a range of discourse devices and cultural assumptions distinct from the ones associated with the native varieties of English. One must extend the scope of the historical dimension and cultural traditions from that of Judeo-Christian traditions to the different heritages of Africa and Asia. This kind of historical and cultural expansion results in a special type of linguistic and literary phenomenon: such texts demand a new literary sensibility and extended cultural awareness from a reader who is outside of the speech fellowship which identifies with the variety.

It is in this sense that English writing has become, to give an example, 'our national literature', and English 'our national language' in Nigeria as claimed by Nnamdi Azikiwe, the first President of Nigeria (quoted in Thumboo, 1976: vii). The same is, of course, true of most of the former British and American colonies or areas of influence, such as India, Singapore, and the Philippines.

Thumboo (1976: ix) is making the same point in connection with Commonwealth writers in English when he says that

> language must serve, not overwhelm, if the Commonwealth writer is to succeed. Mastering it involves holding down and breaching a body of habitual English associations to secure that condition of verbal freedom cardinal to energetic, resourceful writing. In a sense the language is remade, where necessary, by adjusting the interior landscape of words in order to explore and mediate the permutations of another culture and environment.

And discussing the problems of such writers, Thumboo adds (xxxiv):

> The experience of peoples crossing over into a second language is not new, though the formalization of the move acts as a powerful rider. What amounts to the re-location of a sensibility nurtured by, and instructed in one culture, within another significantly different culture, is complicated in the outcome.

DISCOURSAL THOUGHT PATTERN AND LANGUAGE DESIGN

The relationship between underlying thought patterns and language designs has been well illustrated by Achebe in a very convincing way. In his *Arrow of God*, Achebe (1969) provides two short texts as an illustration – one nativized (Africanized) and the other Englishized – and then gives reasons for choosing to use the former. In explaining his choice he says that it will '. . . give some idea of how I approach the use of English'. In the passage, the Chief Priest is telling one of his sons why it is necessary to send him to church. Achebe first gives the Africanized version:

> I want one of my sons to join these people and be my eyes there. If there is nothing in it you will come back. But if there is something then you will bring back my share. The world is like a mask, dancing. If you want to see it well, you do not stand in one place. My spirit tells me that those who do not befriend the white man today will be saying, 'had we known', tomorrow.

Achebe then asks, 'supposing I had put it another way. Like this for instance:

> I am sending you as my representative among those people – just to be on the safe side in case the new religion develops. One has to move with the times or else one is left behind. I have a hunch that those who fail to come to terms with the white man may well regret their lack of foresight.

And he rightly concludes: 'The material is the same. But the form of the one is in character and the other is not. It is largely a matter of instinct but judgement comes into it too.'

It is thus a combination of creative *instinct* and formal *judgement* which makes a text language- or culture-specific within a context of situation (e.g. Yoruba speech, Chicano English, Kannada influence, Punjabi English).[15]

Furthermore, if we accept Kaplan's claim that the preferred dominant 'thought patterns' of English are essentially out of 'the Anglo-European cultural patterns' based on 'a Platonic-Aristotelian sequence', the logical next step is to recognize that in the case of, for example, Raja Rao or Mulk Raj Anand, the underlying thought patterns reflect the traditions of Sanskrit and the regional or national oral lore. And in the case of Amos Tutuola and Chinua Achebe they stem from Yoruba and Igbo traditions, respectively.

Raja Rao makes it clear that such transfer of tradition is part of his creativity.

> There is no village in India, however mean, that has not a rich *sthala-purana* or legendary history, of its own. . . . The *Puranas* are endless and innumerable. We have neither punctuation nor the treacherous 'ats' and 'ons' to bother us – we tell one interminable tale. Episode follows episode, and when our thoughts stop our breath stops, and we move on to another thought. This was and still is the ordinary style of our story telling. I have tried to follow it myself in this story [*Kanthapura*] (Rao, 1963: vii–viii).

Raja Rao's narration of an 'interminable tale' results in breaking the Western norms of punctuation and prose rhythm, and he shares it, for example, with the writers on another continent, West Africa. Tutuola has a 'peculiar use of punctuation, resulting in an unending combination of sentences', which he 'owes to his Yoruba speech' (Taiwo, 1976: 76).

> When he tried all his power for several times and failed and again at that moment the smell of the gun-powder of the enemies' guns which were shooting repeatedly was rushing to our noses by the breeze and this made us fear more, so my brother lifted me again a very short distance, but when I saw that he was falling several times, then I told him to leave me on the road and run away for his life perhaps he might be safe so that he would be taking care of our mother as she had no other sons more than both of us and I told him that if God saves my life too then we should meet again, but if God does not save my life we should meet in Heaven (*Bush of Ghosts*, p. 20; quoted in Taiwo, 1976: 76).

In addition to this characteristic, Taiwo (1976: 111) argues that Tutuola and his compatriot Achebe 'exhibit in their writings features which may be described as uniquely Nigerian'. Taiwo further explains (1976: 75) that Tutuola 'has carried Yoruba speech habits into English and writes in English as he would speak in Yoruba. . . . He is basically speaking Yoruba but using English words.' And 'the peculiar rhythms of his English are the rhythms of Yoruba speech' (1976: 85). With regard to Achebe, Taiwo (1976: 116–117) observes that in the following scene which he quotes from *Things Fall Apart*, Achebe 'has had to rely heavily on the resources of Igbo language and culture to dramatise the interrelation between environment and character:'

> 'Umuofia kwenu!' shouted the leading *egwugwu*, pushing the air with his raffia arms.
> The elders of the clan replied, 'Yaa!'
> 'Umuofia kwenu!'
> 'Yaa!'
> 'Umuofia kwenu!'
> 'Yaa!'
> Evil Forest then thrust the pointed end of his rattling staff into the earth. And it began to shake and rattle, like something agitating with a metallic life. He took the first of the empty stools and the eight other *egwugwu* began to sit in order of seniority after him.

THE BILINGUAL'S GRAMMAR: SOME HYPOTHESES

It seems to me that for understanding the bilingual's creativity one must begin with a distinct set of hypotheses for what has been termed 'the bilingual's grammar' (or multilingual's grammar). I am, of course, not using the term 'grammar' in a restricted sense: it refers to the productive linguistic processes at different linguistic levels (including discourse and style) which a bilingual uses for various linguistic functions.

The bilingual's grammar has to be captured in terms of what sociolinguists term 'verbal repertoire' or 'code repertoire', with specific reference to a speech community (or a speech fellowship).[16] Such speech communities have a formally and functionally determined range of languages and/or dialects as part of their competence for linguistic interaction (see Kachru, 1981b, 1982a).

A characteristic of such competence is the faculty and ease of mixing and switching, and the adoption of stylistic and discoursal strategies from the total verbal repertoire available to a bilingual.[17] One has to consider not only the blend of the formal features, but also the assumptions derived from various cultural norms, and the blending of these norms into a new linguistic configuration with a culture-specific meaning system. There are several salient characteristics of the creativity of such a person. I shall discuss some of these below.

First, the processes used in such creativity are based on multinorms of styles and strategies. We cannot judge such devices on the basis of one norm derived from one literary or cultural tradition (see Parthasarathy, 1983).

Second, nativization and acculturation of text presupposes an altered context of situation for the language. Traditionally accepted literary norms with reference to a particular code (say, Hindi or English) seem to fail here. A description based on an approach which emphasizes the monolingual 'speaker-hearer' is naturally weak in terms of its descriptive and explanatory power.

Third, the bilingual's creativity results in the configuration of two or more codes. The resultant code, therefore, has to be contextualized in terms of the new uses of language.

Finally, such creativity is not to be seen merely as a formal combination of two or more underlying language designs, but also as a creation of cultural, aesthetic, societal and literary norms. In fact, such creativity has a distinct context of situation.

It is this distinctive characteristic which one might say on the one hand formally *limits* the text and on the other hand *extends* it, depending on how one looks at linguistic innovations. The creative processes used in such texts have a *limiting* effect because the conventional 'meaning system' of the code under use is altered, lexically, grammatically, or in terms of cohesion (see Y. Kachru, 1983a, b). A reader-hearer 'outside' the shared or re-created meaning system has to familiarize himself or herself with the processes of the design and formal reorganization, the motivation for innovations, and the formal and contextual implications of such language use. In other words, to borrow Hallidayan terms (1973: 43) one has to see what a multilingual 'can say' and 'can mean'. The *range in saying* and the *levels of meaning* are distinct, and one has to establish 'renewal of connection' with the context of situation.[18]

What is, then, inhibiting (limiting or unintelligible) in one sense may also be interpreted as an extension of the codes in terms of the new linguistic innovations, formal experimentation, cultural nuances, and addition of a new cultural perspective to the language.[19] If the linguistic and cultural 'extension' of the code is missed, one also misses the interpretation at the linguistic, literary, socio-linguistic and cultural levels. One misses the relationship between *saying* and *meaning*, the core of literary creativity.

What does it take from a reader to interpret such creativity? It demands a lot: it almost demands an identification with the literary sensibility of the bilingual in tune with the ways of *saying* and the levels of new *meaning*.

LINGUISTIC REALIZATION OF DISTINCTIVENESS

This altered 'meaning system' of such English texts is the result of various linguistic processes, including nativization of context, of cohesion and cohesiveness, and of rhetorical strategies.

Nativization of context

One first thinks of the most obvious and most elusive process which might be called *contextual* nativization of texts, in which cultural presuppositions overload a text and demand a serious cultural interpretation. In Raja Rao's *Kanthapura*, to take a not-so-extreme example, such contextualization of the following exemplary passage involves several levels.

> 'Today,' he says 'it will be the story of Siva and Parvati.' And Parvati in penance becomes the country and Siva becomes heaven knows what! 'Siva is the three-eyed,' he says, 'and Swaraj too is three-eyed: Self-purification, Hindu-Moslem unity, Khaddar ' And then he talks of Damayanthi and Sakunthala and Yasodha and everywhere there is something about our country and something about Swaraj. Never had we heard *Harikathas* like this And he can sing too, can Jayaramachar. He can keep us in tears for hours together. But the *Harikatha* he did, which I can never forget in this life and in all lives to come, is about the birth of Gandhiji. 'What a title for a *Harikatha*!' cried out old Venkatalakshamma, the mother of the Postmaster.
>
> 'It is neither about Rama nor Krishna.' – 'But,' said her son, who too has been to the city, 'but, Mother, the Mahatma is a saint, a holy man.' – 'Holy man or lover of a widow, what does it matter to me? When I go to the temple I want to hear about Rama and Krishna and Mahadeva and not all this city nonsense,' said she. And being an obedient son, he was silent. But the old woman came along that evening. She could never stay away from a *Harikatha*. And sitting beside us, how she wept! . . . (Rao, 1963: 10).

In this passage it is not so much that the underlying narrative technique is different or collocational relationships are different, but the 'historical' and 'cultural' presuppositions are different from what has been traditionally the 'expected' historical and cultural milieu for English literature. One has to explain Siva and Parvati with reference to the multitude of the pantheon of Hindu gods, and in that context then *three-eyed* (Sanskrit *trinetra*) makes sense: it refers to Lord Siva's particular manifestation when he opens his 'third eye', located on his forehead, spitting fire and destroying the creation. Damayanthi [Damayantī], Sakunthala [Sakuntalā], and Yasodha [Yasodā] bring forth the epic tradition of Indian classics: Damayanthi, the wife of Nala; Sakunthala, who was later immortalized in Kalidasa's [Kālidāsa: 5th century AD?] play of the same name; and Yasodha, the mother of Krishna, the major character of the epic *Mahābhārata*. The contemporariness of the passage is in reference to Gandhi (1869–1948), and the political implications of Hindu-Muslim unity and *khaddar* (handspun cloth). The *Harikatha* man is the traditional religious storyteller who has woven all this in a fabric of story.

Now, this is not unique: this is in fact characteristic of context-specific texts in general.[20] But that argument does not lessen the *interpretive* difficulties of such texts. Here the presupposition of discourse interpretation is at a level which is not grammatical. It is of a special lexical and contextual nature. It extends the cultural load of English lexis from conventional Greek and Roman allusions to Asian and African myths, folklore, and traditions. It universalizes English, and one might say 'de-Englishizes' it in terms of the accepted literary and cultural norms of the language.

Nativization of cohesion and cohesiveness

The second process involves the alteration of the native users' concept of *cohesion* and *cohesiveness*: these concepts are to be redefined in each institutionalized variety within the appropriate universe of discourse (see Y. Kachru, 1983a, b). This is particularly true of types of lexicalization, collocational extension and the use or frequency of grammatical forms. A number of such examples are given in my earlier studies.[21]

The lexical *shift*, if I might use that term, is used for various stylistic and attitudinal reasons.[22] The lexicalization involves not only direct lexical transfer but also entails other devices, too, such as hybridization and loan translation. Such English lexical items have more than one interpretive context: they have a surface 'meaning' of the second language (English) and an underlying 'meaning' of the first (or dominant) language. The discoursal interpretation of such lexicalization depends on the meaning of the underlying language – say Yoruba, Kannada, Punjabi, Malay, etc.

Nativization of rhetorical strategies

The third process is the nativization of rhetorical strategies in close approximation to the devices a bilingual uses in his or her other code(s). These include consciously or unconsciously devised strategies according to the patterns of interaction in the native culture, which are transferred to English.

A number of such strategies are enumerated below. First, one has to choose a style with reference to the stylistic norms appropriate to the concepts of 'high culture' and 'popular culture'. In India, traditionally, high culture entails Sanskritization, and in certain contexts in the north, Persianization. We see such transfer in the much-discussed and controversial work of Raja Rao, *The serpent and the rope*. On the other hand, in *Kanthapura*, Rao uses what may be called a 'vernacular style' of English. His other work, *The cat and Shakespeare*, introduces an entirely new style.[23] In devising these three styles for Indian English, Rao has certainly demonstrated a delicate sense for appropriate style, but such experimentation has its limitations, too. These innovations make his style linguistically 'deviant' from a native speaker's perspective, and culturally it introduces into English a dimension alien to the canons of English literature.[24]

In the expansion of the style range, the African situation is not different from the South Asian. In Achebe we find that 'he has developed not one prose style but several, and in each novel he is careful to select the style or styles that will best suit his subject' (Lindfors, 1973: 74). It is for this reason that, as Lindfors says, 'Achebe has devised an African vernacular style' (74).[25]

Once the choice of the style is made, the next step is to provide authenticity (e.g. *Africanness*, *Indianness*) to the speech acts, or to the discourse types. How is this accomplished? It is achieved by 'linguistic realization' of the following types:

(1) the use of native similes and metaphors (e.g. Yoruba, Kannada, Malay) which linguistically result in collocational deviation;
(2) the transfer of rhetorical devices for 'personalizing' speech interaction;
(3) the translation ('transcreation') of proverbs, idioms, etc.;
(4) the use of culturally dependent speech styles; and
(5) the use of syntactic devices.

Let me now illustrate these five points one by one. First the use of native similes and metaphors. It is through such similes that Achebe, for example, is able to evoke the cultural milieu in which the action takes place (Lindfors, 1973; 75). Examples of such similes are: *like a bush-fire in the harmattan*, *like a yam tendril in the rainy season*, *like a lizard fallen from an iroko tree*, *like pouring grains of corn into a bag full of holes* (also see B. Kachru, 1965 [1983: 131 ff]).

Second, the transfer of rhetorical devices for contextualizing and authenticating speech interaction. Such devices provide, as it were, the 'ancestral sanction' to the interaction, a very important strategy in some African and Asian societies. It is one way of giving 'cultural roots' to English in African and Asian contexts, particularly to its 'vernacular style'. One might say it is a device to link the past with the present. Onuora Nzekwu (*Wand of noble wood*) accomplishes this by the use of what may be called 'speech initiators' which appear 'empty' to one who does not share the cultural and linguistic presuppositions. But for contextualizing the text, these are essential. Consider among others the following: *our people have a saying*; *as our people say*; *it was our fathers who said*; *the elders have said*. Stylistically this also preserves the 'orality' of the discourse.

A third strategy is that of 'transcreating' proverbs and idioms from an African or Asian language into English. The culture-embeddedness of such linguistic items is well recognized and, as Achebe says, they are 'the palm-oil with which words are eaten' (1964: viii). The function of such expression is to universalize a specific incident and to reduce the harshness of an utterance. Achebe's use of proverbs, in Lindfors' view (1973: 77), sharpens character-ization, clarifies conflict, and focuses on the values of the society. In other words, to use Herskovits' term (1958), the use of such a device provides a 'grammar of values'. Consider, for example, the use of the following proverbs by Achebe: *I cannot live on the bank of the river and wash my hand with the spittle*; *if a child washed his hands he could eat with kings*, and *a person who chased two rats at a time would lose one*. It is through the proverbs and word play that the wit and wisdom of the ancestors is passed on to new generations. I have shown earlier (B. Kachru, 1965, 1966) how this device is used to nativize speech functions such as abuses, curses, blessings, and flattery.

A fourth characteristic is to give the narrative and the discourse a 'naive tall-tale style' typical of the earthy folk style (Lindfors, 1973: 57). This is typical of Tutuola, or of Raja Rao's *Kanthapura*. This, as Jolaoso observes (quoted by Lindfors, 1973: 57), 'reminds one very forcibly of the rambling old grand-mother telling her tale of spirits in the ghostly light of the moon' (see also Afolayan, 1971 and Abrahams, 1983: 21–39).

The fifth strategy is the use of particular syntactic devices. An example is the enhancement of the above folk style by using the device of a traditional native village storyteller and occasionally putting questions to the audience for participation. This assures a reader's involvement. Tutuola makes frequent use of asking direct questions, or asking rhetorical questions in the narration. In Raja Rao's case the Harikathaman or the grandmother uses the same devices, very effective indeed for passing on the cultural tradition to new generations and for entertaining other age groups.

One might ask here: Is there evidence that the discourse of Indians reflects features which according to Lannoy represent a 'culture of sound'? (1971: 275) Would one agree with him that one consequence of belonging to such a culture is 'the widespread tendency of Indians to use language as a form of incantation and exuberant rhetorical flourish on public occasions. Orators rend the air with verbose declamations more for the pleasure of the sound than for the ideas and facts they may more vaguely desire to express'? (176). One wonders, is Babu English (see Widdowson, 1979: 202–211) a manifestation of such 'culture of sound' in the written mode?

LINGUISTIC REALIZATION OF THOUGHT PATTERNS

The above-discussed characteristics are essentially related to what may be called the texture of discourse or the nativized cohesive characteristics of various Englishes. The question of linguistic realization of the underlying thought pattern in the bilingual's creativity still remains. I shall now return to that aspect and briefly explore it with reference to South Asia.

Let me begin with two recent studies, both on Indo-Aryan languages of South Asia: Hindi, and Marathi. In Hindi discourse, according to Y. Kachru (1983b: 58), there is a 'spiral-like structure', and there is a greater degree of tolerance for digressions in an orthographic paragraph in Hindi as compared with English, provided the digressions link various episodes in discourse paragraphs in a spiral-like structure.

The paragraph structure of Marathi has been labelled 'circular' (from the point of view of an English speaker) by Pandharipande (1983: 128). Contrasting what Kaplan (1966, 1983) calls the 'linear' paragraph structure of English with the 'circular' structure of Marathi, Pandharipande further points out that

(a) . . . a paragraph in English begins with a general statement of its content, and then carefully develops that statement by specific illustrations; (b) while it is discursive, a paragraph is never digressive; (c) the flow of ideas occurs in English in a straight line from the opening sentence to the last sentence. In contrast to this, the paragraph structure in Marathi is full of digressions. The paragraph opens with a hypothesis and proceeds with arguments to either support or to oppose the hypothesis. Finally, the validity of the hypothesis is confirmed. Thus a paragraph in an expository discourse in Marathi begins and ends roughly at the same point.

We find an identical position in Heimann, who believes that an Indian 'thinks' in 'a circle or a spiral of continuously developing potentialities, and not on the straight line of progressive stages' (quoted in Lannoy, 1971: 278). In Lannoy's view a characteristic trait of Indian minds is 'indifference to the logical procedure defined in Aristotle's law of the excluded middle' (Lannoy, 1971: 277). The Indian preference then is for 'non-sequential logic' (279). However, Lannoy assures us that 'this is not to suggest that India is unconcerned with logic, but that it employs a different system of logic from the West' (277; also see Nakamura, 1964).

Here the *difference* between the two systems, the Aristotelian and Indian, should interest us. This important difference between the two has clearly been brought out by Basham (1954: 501–502); I cannot resist the temptation to quote the relevant passage here.

A correct inference was established by syllogism, of which the Indian form (pañcāvayava) was somewhat more cumbrous than the Aristotelian. Its five members were known as proposition (pratijñā), reason (hetu), example (udāharana), application (upanaya), and conclusion (nigamana). The classical Indian example may be paraphrased as follows:
   (1) There is fire on the mountain,
   (2) because there is smoke above it,
   (3) and where there is smoke there is fire, as, for instance, in a kitchen;
   (4) such is the case with the mountain,
   (5) and therefore there is fire on it.
The third term of the Indian syllogism corresponds to the major premise of that of Aristotle, the second to Aristotle's minor premise, and the first to his conclusion. Thus the Indian syllogism reversed the order of that of classical logic, the argument being stated in the first and second clauses, established by the general rule and example in the third, and finally clinched by the virtual repetition of the first two clauses.[26]

On the basis of the above illustrations one can argue that distinct African, Indian, Chinese, or Thai thought processes manifest themselves in distinct English types.[27] Before one comes to that conclusion, a word of warning is in order here: I am not claiming that such 'transfer in contact' is limited to literary texts or that such 'creativity' appears in literature only. Rather these apply to all linguistic interactions in which multilinguals participate.[28] It is, in fact, part of being an Indian, an African, or a Singaporean.

It is, of course, evident that for understanding such texts, the barriers to intelligibility have to be broken at a minimum of two levels: (1) at the surface level of structural relationships which provide culture-specific text-design or cohesion to the text, e.g. collocational, lexical, or grammatical, and (2) in the reinterpretation of a text within the extended (or altered) sociosemantic and pragmatic system. The structural relationships are just the visible part of such a discoursal iceberg. There is more to it which is beyond the monolingual interpreter's ken – especially for a monolingual who has made no effort to cross the barriers created by monoculturalism and monolingualism.

This then takes us to a related research area, that of contrastive discourse (or contrastive stylistics). But this research must venture beyond its present concerns into contrastive pragmatics, relating linguistic realization to the cultural norms and the 'meaning system' of a society which uses English.[29] The discourse strategies in contact literatures should be seen as linguistic realizations of a new sociosemiotic and linguistic phenomenon which is being added to the canons of literatures in English.

CONCLUSION

The study of the bilingual's creativity has serious implications for linguistic theory, and for our understanding of culture-specific communicative competence. It is of special interest for the study and analysis of the expanding body of the non-native literatures in English and of the uses of English in different cultures.

The universalization of English may be a blessing in that it provides a tool for cross-cultural communication. But it is a double-edged tool and makes several types of demands: a new theoretical perspective is essential for describing the functions of English across cultures. In other words, the use of English is to be seen as an integral part of the socio-cultural reality of those societies which have begun using it during the colonial period and, more important, have retained it and increased its use in various functions in the post-colonial era.

In recent years many such proposals for a theoretical reorientation have been made, not necessarily with reference to international uses of English, by Gumperz (1964), Halliday (1973), Hymes (1967) and Labov (1972), among others. And in 1956, when Firth suggested (in Palmer, 1968: 96–97) that 'in view of the almost universal use of English, an Englishman must de-Anglicize himself', he was, of course, referring to the implications of such universalization of the language. In his view, this de-Anglicization was much more than a matter of the readjustment of linguistic attitudes by the Englishmen; it entailed linguistic pragmatism in the use of English across cultures.

The diaspora varieties of English are initiating various types of changes in the English language. More important is the decanonization of the traditionally recognized literary conventions and genres of English. This change further extends to the introduction of new Asian and African cultural dimensions to the underlying cultural assumptions traditionally associated with the social, cultural, and literary history of English. The shared conventions and literary milieu between the creator of the text and the reader of English can no more be taken for granted. A text thus has a unique context. English is unique in another sense too: it has developed both national English literatures, which are specific and *context-bound*, and certain types of *context-free* international varieties. The national varieties show more localized organizational schemes in their texture, which may be 'alien' for those who do not share the canons of literary creativity and the traditions of underlying culture which are manifest in such varieties.

The national English literatures are excellent resources for culture learning through literature, a topic which has attracted considerable attention in recent years.[30] However, for such use of these texts one has to acquire the appropriate interpretive methodology and framework for identifying and contextualizing the literary creativity in English, especially that of its non-native bilingual users. It is only by incorporating such pragmatic contexts, as has been recently shown, for example in Chishimba (1983),[31] that the functional meaning and communicative appropriateness of the new discourse strategies and discourse patterns will be understood and appreciated.[32]

Notes

This chapter is a slightly modified version of 'The bilingual's creativity and contact literatures', in *The Alchemy of English: The Spread, Functions and Models of Non-Native Englishes*, by Braj B. Kachru; Oxford: Pergamon Institute of English, 1986, pp. 159–173. An earlier version appeared in *Studies in the Lingusitic Sciences*, 1983, 13.2.37–55.

1. In this chapter I have used the term 'bilingualism' to include 'trilingualism', 'multi-lingualism', and 'plurilingualism'. The 'bilingual's creativity' refers to linguistic creativity exhibited by non-monolinguals in all these situations.
2. Strevens (1982: 419) claims that English has 400 million non-native speakers and 300 million native speakers.
3. This term was suggested to me by Michael G. Clyne. It was, however, first used by Heinz Kloss. I have earlier used the term 'polymodel' in roughly the same sense. See B. Kachru, 1977 and 1981a.
4. The issues related to the models and norms of English and the implications of these issues have been discussed in B. Kachru, 1982b and 1983.
5. For discussion of this topic see, e.g., Prator, 1968, and my response to Prator in B. Kachru, 1976. Also see relevant studies in Smith, 1981, 1983, and Noss, 1983.
6. Ferguson (1978) raises several interesting questions concerning 'multilingual grammars', and summarizes several attempts for describing multilinguals' linguistic interaction. Also see Hymes, 1967.
7. See, e.g., Jakobson (quoted in Erlich, 1965: 172): 'The subject of literary scholarship is not literature in its totality, but literariness (*literaturnost*), i.e. that which makes of a given work a work of literature.' For the relationship of *context* and *text* see also Seung, 1982.
8. See B. Kachru, 1982b: 330 and 341.
9. However, there are some exceptions to this. An excellent study is Chishimba, 1983. See also Lowenberg, 1984 and Magura, 1984 regarding contact literatures in Southeast Asia and Africa, respectively. For further references see B. Kachru, 1983; Pride, 1982, 1983; Sridhar, 1982.
10. For lexical evidence see Serjeantsen, 1961.
11. For further discussion see Parthasarathy, 1983.
12. I am grateful to Wimal Dissanayake for pointing out to me that the Platonic and Aristotelian *sequences* are not identical, and that Kaplan's coupling of these two together is misleading.
13. A discussion of the bilingual's discourse strategies in educated English, and specific illustrations of some cohesive characteristics of educated Indian English are given in Y. Kachru, 1983a, b.
14. See the following for discussion and illustrations of contrastive discourse: for Hindi, Y. Kachru, 1983a, b; for Japanese, Hinds, 1983; for Korean, Chang, 1983; for Mandarin, Tsao, 1983; and for Marathi, Pandharipande, 1983.
15. See B. Kachru, 1983; Pride, 1983; Sanchez, 1983.
16. In this context one might mention the insightful work of John Gumperz, Dell Hymes and several other scholars. For references and further discussion see Chishimba, 1983 and B. Kachru, 1982c.
17. See B. Kachru, 1978 for references, illustrations, and further discussion. Also see Sridhar and Sridhar, 1980.

18. The relationship of sociolinguistic context and the 'meaning potential' of non-native Englishes, with specific reference to African varieties of English, has been discussed extremely well by Chishimba, 1983 and Magura, 1984. Also see B. Kachru, 1982b, 1983a; Lowenberg, 1984.
19. Nelson (1982, 1984) discusses several issues related to intelligibility of non-native Englishes. Also see Smith, 1983.
20. One also finds this in James Joyce, Walter Scott or Thomas Hardy, to give just three examples. But all these were still experimenting within the Western cultural and literary traditions.
21. See B. Kachru, 1965 and later, reproduced with an extensive bibliography, in B. Kachru, 1983.
22. For example, consider Yorubaization in Amos Tutuola, Sanskritization in Raja Rao, and Hindiization and Punjabiization in Mulk Raj Anand. For references and discussion, see B. Kachru, 1983.
23. See Parthasarathy, 1983.
24. A recent example of such stylistic experimentation is provided by another acclaimed South Asian writer, Salman Rushdie, in his novels *Midnight's children* (1980), which won the Booker Prize, and *Shame* (1983).
25. Also see Chinweizu, J. O. and Madubuike, I, 1983; Moore, 1962; Mphahlele, 1964; and Sridhar, 1982.
26. For discussion on this topic see also a very insightful discussion in Nakamura, 1964.
27. For Chinese see Cheng, 1982, and for Thai see studies by Mayuri Sukwiwat, 1983.
28. See, e.g. Gumperz, 1964; B. Kachru, 1981a; Sridhar and Sridhar, 1980; Pandharipande, 1982 and 1983.
29. The term 'meaning system' is used here in a wider sense, more or less as used by Halliday.
30. See, e.g., Amirthanayagam, 1976, and Sharrad, 1982. Sharrad provides a useful list of relevant references.
31. See also relevant chapters in Kachru (ed.), 1982b & d; Lowenberg, 1984; Magura, 1984; and Pride, 1983.
32. As an important afterword, I should point out that the issues raised here have several parallels in situations of bi- or multi-dialectism (for example, Scottish, Welsh, and Irish literatures, or what are termed 'dialect' literatures in other languages). A reader who does not share the linguistic and cultural norms of such writers is therefore at a disadvantage. True, a text does provide its own context, but it does not necessarily provide its culture-specific or language-specific interpretive context.

References

ABRAHAMS, ROGER D. (1983) *The man-of-words in the West Indies: performance and the emergence of creole culture*. Baltimore: Johns Hopkins University Press.
ACHEBE, CHINUA (1964) Foreword. In W. H. Whitley, *A selection of African prose*. Oxford: Clarendon Press.
ACHEBE, CHINUA (1969) *Arrow of God*. New York: Doubleday
AFOLAYAN, A. (1971) Language and sources of Amos Tutuola. In *Perspectives on African literature: selections from the proceedings of the Conference on African Literature* held at the University of Ife, 1968, edited by Christopher Heywood. London: Heinemann.
AMIRTHANAYAGAM, GUY (1976) *Culture learning through literature*. Honolulu: East-West Center.
BASHAM, A. L. (1954) *The wonder that was India*. London: Sidgwick and Jackson.
CHANG, SUK-JAN (1983) Linguistics and written discourse in English and Korean. In Kaplan *et al.*, 1983.
CHENG, CHIN-CHUAN (1982) Chinese varieties of English. In Kachru, 1982b.
CHINWEIZU, ONWUCHEKWA JEMIE and IHECHUKWU MADUBUIKE (1983) *Toward the decolonization of African literature*. Washington, DC: Harvard University Press.
CHISHIMBA, MAURICE (1983) African varieties of English: text in context. Unpublished doctoral dissertation, University of Illinois.

ERLICH, VICTOR (1965) *Russian formalism: history–doctrine*. The Hague: Mouton.

FERGUSON, CHARLES A. (1978) Multilingualism as object of linguistic description. In *Linguistics in the seventies: directions and prospects*, edited by Braj B. Kachru. Special issue of *Studies in the Linguistic Sciences* 8(2): 97–105.

GUMPERZ, JOHN J. (1964) Linguistic and social interaction in two communities. In *The ethnography of communication*, edited by John J. Gumperz and Dell Hymes. Special publication, *American Anthropologist* 66(2): 137–153. Washington, DC: American Anthropological Association.

HALLIDAY, M. A. K. (1973) *Explorations in the functions of language*. London: Edward Arnold.

HERSKOVITS, M. J. (1958) *Dahomean narrative*. Evanston: Northwestern University Press.

HINDS, JOHN (1983) Linguistics and written discourse in English and Japanese. In Kaplan *et al.*, 1983.

HYMES, DELL (1967) Models of the interaction of language and social setting. *Journal of Social Issues* 23(2): 8–28.

KACHRU, BRAJ B. (1965) The *Indianness* in Indian English. *Word* 21: 391–410 (also in B. Kachru, 1983).

KACHRU, BRAJ B. (1966) Indian English: a study in contextualization. In *In memory of J. R. Firth*, edited by C. E. Bazell *et al.* London: Longmans (also in B. Kachru, 1983).

KACHRU, BRAJ B. (1976) Models of English for the Third world: White man's linguistic burden or language pragmatics?; *TESOL Quarterly* 10(2): 221–239.

KACHRU, BRAJ B. (1977) The new Englishes and old models. *English Language Forum* (July). pp. 29–35.

KACHRU, BRAJ B. (1978) Code-mixing as a verbal strategy in India. In *International dimensions of bilingual education*, edited by J. E. Alatis. Georgetown Monograph on Languages and Linguistics. Washington, DC: Georgetown University Press.

KACHRU, BRAJ B. (1980) The new Englishes and old dictionaries: directions in lexicographical research on non-native varieties of English. In *Theory and method in lexicography: a Western and non-Western perspective*, edited by L. Zgusta (also in B. Kachru, 1983).

KACHRU, BRAJ B. (1981a) The pragmatics of non-native varieties of English. In Smith, 1981.

KACHRU, BRAJ B. (1981b) Socially-realistic linguistics: the Firthian tradition. *International Journal of the Sociology of Language* 31: 65–89.

KACHRU, BRAJ B. (1982a) The bilingual's linguistic repertoire. In *Issues in international bilingual education: the role of the vernacular*, edited by B. Hardford *et al.* New York and London: Plenum Press.

KACHRU, BRAJ B. (ed.) (1982b) *The other tongue: English across cultures*. Urbana: University of Illinois Press.

KACHRU, BRAJ B. (1982c) Models for non-native Englishes. In B. Kachru, 1982b.

KACHRU, BRAJ B. (1982d) Meaning in deviation: toward understanding non-native English texts. In B. Kachru, 1982b.

KACHRU, BRAJ B. (1983) *The Indianization of English: the English language in India*. New Delhi and New York: Oxford University Press.

KACHRU, YAMUNA (1983a) Cross-cultural texts, discourse strategies and discourse interpretation. Paper presented at the Conference on English as an International Language: Discourse Patterns Across Cultures. East-West Center, Honolulu, 1–7 June (manuscript).

KACHRU, YAMUNA (1983b) Linguistics and written discourse in particular languages: contrastive studies: English and Hindi. In *Annual review of applied linguistics*, edited by R. Kaplan *et al.* Rowley, MA: Newbury House.

KAPLAN, ROBERT B. (1966) Cultural thought patterns in intercultural education. *Language Learning* 16: 1–20.

KAPLAN, ROBERT B. *et al.* (eds) (1983) *Annual review of applied linguistics*. Rowley, MA: Newbury House.

LABOV, WILLIAM (1972) *Sociolinguistic patterns*. Philadelphia: University of Pennsylvania Press.

LANNOY, RICHARD (1971) *The speaking tree: a study of Indian culture and society*. New York: Oxford University Press.

LINDFORS, BERNTH (1973) *Folklore in Nigerian literature*. New York: Africana.

LOWENBERG, PETER (1984) Language contact and change: English in the Malay Archipelago. Unpublished Ph.D. dissertation, University of Illinois.

MAGURA, BENJAMIN (1984) Style and meaning in African English: a sociolinguistic study. Unpublished Ph.D. dissertation, University of Illinois.

MOORE, GERALD (1962) *Seven African writers*. London: Oxford University Press.

MPHAHLELE, EZEKIEL (1964) The language of African literature. *Harvard Educational Review* **34**: 90–101.

NAKAMURA, HAJIME (1964) *Ways of thinking of Eastern peoples*. Edited by Philip P. Wiener. Honolulu: The University Press of Hawaii.

NELSON, CECIL (1982) Intelligibility and non-native varieties of English. In B. Kachru, 1982b.

NELSON, CECIL (1983) Syntactic creativity and intelligibility (manuscript).

NELSON, CECIL (1984) Intelligibility: the case of non-native varieties of English. Unpublished Ph.D. dissertation, University of Illinois, Urbana.

NOSS, R. B. (ed.) (1983) *Varieties of English in Southeast Asia*. Anthology Series 11. Singapore: SEAMEO Regional Language Center.

PALMER, F. R. (ed.) (1968) *Selected papers of J. R. Firth, 1952–59*. Bloomington: Indiana University Press.

PANDHARIPANDE, RAJESHWARI (1982) Dimensions of multilingualism: language pluralism in India (manuscript).

PANDHARIPANDE, RAJESHWARI (1983) Linguistics and written discourse in English and Marathi. In Kaplan *et al.*, 1983.

PARTHASARATHY, R. (1983) South Asian literature in English: culture and discourse. Paper presented at the Conference on English as an International Language: Discourse Patterns Across Cultures. East-West Center, Honolulu, 1–7 June (manuscript). A revised version in this volume.

PRATOR, CLIFFORD H. (1968) The British heresy in TESOL. In *Language problems of developing nations*, edited by J. A. Fishman *et al*. New York: Wiley.

PRIDE, JOHN B. (1982) *New Englishes*. Rowley, MA: Newbury House.

PRIDE, JOHN B. (1983) Linguistic competence and the expression of cultural identity. In Noss, 1983.

RAO, RAJA (1963) *Kanthapura*. New York: New Dimensions (first published in 1938, London: Allen & Unwin).

RUSHDIE, SALMAN (1980) *Midnight's Children*. New York: Alfred A. Knopf.

RUSHDIE, SALMAN (1983) *Shame*. New York: Alfred A. Knopf.

SANCHEZ, ROSAURA (1983) *Chicano discourse: socio-historical perspective*. Rowley, MA: Newbury House.

SERJEANTSEN, M. S. (1961) *A history of foreign words in English*. New York: Barnes & Noble.

SEUNG, T. K. (1982) *Semiotics and thematics in Hermeneutics*. New York: Columbia University Press.

SHARRAD, PAUL (1982) Culture learning through literature. *East–West Culture Learning Institute Reporter* **8**(1): 1–11.

SMITH, LARRY, E. (1981) *English for cross-cultural communication*. London: Macmillan.

SMITH, LARRY E. (1983) *Readings in English as an international language*. London: Pergamon Institute of English.

SRIDHAR, S. N. (1982) Non-native English literatures: context and relevance. In B. Kachru, 1982.

SRIDHAR, S. N. and K. SRIDHAR (1980) The syntax and psycholinguistics of bilingual code-mixing. *Canadian Journal of Psychology/Revue Canadienne de Psychologie* **34**: 407–416.

STREVENS, PETER (1982) World English and the world's English: or, whose language is it anyway? *Journal of the Royal Society of the Arts*, London, 8 March.

SUKWIWAT, MAYURI (1983) Interpreting the Thai variety of English: a functional approach. In Noss, 1983.

TAIWO, OLADELE (1976) *Culture and the Nigerian Novel*. New York: St Martin's Press.

THUMBOO, EDWIN (1976) *The second tongue: an anthology of poetry from Malaysia and Singapore*. Singapore: Heinemann Educational Books.

TSAO, FENJ-FU (1983) Linguistics and written discourse in English and Mandarin. In Kaplan *et al.*, 1983.

WIDDOWSON, HENRY (1979) *Pidgin and babu. Explorations in applied linguistics*. London: Oxford University Press.

11

Poetic Imperialism or Indigenous Creativity?: Philippine Literature in English

ANDREW GONZALEZ

PHILIPPINE literature in English began as early as the first decade of this century (Dato, 1924), a little after a decade of American colonial rule, which began in 1898.

It is quite indicative of the Filipino's almost embarrassing eagerness to learn the foreign language of the new colonial masters that, as early as 1903, a group of talented Filipino males was ready to be sent as pensionados to the United States. They had learned to speak and write English in less than five years, initially, under the tutelage of the American soldiers who set up make-shift schools near their barracks and subsequently, from the Thomasites (American public school teachers who began to arrive aboard the *USS Thomas* in 1901) after the Organic Act of 1902 establishing the Philippine educational system.

From a population with no knowledge of English, officially counted for the first time in the census of 1903, as many as 885,854 out of a literate population of 3,138,634 or 28 per cent, were listed as being able to read English by the next census of 1918 (see Gonzalez and Alberca, 1978: 1).

Shortly after the opening of the University of the Philippines in 1908, poems in English written by young college students were published in the *Philippine Free Press* (1909) and in the *College Folio* (1910), the literary magazine of the university. The first Philippine novel in English (Galang's *Child of Sorrow*) appeared in 1921. In 1925 Paz Marquez Benitez published the first Philippine short story in English entitled 'Dead stars' (see Yabes, 1981).

Thus began Philippine literature in English, which initiated the Filipino literary artist's second apprenticeship under a foreign mentor in a new tongue. The first apprenticeship was under the Spaniards, and flourished for a bare 25 years, during the last decade of the 19th century.

In expressing his vision in a second language, the lowland, Christianized Filipino was repeating an experience his forbears had shared for nearly 400 years under the Spanish occupation. The Spanish had never systematically taught the Filipino their language until near the end of the period (1863). In spite of this, the Filipino learned his lessons readily and was about to begin a golden era of literature before it was aborted by the arrival of a new set of masters, under whom he began his literary apprenticeship once more. What is important to emphasize is that the Filipino was coming from a Spanish tradition and not a totally indigenous one; it was an indigenous tradition with Hispanic influence, so that the tradition was no longer Austronesian but Hispanicized Austronesian.

Under the Spaniards the Filipino had learned Western, specifically Hispanic, literary forms; for the most part he wrote about Judaeo-Christian subject matter in his native tongue. There is a rich Christian vernacular literature among the lowland, Christianized groups. Among these are: ethnic versions of the *Pasyon* (the story of the Passion of Christ and the Easter Story), *awits* (songs), *corridos* (roundels), plays based on the Bible (comparable to the western medieval church's mystery plays), and plays based on the lives of the saints (comparable to the western medieval church's miracle plays). All these were done in the local vernacular using the poetic conventions of these vernaculars. Perhaps the only indigeneous literary feature that remained (besides the language, of course) was the poetic convention of versification found in these works. It is only among the cultural minority groups and the highland tribes that were not reached by Christianity that the ancient indigenous literary art forms (oral discourse, except for the *ambahans* [love poems] of the Mangyans of Mindoro written on their bamboo tubes with a local South-Indian base syllabary) have survived through riddles, proverbs, songs, fables, legends, and long narratives (epics).

As early as the time when Filipinos began to write in Spanish, these traditions maintained in the highlands and among other cultural communities had been lost, especially in the urban centre, Manila, where the bulk of the writers in Spanish lived. And since it was also in the Manila area where writing in English began, in an academic setting, one can predict almost *a priori* that the traditional discourse patterns were no longer retrievable.

TRANSFERS ACROSS CULTURES

When a first-language speaker begins to learn a second language, the most immediate transfers noticeable are in the area of phonology. There is enough literature on contrastive analysis and error analysis to show that many of these phonological features and rules of the first language are transferred to the second or target language and constitute what in layman's language we call 'accent'.

It is not only in the area of phonology but also in the areas of vocabulary and syntax that this transfer takes place. Language learners are warned about *anis faux*, seeming cognates with different meanings. Syntactic features of word order and morphology are carried across and semantic features, tense/aspect, gender, categorizations and subcategorizations, though less overt, are nonetheless transferred. As the learner advances, he begins to translate and, unless he learns otherwise, he soon translates first-language collocations literally into the target language (calques).

The features of the transitional language, often fixated when the learner stops learning or when his learning reaches a plateau, are considered as features of the interlanguage under a new rubric.

Less well described, but still operative, are transfers of presuppositions, and knowledge of the world arising from one's culture, society, and personal history. These non-overt features soon become inferrable from the linguistic thematizations of somebody else's world. These transfers continue in the case of an individual living in a different society and culture than his own until the person attains some degree of biculturalism. This aspect of 'transfer' is well illustrated, for example, in Chapters 7, 9, 10 and 12 in this volume.

However, in a social setting such as the Philippines, India, and Singapore, we notice other things too: an alien tongue or code becomes a superposed variety during the country's historical period of colonization, and even attains the status of a lingua franca. The imposed code, then, is competing with a native lingua franca or legally selected code. The result of this is that the second language undergoes not only transfers but, through long use, becomes nativized (or indigenized). It also develops subvarieties (pidgins) and can even become the first language of a small élite, side by side with a native language. In such a situation, all that one really has is the code with the cultural presuppositions and assumptions of the world view left behind in their usual matrix. Since this process of code transfer into another culture has not been sufficiently studied in depth, much of the discussion and study thus far has been anecdotal in character. Clearly, this is a fertile area for the study of transfers. For clarification, see Figure 1.

This deracination or de-rooting of a code (Code 1) and its placement in Cultural matrix 2 results not only in a disturbance of the presuppositions, world-views, *Volksgeist*, behavioural patterns, values, beliefs, and referents of Cultural matrix 2 (where there is a natural fit between cultural matrix and

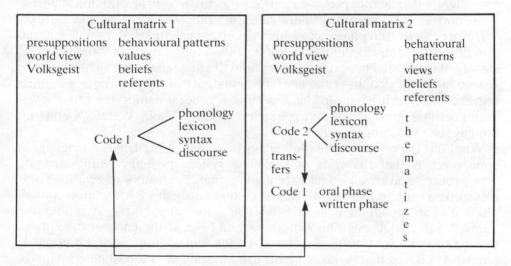

Figure 1

code) but, likewise, a mixing and influence of many features of Code 2 on Code 1. This kind of cultural diffusion is inevitable, as Code 1 becomes more and more distant from its roots (because of nationalism, independence, lack of close contact between speakers of Code 1 and Code 2 and the disappearance of Code 1 speakers from the teaching cadres of the country's educational system). Code 1 either suffers linguistic death or linguistic acculturation/nativization into a new variety of the language, assuming that a social and political decision has been made to retain it side by side with an indigenous language which has been selected as the linguistic symbol of unity and nationhood. Initially through the restriction of domains and gradually through its use only for international purposes, Code 1 is extinguished except among a small élite.

The above paradigm seems to be an approximation of what has happened to English in once-colonized countries of Britain and the United States, certainly of English in the Philippines. It has given rise to what are referred to in the literature now as 'the new Englishes' or more soberly 'new varieties of English' and more specifically, 'Philippine English', or, to use Llamzon's (1969) term, 'Standard Filipino English'.

There have been detailed descriptions of the distinctive features of Philippine English (Gonzalez and Alberca, 1978), at least one variety of it (English in the Philippine mass media), but these descriptions have delved into basic structural features (phonology, lexicon, syntax) and the beginnings of style (defined here using Joos' (1969) definition of style as varieties arising from the solidarity relations between interlocutors [intimate, casual, consultative, formal, frozen]). Linguistic units larger than the sentence, however, giving rise to different types of discourse serving various functions, have not been described for Philippine English (except for English in the printed media; Gonzalez, 1982). On the other side of the spectrum, approaching the subject less from a linguist's viewpoint and more from a literary viewpoint, are studies on one type of discourse in English in the Philippines, the discourse of narrative and lyrical expression, carried out in two surface manifestations, prose and poetry – under the general rubric of Philippine literature in English.

Before the written phase is considered, certain examples of discourse in the oral phase to exemplify this transfer of discourse across cultures should be cited by way of contrast. These transfers are from the first language (Tagalog) to the second language (English) and are representative not only of Tagalog culture but Philippine, Christian, lowland culture in general among the other seven major ethnic groups: Ilocano, Kapampangan, Bicol, Waray, Cebuano, Hiligaynon, and Pangasinense.

What has happened in the Philippines, in so far as the English language is concerned, is that the code or signalling system (sounds, sound-meaning correlations, and to a certain extent the semantic clusters of features) was transferred without its cultural matrix. Undoubtedly this is a common enough phenomenon in similar colonial situations and, refreshingly, it refutes the Sapir-Whorf hypothesis. This hypothesis had been at the back of thinking of the majority of Americans who favoured the annexation of the Philippines, and who believed that it was only through knowledge of the English language that Filipinos could learn the ideals of American democracy and progress.

In actual language use, the Filipinos took in parts of the signalling system (the sound units and their combinations), made the expected phonological adaptations, but never quite mastered the American English sound system in its integrity. The Filipino took over the lexical inventory but added his own loan words, his calques, his own semantic connotations to certain vocables, even his own meanings. He assumed the syntactic rules (again with some adaptations, never quite mastering the article system, the tense/aspect system, and the prepositions as well as their combinations with verbs). More telling were the adaptations of the discourse rules, for in his greetings, leave-takings, phatic expressions, and argumentation, the Filipino never quite gave up his native expressions, although he substituted seemingly English forms for his local ones. This again is not different from what happened in, for example, India as has been shown (in Chapters 7, 10 and 12).

Thus, American English-type introductions (with the ritual shaking of hands in American and Anglo Saxon culture) were not really mastered by the Filipino: the typical Filipino, on being introduced to a fellow Filipino, does not do it exactly the American way. Unless there is an American, or it is an American-type business situation, ritual shaking of hands is not *de rigueur*; in fact a smile, a raising of eyebrows in greeting, or a hand-gesture with 'Kumusta? (How are you?)' is more authentic than the American ritual.

Saying goodbye is carried out likewise in Filipino ways with accompanying behavioural patterns. Between the time goodbye is expressed with literal translation of Tagalog 'ma-una na kami' (We are going to be the first = We're leaving first) and the actual farewell, from the dining area to the front door or gate can take half an hour to an hour. The signal for everyone to leave politely at the end of a party is given by the guest of honour, who is the first one to stand up after a meal. He too is constrained to allow a decent interval after the last course so as not to be impolite. One can rush things if one has an excuse (e.g. another appointment, someone sick in the family, a person who is waiting).

Reprimanding exemplifies typical Filipino indirection – usually not in English but in Pilipino – with clitic expressions (placed after the main verb) like *yata* (it seems), *naman* (an impact reducer 'No *naman* Please, it's not quite that way)', dual expressions for 'you and I (let us, shall we, let us not . . .)'.

Interrupting a conversation can be done politely without any social formulae, one's presence and proximity and decent interval of waiting being considered sufficient justification for interrupting.

Apologies do not take the same simple formulae that they do in American English; when one has to pass between two people talking directly to each other, one stoops and walks across so as not to break the eye contact between the interlocutors unless of course there is enough space to by-pass interlocutors, in which case one goes around them rather than between them. If one must ask someone to make room, one says, 'Excuse me'. And when one accidentally bumps against someone, one also says 'Excuse me' (rather than American 'Sorry'). 'Sorry' is reserved for other types of apologies necessitated by having committed graver inconvenience (e.g. making someone wait unduly).

Probes are usually done in Pilipino rather than English (see Bautista, 1979, for examples in Pilipino). What is interesting to observe from the Philippine situation is that where a society has more than one language to call on as part of its linguistic resources, then one language need not be used for all functions; rather, the two languages may play complementary roles and even be mutually exclusive for certain roles and domains, so that probing is done through indirection, especially when the solidarity dimension is describable as intimate or familiar; it is done in Pilipino more than in English, and is usually carried out by means of openings using the clitic *yata* (it seems).

Requests are typically expressed using the clitic *nga* (request marker) in Pilipino. In English, where the Filipino speaker is more used to expressing the ideational functions of language, one is sometimes faced with declarative statements which are clearly requests for permission: 'I will go out', meaning 'May I go out?' 'I am going to the market', meaning 'May I go to the market?'

An area still needing further research is natural logic within a culture and the processes of argumentation/persuasion, which are clearly culture-bound. Hence notions of causality, ratiocination, justification will undoubtedly be based on Pilipino styles of thought although expressed in English. For example, there was the remark of one devotee of the Santo Niño (the child Jesus) to an anthropologist one day: 'The Santo Niño is all powerful, so powerful in fact that Jesus Christ would not have been crucified if he had prayed to the Santo Niño!!!' (an anecdote of F. Landa Jocano). Undoubtedly, in attempting to persuade a fellow Filipino in English with indigenous thought patterns and rhetorical structures, one will use family ties (spoken or unspoken), formal *utang na loob* debts (debt of inner self), position and power, blood or affinal relationship as reasons which will hold little validity in an American context.

One other area of the oral phase of English is the area of public speaking, mostly in remarks for social occasions and occasional speeches. Although the English language is used in a Victorian style of rhetoric, delivery is quite Filipino in gesticulation, in the elevation of pitch (almost chanted), in the sing-song manner of speaking, and in the floridity of expression (with undoubted influence from Spanish culture and Philippine ceremonial poetry called *Balagtasan*, after the 19th-century Master of the Craft, Francisco Balagtas). This is true of India too which uses an institutional variety of English (see Chapter 10 in this volume). On such occasions high praise is given in superlative terms so that one uses a code for a rhetorical style that is completely alien to American speaking style.

These important manifestations of discourse patterns preserved from the native languages and transferred into a culture-isolated code such as English have been highlighted to contrast the oral phase from the written phase, which manifests an altogether different development.

DISCOURSE PATTERNS: WRITTEN PHASE (PHILIPPINE ENGLISH)

I will first discuss poetry and then come to prose. Mention has already been made that Philippine literature in English arose out of an academic setting, more specifically at the University of the Philippines, which began in 1908. The young Filipino writers were taught by American university teachers at the University of the Philippines and were indoctrinated in the Aristotelian principles of the three unities (place, time, action) and the sacrosanct prescription that every literary creation had to have a beginning, a middle, and an end, thus laying the foundation for well-defined, linear structures in both prose and poetry, in essays and narratives as well as in poems. It was academic writing in a second language, following American and British patterns, and arising from a classroom register of English composition writing which is still very much alive today in Philippine school rooms.

Considering that the lowland, Christian Filipinos who cheerfully left their Spanish language and their literature (except for the few writers in Spanish who continued to write in the Castilian tongue) were already quite removed from the indigenous tradition of poetry, one is not surprised that in this early writing in English there are no traces, for practical purposes, of the native traditions of writing.

There is a rich tradition of lyric expression in verse in Tagalog and the Philippine languages. Over the years, especially during the 19th century, certain conventions began to be used as a result of consensus. End-rhyme in Tagalog poetry is determined primarily by the sameness of the vowel, the variety provided by consonants, which were divided into families of sounds which, based on today's principles of phonology, were intuitively correct. The nasals and liquids were gathered together in one category (sonorants) and the stops separated (all noncontinuants). Metre was determined not so much by stress (louder, greater amplitude; see Gonzalez, 1981) or even by pitch (higher fundamental frequency) but by syllable-counting punctuated by lengthened syllables which under certain circumstances were predictably characterized by accompanying higher pitch and in open syllables by greater amplitude as well. These are the building-blocks of sound patterning in the language, and these were exploited by the Tagalog poet.

On the other hand, for poetry written in English, stress-timing is all, resulting in various types of line-lengths dictated by the number of beats, with internal rhyme arising from assonance and alliteration and end-rhyme by rhyming syllables composed of vowel + consonant of the same phonemes with alternation between lines. There are conventional stanzaic forms, couplets, quatrains, sonnets (fourteen lines), and longer units.

The models of the early Filipino poets in English were the late Victorians and the early Edwardians, and some of the newer American poets who were then emerging and experimenting with their own forms using a more familiar and less 'exalted' or formal vocabulary, in the tradition of Whitman. An early volume, edited by Dato (1924), shows rather faltering steps in a schoolboyish type of poetry with the conventions followed quite mechanically and the vocabulary in the formal ('exalted') style for odes, with embarrassing expressions of loyalty to America. Clearly this was imitative art, commendable but not particularly creative, and certainly removed from the native tradition. About the only thing Filipino in the poems was that they dealt with the romantic themes of the *kundiman* (love songs), referring to the realities of

Filipino life, with its sunset, dusk, dawn, and using Filipino names with an occasional loan word for the name of a flower or a plant. One therefore has here the transplantation of English structures and poetic discourse applied to a new environment, a new cultural matrix, and referring to realities hitherto unfamiliar in English – in so far as the English language had not been used to speak of these realities up to this time in its original contexts of Britain, America, North America, Australia and New Zealand. This characteristic of new *contextualization* of English applies to, for example, Nigerian, Indian, Singaporean and Kenyan English, too.

The lyric poetry of the Filipinos after the first decade embodies a simplification of language (vocabulary) from the formal and archaic (with its use of the archaic *thou* and the *-st* morpheme for the second person singular) to a more colloquial vocabulary, deftness in the use of the language, and a liberation from traditional metric forms followed by an effort to experiment with other forms basically within the tradition of English poetry. However, the themes were Filipino. One does not find attempts at experimentation with the English language and an exploitation of its resources for artistic and contemplative effects of form until one gets to José Garcia Villa and Rafael Zulueta da Costa (Bulosan, 1942).

Zulueta da Costa (1940) began to exploit the compounding and nominalizing resources of English in the manner of Gerard Manley Hopkins. In the postwar era the poetry of Amador Daguio (1973) evidences some novel attempts at rhyming. Whether or not this was consciously from the Tagalog tradition, or merely a discovery of the possibilities of English, cannot be ascertained without more access to details of his life.

Experimentation in pure form comes with José Garcia Villa (1922), perhaps the most consummate craftsman among the pre-war poets of the Philippines, with his experiments, undoubtedly very much influenced by the experimentation in verse and poetry going on in the United States (summarized by Archibald Macleish's famous dictum 'a poem should not mean but be'). Villa's poems in the late 1930s, and the postwar ones, play with two techniques: metathesis (or reversed consonance) which consists of inversion of consonant$_1$ + consonant$_2$ combinations to a consonant$_2$ + consonant$_1$ sequence in alternating lines, and prolonged sprung rhythm (to use Gerard Manley Hopkins' term). In his famous poems Villa diverges from the sing-song rhythm of the favourite English metre, the iamb, and forces pauses which result in a version of continuing sprung-rhythm through a succession of stressed syllables. Perhaps more than these novelties is Villa's insistence to his Philippine audiences, and later to his American audiences, that in poetry, form is all. He was the first Filipino poet who took art for art's sake to its logical conclusion and used the resources of a second language to begin innovating with these resources much as a first language speaker does. In the process, although his role in the history of verse and poetry in America is rarely acknowledged since he did not belong to the mainstream of English poetry, he embodied the Filipino having perfected his art as form and his mastery of the English language. He followed his own lights in poetry and as a non-native speaker experimented with the potentialities of the language in the manner of Joyce.

In the postwar period, in the 1960s, largely as a result of the initiatives of Rolando Tinio, attempts were made to write what the critic Eric Torres (1975) called 'bagay-poetry' (from Tagalog bagay [suitable], hence fitting poetry), suitable to the nationalism of the period. This movement was short-lived and was really inspired by the nationalism of the times. Basically it consisted of bringing loans and whole collocations and even sentences into the English text (otherwise traditional) to give an effect of nativeness. It would be too simplistic to consider this a case of macaronic verse or even Taglish – it was an attempt to create a unity out of two main linguistic strands and to capture in poetry a special code-switching variety of English and Pilipino used among educated Filipinos in informal transactions to establish rapport. Apparently the movement did not catch on, however.

In the postwar period, as a successor to Villa in his versatility and facility with the English language, is Cirilo F. Bautista, largely through the first two volumes of his proposed trilogy, *The Archipelago* (1970, 1981). A superb craftsman, Bautista is fully in command of his medium, the English language, and its potentialities. He experiments with various forms of rhyme, metre, and register (or tone), capturing many voices in reflecting on the history and the physiognomy of the country. Innovations in stanzaic forms, rhythms, metres, line lengths, tones and symbolism abound. One finds the same richness of association and connotation, and reference to a rich background of literature (both Eastern and Western), and of history, in Bautista as in T. S. Eliot. In Bautista the Filipino has come of age. In his use of English, and in technical mastery and techniques in English, Bautista has surpassed even Villa.

However creative this process is, and showing as it does the Filipino in full command of his second tongue, one cannot say that the contribution has been distinctively Filipino. Even though the poetry in English of Villa, Zuleta da Costa, Daguio and Bautista has reached new peaks, it has been distinctively Filipino only in themes and in authorship. The forms are modern, exploiting the potentials of modern English; the versification or poetry is not Filipino but English. The Filipino has indeed mastered the rules of the language not only in its grammatical structure but in its discourse and poetics. It is poetry in the English language written by Filipinos concerning Philippine topics and realities and themes, but there is no Filipino art form to speak of as transferred from the indigenous culture to the new tongue. There are no traces in this literary language born of academia and English schooling and modelled on the poetic experiments of America, of the local traditions of versification and poesy. The assumption of a non-indigenous art form, albeit applied to local themes, is complete, with hardly any traces left of the local forms.

Let me now turn to prose. In addition to versified narratives there are likewise prose narratives, usually of a shorter nature, consisting of folktales, legends, and fables. Eugenio (1981) classifies them into myths, folk epics, legends (aetiological and non-aetiological), and folktales (animal tales, fables, tales of magic, trickster tales).

An attempt at a comprehensive cross-linguistic study has been made of these narratives to come up with a typology of Philippine discourse structures (Longacre, 1968). There have likewise been incisive observations made in editions of folk literature of various languages (especially those of the cultural communities) as well as intensive study of different discourse types of specific languages done by the Summer Institute of Linguistics (see, e.g. Longacre, 1968 and Grimes, 1975). These studies, however, deal with the first languages of smaller ethnic groups in the Philippines, and do not deal with the literature of the eight major ethnic groups whose languages are considered major. These languages were those of lowland Filipinos (who had been Christianized and who had been under Spanish influence) and were subsequently under similar American influence as a result of schooling. It is precisely among these groups that the oral traditions of the Filipinos have, for the most part, disappeared. It is also from these groups, who had been educated in American-type schools, where the first writers of Philippine literature in English emerged. One is therefore not surprised that in their writings in English there is little of the native tradition and hence little transfer of indigenous discourse conventions and techniques.

Perhaps as indicator of how much of the original indigenous tradition has been lost is that there are few long narrative poems done by a Filipino in English: to my knowledge, among significant ones, there is only Cirilo F. Bautista's (1970, 1981) projected three-volume trilogy, *The Archipelago*, and Nick Joaquin's (1981) *The Ballad of the Five Battles*.

However, Bautista's masterpiece is not a narrative poem in the real sense of the term, but a series of reflections from different viewpoints, in the style of Virginia Woolf, ending up with a series of verbal collages. It is really expressive and ideational more than narrative in function, the narrative being embedded in the revelatory monologues. Mention has been made of its verbal richness and innovation; little of the original Filipino tradition of narrative discourse comparable to folk literature narrative or even the epic tradition is present in this poem, however.

Similarly, Joaquin's narrative on *La Naval de Manila* (a fiesta com-memorating Spanish victory over the Dutch in Manila through the intercession of the Virgin) follows the classical metre and rhyme of the ballad, and is modelled on Chesterton's own narrative of the Battle of Lepanto.

The field work of the Summer Institute of Linguistics analysts has resulted in studies of discourse and paragraph structures on various minority languages. This work has included the prediction of discourse genres on the basis of paragraph types, as well as in-depth studies on cohesion, transitivity, effectiveness, and the conventions of narrative in some groups (Benn, 1983). For example, Wrigglesworth (1981) sets down the verbal conventions in Ilianen Manobo for introducing an entire narrative (with set formulae); verbal conventions for introducing individual scenes (needed in oral recitation to give the listeners warning that something new will be told through employing similar conventional settings for each new scene which formally introduces or reintroduces the key participants, using deictic 'here'), verbal conventions for introducing immortal characters within a scene by means of magic formulae; verbal conventions and closures to the tale, using variations of 'end', 'completion'; techniques for alerting the audience to peak points (to heighten vividness and to add excitement) by means of parallelism, and concentration of participants (a crowded scene). In quoting characters there is frequent use of 'he said' as a vital part of the dialogue resulting in broken quotation; there is also a shift to a more specific person (from third person to second person to highlight the action of a key participant, and a shift to the second person 'you' to refer to the narrator's audience or a shift to the dual ('you and I') to tie the speaker more closely with the listeners).

These conventions and practices belong more properly to a non-literate society which capitalizes on memory to carry on its story-telling activities. Such linguistic conventions therefore pertain more exactly to oral rather than written narration. Their absence in Philippine short stories in English, apart from the long divorce from the oral tradition, is not surprising in a society of lowlanders which has learned to read and to write, and which relies on the written/printed word to carry on its transmission of culture.

Thus, none of these conventions is present in the major short-story writers who are the subjects of anthologies of Philippine literature in English, and who are considered the chief exponents of Philippine literary forms.

The broad humour found in Carlos Bulosan, largely through exaggerations, is reminiscent of some Philippine folktales. The tall story has cross-cultural manifestations and is also found in the *aswang* (evil spirits) stories of I. V. Mallari (1951), the cockfighting stories of Alejandro Roces (1959), and the exaggerations of the early Bulosan (1942) before he left for the USA and talked about the more serious plight of the poor Filipino in exile.

In a more serious vein, the short stories of Paz Marquez Benitez (1925), the early Villa (1928) and Manuel E. Arguilla (1940), all based on rustic scenes of the simple lives of farmers and couples close to the soil, use conventions that are clearly American English, although the referents, and subject-matter and themes, are Filipino. It seems to me that Pike's (1981) distinction between grammatical and referential hierarchy in the analysis of discourse is applicable here.

Among the pre-war, short-story writers, perhaps the most versatile was Manuel E. Arguilla, whose stylistic range went from the almost lyrical, rustic desription of farm life in the Ilocos to the realistic, almost cynical, views of Manila and its politics. Arguilla mastered various tones, from the lyrical and evocative to the sarcastic, and in one short story, 'Imperfect farewell', experimented with a form of the dramatic monologue. His mastery of English is perhaps best manifested in his sarcastic and bitter stories, for only when one has mastered a second language can one express its rich nuances of tone. However, interesting as these experiments are, and evidence as they are of Arguilla's versatility, they show mastery of the traditional techniques of the short story on Western terms, not Filipino.

Beginning to show promise at the outbreak of the war was Arturo B. Rotor (1936), who, although he eventually became a medical doctor, showed signs of a conscious attempt at form and experimentation in his short stories of this period.

Rotor is remarkable in his use of common, everyday language, a colloquial form of Philippine English, as opposed to the formal almost neo-Victorian style of writing and vocabulary of most Philippine fiction writers of the time.

He experimented with points of view using multiple, or sometimes single, viewpoints, and maintained consistency in these experiments. There is a skilful shifting of past and present tense to differentiate between the narrative – what is reminisced – and generalizations about life – what is reflected upon. Sometimes, however, in the early stories, this shifting is done none too skilfully, and leads to tense inconsistency, a characteristic of Philippine English writing. In this experimentation of point of view, what Sean O'Faolain calls *manière de voir*, Rotor often addresses an undifferentiated generic 'you', and sometimes a conspiratorial 'we (you and I)' or dual, reminiscent of a technique in oral literature that the local, ethnic poets use to heighten audience participation. It is not clear whether Rotor deliberately transferred this technique from Philippine literature. The indications are that he did not, although a case can be made for the parallelism. Perhaps his use of an imagined interlocutor is indicative of more universal techniques found in all narrative literature, certainly in writers like Ring Lardner who set up an imaginary interlocutor, although not as blatantly as Victorian novelists such as William Makepeace Thackeray, who addressed his reader directly as 'Dear Reader'.

In these prose narratives the authors usually observed unity of place, time and action, with the action ordinarily confined to the events near the climax, or if writing about events stretching across time, the authors used the flashback technique and transitional markers to mark passage of time. Because these stories are meant to be read, and are short, the repetitive pattern of narrative folk tales (a seriality of design) is not evident. Instead, the designs are quite traditional, similar to the short stories of American and British writers. There is usually an omniscient viewpoint taken, with freedom on the part of the writer to delve by introspection into the thoughts and sensibilities of the characters, but not freedom to intrude by an editorial 'we', nor freedom to editorialize, nor freedom to address the reader as 'you', all of which are taboo in modern fiction even though they were widely indulged in by the Victorian novelists.

Hence, in techniques and in presentation, there is no innovation but complete acceptance of American English standards. There is no transfer here of the first language discourse patterns into the English output in so far as the conventions and techniques of fiction writing are concerned.

Where the Filipinism comes in is not with regard to the style or to the fiction conventions, but in the use of a new code to speak about realities in a totally different culture.

Clearly the references are to Filipino reality: persons with local names and titles transferred as collocations, place names in the Philippines, realia or objects specific to Philippine culture, situations, behaviour, customs, introspective reactions and sensibilities, completely Filipino, and quoted speech manifesting speech patterns in English almost directly translated from the local language or full sentences in Tagalog or in Spanish (still the language of the élite during the period). The English language's resources are thus extended to a new horizon, to new realities, to thematize these new realities in a totally new code (with its sounds, meaning system, vocabulary, syntax) internalized by a non-native speaker. For these authors being cited, the Filipinism is in the reference hierarchy and its cultural matrix, but with the grammatical hierarchy or code totally foreign, including the discourse structure.

Perhaps the most outstanding prose writer in English of the Philippines thus far, the Philippine version of Joseph Conrad and Vladimir Nabokov in prose, comparable in stature to José Garcia Villa and Cirilo F. Bautista in poetry, is Nick Joaquin (1963) – his dramatic contributions will not be treated in this study – who has made the main subject of his storytelling Philippine life during the Spanish period, with its peninsular veneer underneath an Austronesian pagan sensibility and unconscious. In his scenes from the Spanish period of Philippine life Nick Joaquin refers to a way of life, ethos, mores, and characters, thoroughly Filipino, with their language interspersed with Hispanisms and whole collocations and sentences in Spanish, their names and titles Hispanic Filipino and, of course, their outlook, beliefs, even super-stitions, a blend of Spanish Catholicism and Philippine animism.

Yet the mode of narration is entirely Western, following the conventions of the short story. Joaquin's use of archetypal myths and neo-pagan rituals is within the tradition of D. H. Lawrence; in addition, he introduces Gothic elements of the 19th-century Victorian novel into a tropical setting. The clear innovation in language is his use of long, run-on sentences – sentence-para-graphs – which, while following the conventions of English orthography and mechanics in capitalization and punctuation, do not follow normal canons of good writing. Here one is almost tempted to think that Nick Joaquin is using a Faulknerian syntax. There is a piling up of participial phrases, usually using right-branching adjunctions (to use the terminology of transformational generative grammar), creating an almost mesmerizing effect and leading to a crescendo of emotional pitch. Again, however, this experimentation is within the potentialities of the English language and is not a carry-over from any native tradition or a transfer in discourse structure from Tagalog to English.

Joaquin began writing during the Japanese period and continued his literary activity during the postwar period, mastering his craft, temporarily suspending publications in fiction in the 1970s, although he is now resuming his literary activities in the 1980s.

Among the postwar, Filipino, short-story writers who should be mentioned are N. V. M. Gonzalez, Bienvenido N. Santos, and F. Sionil José (the latter, one of the more productive novelists in contemporary times).

N. V. M. Gonzalez (1959) speaks of his *kaingeros* (shifting agricultural planters) in Mindoro in sentences with almost transparently overt adjunctive structures. He speaks of the recurring life cycle of these non-Westernized Filipinos, their world-view, their lifestyles and values, in a simple vocabulary (non-Victorian but nonetheless formal). Plot or dramatic action is secondary to the sensibilities and perceptions of his characters caught up within their cyclical way of life with its predictabilities. The writing and the manner of forming the narrative is, however, Western–not transferred from local forms.

The same goes for Bienvenido N. Santos (1965), writing like Carlos Bulosan but with less proletarian leanings about the Filipino in exile; not the Filipino workers in Alaska or the vineyards of Stockton but Filipinos in exile in the cities. However, Bienvenido N. Santos' prose breaks no new ground, nor does it harken to an indigenous tradition of narrative; indeed, his mastery of English grammar is less secure than some of his contemporaries. His use of symbols, reminiscent of Henry James, is interesting but hardly original.

F. Sionil José (1962), perhaps the most prolific Filipino fiction writer at present, has mastered the idiom of informality, even slang, to capture the speech of upper-class westernized Filipinos. His situations are totally Filipino, with all their political overtones and references. When he is not writing about his boyhood in his native Rosales, with the history of exploitation between social classes (reminiscent of Faulkner's Yoknapatawpha County) or village life among the cultural communities of the north and their particular mores and values as well as beliefs, than he writes about contemporary, high-class life among Manila's élite and their social mores. While the language is contemporary and no longer Victorian, even slangish, the style of narration is quite Western and again shows no cultural transfers from the first language (Pangasinense and Ilocano). In José F. Sionil one can likewise say that the Filipino has learned his craft of fiction well from his American and British models, and in the process has thoroughly internalized this craft of fiction on the foreigner's own terms. Like Santos, Sionil José's use of symbolism is likewise interesting, though again not original.

CONCLUSION

In assessing the experience of Philippine literature in English, therefore, one must pose the question, in these days of nationalism and self-conscious efforts on the part of the Filipino to liberate himself not only politically and economically but above all culturally from the experience of colonialism and the imperialistic past: is there a case here of poetic imperialism or indigenous creativity?

That there has been indigenous creativity seems evident – the writing of Philippine literature in English continues as a lively tradition although it is élitist and is confined to the segment of Philippine society most at home in English – those in Philippine academia and business. What is remarkable is that the creativity of Filipino writers, both poets and short-story writers, although derivative from American and British tradition, shows innovation within the traditions of American and British literary creation. The resources of the English language itself, as this language has been adapted to indigenous soil, have been expanded and enriched. Filipino writers, in their creative experiments, although small in number, have taken the American and British practices of craftsmanship to heart and are producing innovations within these traditions on the West's terms rather than the East's, without closing the door to the future to a creative blending of both Western and Eastern traditions.

On the other hand the loss of Philippine indigenous traditions, lost even before the coming of the Americans, at least among the Philippine educated élite, is a negative development. In fact, it seems that together with manifstations of linguistic, intellectual, scientific and artistic imperialism, one must recognize the reality of literary imperialism as well, for little of the indigenous tradition survives. So total has the takeover been, as a result of the academic roots of this type of writing, that barely anything of native literary forms in both structure and techniques has been transferred; only subject-matter and themes are local; the techniques are foreign.

In the Philippine search for a usable past the Filipino must continue to attempt to retrieve what of his oral and indigenous traditions is worth preserving. If indeed the Philippines will continue to be a bilingual nation, then these traditions, while revived in the writing of literature in Tagalog (Pilipino) and the other vernacular languages, might fruitfully be transferred into English and fructify the tradition of the presently all-too-American, Philippine writing going on in English.

References

ARGUILLA, M, E. (1940) *How my brother Leon brought home a wife and other stories*. Manila: Philippine Book Guild.

BAUTISTA, C. F. (1970) *The archipelago*, Manila: San Beda College.

BAUTISTA, C. F. (1981) *Telex moon*. Manila: Integrated Research Center, De La Salle University.

BAUTISTA, M. L. S. (1979) Apologies, compliments and probes in Pilipino radio drama: an exploratory analysis of Pilipino speech acts. *Philippine Journal of Linguistics*, **10**(1 and 2): 45–62.

BENITEZ, P. M. (1925) Dead stars. Manila: *The Philippines Herald*, 20 September. See Yabes, 1981.

BENN, K. (1983) Discourse approaches to cohesion: a study of the structure and unity of a Central Bontoc exhortatory text. Master's thesis, De La Salle University.

BULOSAN, C. (ed.) (1942) *Chorus for America: six Philippine poets*. Los Angeles: Wagon & Stars Publishers and Harvey Parker & Craftsman.

BULOSAN, C. (1978) *The Philippines is in the heart: a collection of stories (1914–1956)*. Quezon City: New Day.

DAGUIO, A. (1973) *Bataan harvest: War poems*. Manila: Alberto S. Florentino.

DATO, R. (1924) *Filipino poetry (1909–1924)*. Manila: J. S. Agustin.

EUGENIO, D. L. (compiler) (1981). *Philippine folk literature: an anthology*. Quezon City: Folklore Studies Program, University of the Philippines, and the UP Folklorists.

GALANG, Z. M. (1921) *A child of sorrow*. Manila: The Author; (1924) Manila: Philippine Education Co.; (1952) third edition revised and abridged, Manila: Bardavon; (1955) Manila: Abiva.

GONZALEZ, A. (1981) Tagalog accent revisited: Some preliminary notes. In *Linguistics across continents: Studies in honor of Richard S. Pittman*, edited by A. Gonzalez and D. Thomas, pp. 27–45. Manila: Summer Institute of Linguistics and Linguistic Society of the Philippines.

GONZALEZ, A. (1982 English in the Philippines mass media. In *New Englishes*, edited by J. B. Pride, pp. 211–226. Rowley, Mass.: Newbury House.

GONZALEZ, A. and W. ALBERCA (1978) *Philippine English of the mass media*. Manila: Linguistic Society of the Philippines.

GONZALEZ, N. V. M. (1959) The bamboo dancers. *The Diliman Review*. Manila: Benipayo Press.

GRIMES, J. E. (1975) *The thread of discourse*. The Hague: Mouton.

JOAQUIN, N. (1963) *Prose and poems*. Manila: Alberto S. Tolentino.

JOAQUIN, N. (1981) *The ballad of the five battles*. Makati, Metro Manila: Arts Unlimited. Inc.

JOOS, M. (1969) *The five clocks*. New York: Harcourt Brace.

JOSÉ, F. S. (1962) *The pretenders and eight short stories*. Manila: Regal.

JOSÉ, F. S. (1980) *Waywaya and other short stories from the Philippines*. Hong Kong: Heinemann Educational.

LLAMZON, T. (1969) *Standard Filipino English*. Quezon City: Ateneo de Manila Press.

LONGACRE, R. E. (1968) *Philippine languages: discourse, paragraph and sentence structure*, vol. 1: *Discourse and paragraph structure*. Glendale, Calif.: Church Press.

MALLARI, I. V. (1951) *When I was a little boy: stories for children based on Filipino customs and superstitions*. Manila: Bookman.

PIKE, K. L. (1981) Grammar versus reference in the analysis of discourse. In his *Tagmemics, discourse, and verbal act*, pp. 47–64. Ann Arbor, Mich.: University of Michigan.

ROCES, A. R. (1959) *Of cocks and kites, and other short stories*. Manila: Regal Publishing.

ROTOR, A. B. (1936) *The wound and the scar*. Manila: Philippine Book Guild.

SANTAROMANA, M. L. (ed) (1975) *Sinaglahi: an anthology of Philippine literature published by the Writers Union of the Philippines in celebration of the Afro-Asian Writers Symposium, 1975*. Philippines: Writers Union of the Philippines.

SANTOS, B. N. (1965) *Villa Magdalena*. Manila: Erehwon.

TORRES, E. (ed.) (1975) *An anthology of poems 1965–1974*. Manila: Department of Public Information.

VILLA, J. G. (1922) Poem in *Never Mind*. Manila: Procopio.

VILLA, J. G. (1928) *Philippine short stories: the best 25 stories of 1928*. Manila: The Writers Club.

WRIGGLESWORTH, H. J. (1981) *An anthology of Ilianen Manobo folktales*. Cebu: San Carlos Publications.

YABES, L. (1981) *Philippine short stories (1925–1955): Parts I and II*. Quezon City: University of the Philippines.

ZULUETA DA COSTA, R. (1940) *Like the Molave*. Philippines, Tirso Obispo.

12

Tradition and Creativity: Stylistic Innovations in Raja Rao

R. PARTHASARATHY

ONE of the difficulties a reader encounters in the presence of South Asian literature in English is that of understanding the nature of the world projected by the text, and by implication the strategies of discourse adopted by the writer to nativize the English language. Not enough attention has so far been paid to this in the South Asian context, with the exception of Kachru's (1983) comprehensive study. Kachru examines the problem from the perspective of a sociolinguist. I will, however, try to explore its implications generally in the context of South Asian literature in English, and specifically in the context of the fiction of Raja Rao (b. 1908). His fiction offers a paradigm of South Asian literature in English with all its contradictions and inconsistencies.

The Foreword to *Kanthapura* (1938) is revolutionary in its declaration of independence from English literature. It was Rao who, more than any other writer of his generation, which includes Mulk Raj Anand (b. 1905), R. K. Narayan (b. 1906), and Bhabani Bhattacharya (b. 1906), established the status of South Asian literature in English during India's struggle for freedom from British rule. He is one of the most innovative novelists now writing in English. Departing boldly from the European tradition of fiction, he indigenized the novel in the process of assimilating material from the Indian literary tradition. The Foreword is explicit about this.

> There is no village in India, however mean, that has not a rich *sthala-purana*, or legendary history, of its own. Some god or god-like hero has passed by the village . . . the Mahatma himself, on one of his many pilgrimages through the country, might have slept in this hut, the low one, by the village gate. In this way the past mingles with the present, and the gods mingle with men to make the repertory of your grandmother always bright. One such story from the contemporary annals of my village I have tried to tell. (1963: vii)

Kanthapura is the story of how Gandhi's struggle for independence from the British came to an unknown village in South India. References to specific events in India in the late 1920s and the early 1930s suggest that the novel has grown out of a distinct historical context. The story is told by an old woman, Achakka, and it evokes the spirit of India's traditional folk narratives, the puranas. It is almost fifty years since Rao wrote that Foreword. In an attempt to elucidate Rao's intentions, I shall examine the Foreword as an introduction to his own fiction.

Since the rise of the novel in the 18th century, its philosophical bias has been towards the particular; hence its focus on the individual in an objective world. An entirely opposite view is expressed in *The Serpent and the Rope* (1960:330): India is 'perhaps the only nation that throughout history has questioned the existence of the world – of the object'. When a writer from the Third World, like Rao, chooses this specific genre rather than one that is traditional to his own culture, like the epic, for instance, and further chooses to project this genre in a language not his own, he takes upon himself the burden of synthesizing the projections of both cultures. Out of these circumstances Rao has forged what I consider a truly exemplary style in South Asian, in fact in Third World, literature. He has, above all, tried to show how the spirit of one culture can be possessed by and communicated in another language.

English as a code is now universally shared by both native and non-native speakers. What are not always shared or recognized are the manifestations of a specific culture embedded by the writer in the language. Though the language can now be taken for granted, what cannot any longer be taken for granted are the cultural deposits transmitted by the language. To understand them the reader, especially if he is a native speaker, must equip himself with a knowledge of the writer's socio-cultural milieu. Would he not be expected to do so if he were to read an English translation of, say, the *Mahabharata* or, for that matter, the *Iliad*?

THE INDIAN WORLD-VIEW: PHILOSOPHICAL AND LINGUISTIC SPECULATIONS

Culture determines literary form; and the form of the novel from cultures within South Asia has been strongly influenced by those cultures themselves, resulting in something different from the form of the novel in the West. Rao himself is of the opinion that an Indian can never write a novel; he can only write a purana. The puranas are sacred history included in the canon of scripture, and they tell stories of the origin of the universe, the exploits of gods and heroes, and the genealogies of kings. Their impact on the minds and imaginations of the people of India has been profound. Through them the Vedas and the Upanishads and the ideas of the great tradition of Hinduism were communicated by intention and organized effort to the people, and woven into their lives in festivals and rituals. The *Mahabharata* and the *Ramayana* were expressly composed for the same purpose. There is, at least in South India, an unbroken tradition of recitation of the two epics by ruler and teacher in the vernacular languages. The epics were recited in the form of stories by the *sūtapaurāṇikas*, bards who recite the puranas.

Sanskrit is, in fact, an obsession with Rao: 'It is the source of our culture . . . and I have wished a thousand times that I had written in Sanskrit.' Intellectually and emotionally, he is deeply rooted in the Indian tradition, especially in the philosophical tradition of the Advaita Vedanta of Sankara (8th century AD). Sankara was interested in the nature of the relationship of the individual Self (atman) with the universal Self (Brahman). He insisted that these were identical (*tat tvam asi*, 'Thou art that', Chandogya Upanishad,

6.12–14), and that all appearances of plurality and difference arose from a false interpretation of the data presented by the mind and senses. He therefore rejected subject-object dualism. The only reality is Brahman. For Sankara, liberation (moksha) was the ultimate aim, and he defined it as intuitive knowledge of the identity of atman and Brahman, and not, it is to be remembered, union with God.

Rao's ideas of language are formed by the linguistic speculations of the Indians, notably the *Vākyapadīyam* (Of the sentence and the word) of Bhartṛhari (5th century AD). Rao himself observes that:

> to say a flower . . . you must be able to say it in such a way that the force of the vocable has power to create the flower. Unless word becomes *mantra*, no writer is a writer, and no reader a reader. . . . We in India need but to recognize our inheritance. Let us never forget Bhartṛhari. (*Literary Criterion* 1965: 229–31)

In an oral culture, such as that of the Indians, thinking is done mnemonically to facilitate oral recurrence. Thought comes into existence in rhythmic, balanced patterns, in repetitions or antitheses, in epithetic, aphoristic or formulaic utterances, in proverbs, or in other mnemonic forms. Words are therefore invested with power, and this relates them to the sacral, to the ultimate concerns of existence.

In examining Rao's use of English it is important to keep in mind his philosophical and linguistic orientations. The house of fiction that he has built rests on these twin foundations. Among South Asian writers in English he is perhaps unique in his attempt not only to nativize but also to Sanskritize the English language. Sanskritization is used here in the sense it is understood by anthropologists as a process of social and cultural change in Indian civilization. Rao strains to the limit all the expressive resources of the language. As a result, the Indian reality that emerges from his writing is authentic. Foremost among the problems the South Asian writer in English has to wrestle with are, firstly, the expression of modes of thinking and feeling specific to his culture, and secondly, terminology. Rao overcomes the first problem by invariably drawing upon Kannada and Sanskrit, and in the process he uses devices like loan translation, idiomatic and syntactic equivalences, and the imitation of native-style repertoires. He overcomes the second problem of finding words for culturally bound objects by contextualizing them so that their meanings are self-evident. By evoking the necessary cultural ambience these strategies help the writer to be part of the mainstream of the literatures of India.

In an illuminating essay investigating the nature of Osip Mandelstam's Jewishness, Cohen observes:

> A poet's nation is his language and unless one wills to become of no language or of several languages or to put on languages without fixity of place, the poet has no choice but to become the language he speaks and hopefully, if one is great in the use of the language, to change it as profoundly as one is changed. But language by itself is not a nation, however much the experience of the people is transmitted through its unfolding, resonation and echo. Language is abstract until it becomes one's own language and then it is possessed, most particularly. (1974:42)

Among Kannada, Sanskrit, French and English, it is English that Rao most consummately possesses, and it is in that language that his fiction most consummately speaks to us. From the beginning, English is ritually de-Anglicized. In *Kanthapura* English is thick with the agglutinants of Kannada; in *The serpent and the rope* the Indo-European kinship between English and Sanskrit is creatively exploited; and in *The cat and Shakespeare* (1965), English is made to approximate the rhythm of Sanskrit chants. At the apex of this linguistic pyramid is the forthcoming *The chessmaster and his moves*, wherein Rao has perfected an idiolect uniquely and inimitably his own. It is the culmination of his experiments with the English language spanning more than fifty years. *The Chessmaster and his Moves* has none of the self-consciousness in the use of English that characterizes his other work. In it he realizes the style that had eluded him in *The Serpent and the Rope*. Of style, he writes:

> The style of a man . . . the way he weaves word against word, intricates the existence of sentences with the values of *sound*, makes a comma here, puts a dash there: all are signs of the inner movement, the speed of his life, his breath (*prana*), the nature of his thought, the ardour and age of his soul. (1965: 164–5)

I shall now examine some of Rao's discourse strategies that constitute his style.

KANTHAPURA

A peasant society, such as Kanthapura, has a homogeneous outlook and tradition. Its relationship to tradition produces a sense of unity and continuity between the present and past generations. Tradition is therefore an important instrument in ensuring social interdependence. Under the raj, even villages weren't spared the blessings of the Pax Britannica. It triggered socio-economic changes which eventually split up the small communities. The oral tradition itself became fragmented, though it remained the chronicler of the motherland through a poetically gifted individual's repertoire.

   Kanthapura is a mine of information about the socio-cultural life of peasant society in South India. This is usually the perspective from which the novel is read in the West – the little tradition pitted against the great tradition, to use the terms proposed by Robert Redfield in 'Peasant society and culture' (1956). Redfield distinguishes the beliefs and practices of the folk from those of the élite in an agrarian society. The little tradition functions as a symbolic criticism of the great tradition, while at the same time gravitating towards it because of the latter's institutional charisma. Brahmins, for instance, who sit atop the caste hierarchy, owe their status to the belief that they alone are empowered to perform the *saṃskāras*, central rituals, of Hinduism. The recognition by peasants of a great tradition, of which their practices are a variant, implies a stratification of culture. In a complex society, like India, the stratification of culture implies a stratification of power and wealth. The representatives of the great tradition are the gentry, officials, and priests who collectively form a ruling as well as a cultural élite. Relations between the little and great traditions are uneasy, and fraught with tension as their interests are diametrically opposed. The existing cultural hierarchy relegates the peasantry to a status of permanent inferiority. The little tradition lacks the institutional means for a direct confrontation with the great tradition. Colonialism further increased the distance between the little and great traditions by diluting ethnic identities.

The Foreword is, again, a criticism not only of the language of the middle class, but also of its ethnic identity and culture, which are fragmented. This is characteristic of societies under exploitative colonial regimes. The condition gives rise to social protest. In *Kanthapura*, under the influence of Gandhi, social protest becomes, on the one hand, a movement to reform the non-egalitarian Hindu society and, on the other, a movement to end British colonialism. The protest manifests itself as the expression of a critical attitude towards existing institutions and their underlying ethos. Social protest may be initiated by an individual or a community. Individuals play a decisive role in expressing social protest and mobilizing collective support for it, especially charismatic leaders like Gandhi.

Space within an Indian village is cut up and allocated to the different castes. Social relationships are interpersonal but hierarchical, with the brahmin and the pariah at the opposite ends of the spectrum. Into this world steps a young brahmin, Moorthy, who is educated in a town, and is therefore considered modern. He is a figure of authority, because he combines in himself upper-caste status and a college education. He is also a Gandhian, and committed like Gandhi to ending British rule as well as ending the inequalities within Indian society, such as untouchability and the oppression of women. The Gandhian movement was based on satyagraha, firmness in truth. Gandhi added an ethical dimension to what was basically a social and political movement. The Gandhian bias of the novel is obvious: moral revolution takes precedence over social and political revolutions. It is significant that Moorthy enters the untouchable's house in his own village first before his imprisonment as a revolutionary. While the inspiration of the novel is moral and humanistic, its idiom is spiritual and religious. Stress is laid on such values as righteousness, love, non-violence, and on ritual beliefs and practices.

Kanthapura is one long, oral tale told in retrospect. There are other tales interspersed with the main narrative that begin with the oral tags 'Once upon a time', and 'And this is how it all began', but these are usually digressions. Other characteristics of the oral narrative include the use of songs and prayers, proverbs, mythology, and epic lists and catalogues. The novel is, in fact, unthinkable without the oral tradition. The Foreword itself defines *Kanthapura* as an oral, and not a written, text:

> It may have been told of an evening, when as the dusk falls, and through the sudden quiet, lights leap up in house after house, and stretching her bedding on the veranda, a grandmother might have told you, newcomer, the said tale of her village. (1963: viii)

It is within the frame of Kannada that the tale is told. English is made to simulate the 'thought-movement' and idiom of the old woman, Achakka, who is the narrator. One detects here the notion of linguistic relativity associated with the Sapir-Whorf hypothesis that one's conceptualization of the world is partly the product of the form of the language habitually used to describe it and talk about it. Rao's use of English suggests the appropriation of the structural characteristics of Kannada, as a recent study (Patil 1969) shows. Consider the opening sentence as an example of syntactic re-creation.

> High on the Ghats is it, high up the steep mountains that face the cool Arabian seas, up the Malabar coast is it, up Mangalore and Puttur and many a centre of cardamom and coffee, rice and sugar cane. (1963:1)

Janet Gemmill has this translated into Kannada, and again retranslated into English as follows:

> Upon Ghats upon is it, upon steep mountain(s) upon, cool Arabian sea to face making mountain upon, Malabar coast upon is it, Mangalore, Puttur and many cardamom, coffee, rice, sugar cane centre(s) upon is. (1974: 194)

The similarity in the word order is unmistakable, especially the reversal of the word order of subject and verb, and the omission of the verb in the second clause. The deviation is, of course, kept within the bounds of intelligibility. The embedding of Kannada structure in English is done with such finesse as to be almost unnoticeable.

Parataxis and simple co-ordination are syntactic features that generally characterize the oral narrative. They dominate *Kanthapura*. One example will suffice – the celebrated description of the Kartik festival.

> Kartik has come to Kanthapura, sisters – Kartik has come with the glow of lights and the unpressed footsteps of the wandering gods . . . and gods walked by lighted streets, blue gods and quiet gods and bright-eyed gods, and even as they walk in transparent flesh the dust gently sinks back to the earth, and many a child in Kanthapura sits late into the night to see the crown of this god and that god, and how many a god has chariots with steeds white as foam and queens so bright that the eyes shut themselves in fear lest they be blinded. (1963: 81)

Idioms are a fertile area for nativization, and here Rao both transplants from the Kannada, and implants new ones, e.g. 'to stitch up one's mouth' (p. 58); 'to tie one's daughter to the neck of' (p. 35); 'a crow-and-sparrow story' (p. 15); (from 'a cock-and-bull story'); and 'every squirrel has his day' (p. 77) (from 'every dog has his day').

Adjuncts are frequently used in oral narratives for highlighting a word or phrase, e.g. 'And the Swami, who is he?' (p. 41); '. . . my heart it beat like a drum' (p. 182); 'She has never failed us, I assure you, our Kenchamma' (p. 2); and 'Our village – Kanthapura is its name' (p. 1).

In an Indian village, relationships are interpersonal. Social stratification is along caste and occupational lines. Often idiosyncrasies and physical disabilities attach themselves as sobriquets to names of individuals. Examples of these abound in the novel: Patel Rangè Gowda, Pariah Sidda, Post-office Suryanarayana, Husking Rangi, Four-beamed-house Chandrasekharayya, One-eyed Linga, and Waterfall Venkamma.

On ceremonial occasions social relationships are meticulously observed. In a traditional society certain aspects of conversation are ritualized. Elaborate attention is paid, for example, to modes of address. They reflect the use of language as a means of establishing a friendly rapport between speaker and listener, and of reinforcing communal solidarity. Malinowski (1923) refers to this as 'phatic communion'. For instance, in a host-guest interactional situation, Rao hits upon the exact phrase translated from the Kannada to dispel any uneasiness. The guest is coaxed: 'Take it Bhattarè, only one cup more, just one? Let us not dissatisfy our manes' (1963: 21). On the anniversary of a death in a brahmin family other brahmins are invited to a feast, and they are expected to indulge their appetites fully so that the spirits of the dead are pacified. Narasimhaiah remarks: 'With a people like us, used to being coaxed, the English form, 'Won't you have a second helping?' or the mere 'Sure you don't care for more?' will be ineffective, and even considered discourteous.' (1968: 14) Culture-sensitive situations like this are not always grasped by the native speaker of English.

Through a choice of strategies, skilfully deployed, Rao has been able to reconstruct the performance-centred discourse of the traditional oral tales of India. Kanthapura is village India in microcosm – the context that has determined and shaped the expressive devices in the novel.

THE SERPENT AND THE ROPE

Rao considers his entire work as

> an attempt at 'puranic' re-creation of Indian story-telling: that is to say, the story, as story, is conveyed through a thin thread to which are attached (or which passes through) many other stories, fables and philosophical disquisitions, like a *mala* (garland). (Naik 1972: 103)

If Kannada is the prototype for English in *Kanthapura*, Sanskrit is in *The Serpent and the Rope*. Sanskrit is the obvious choice, as the novel has a strong metaphysical bias. It was in Sanskrit that the philosophical speculations of the Indians found their profoundest expression. Rao's Sanskritic English is not unlike Milton's Latinate English in *Paradise Lost*. The intent is the same: to assimilate into English qualities and features of a prestige language the writer admires most. As opposed to the Prakrits, the vernaculars, Sanskrit was the 'perfected' language. The Sanskritization of English should be seen as part of a wider socio-cultural phenomenon that has, historically, characterized Indian civilization. Dumont and Pocock interpret Sanskritization as the 'acceptance of a more distinguished or prestigious way of saying the same things'. Quotations in the original together with English translations, from the classical Sanskrit poets, Kalidasa (fl. 5th century AD) and Bhavabhuti (8th century AD), and from the devotional hymns of Sankara, are skilfully woven into the story, and function as a parallel text. Ramaswamy, the protagonist, relapses into Sanskrit to tell his wife, Madeleine, as delicately as possible what he is unable to tell her openly – his feeling of despair as she increasingly withdraws into herself. He finds a parallel in Bhavabhuti's *Uttararāmacarita* (Rama's later history) to which he draws her attention. The occasion has all the solemnity of a ritual, and it represents his farewell to her.

> ekaḥ samprati nāśitapriyatamastāmadya rāmaḥ katham/ pāpaḥ pañcavaṭiṃ vilokayatu vā gacchatvasaṃbhāvya vā//

> Alone, now, after being the cause of the loss of his dear (wife), how should Rama, sinful as he is, visit that very same Pañcavaṭī, or how pass on regardless of it? (1960: 326)

A powerful recursive device used throughout the novel is the dash (–) to suggest the to-and-fro movement of a thought, its amplitude and density. The dash is used to indicate a break or an interruption in the thought. In between dashes a thought is often insinuated or slipped under the breath, as it were.

> The world is either unreal or real – the serpent or the rope. There is no in-between-the-two – and all that's in-between is poetry, is sainthood. (1960: 333)

Philosophical debates are a part of both the Upanishads and puranas. *The serpent and the rope* resembles both. The novel interprets Vedanta in terms of the discourse of fiction. The philosophy is not an interpolation, but an integral part of the novel – its informing principle.

THE CAT AND SHAKESPEARE

The philosophical bias is even more pronounced in *The Cat and Shakespeare*. It has been described as 'a tale of modern India', and it exhibits none of the communicative strategies of *Kanthapura* or *The Serpent and the Rope*. Unlike the highly individual and expressive idiolects of the earlier novels, the idiolect of *The Cat and Shakespeare* is ordinary in order to express traditional lore. In this process Rao has pitted the symmetry of language against the asymmetry of thought with its indirections and paradoxes. The protagonist, Ramakrishna Pai, describes his moment of illumination thus:

> I saw truth not as fact but as ignition. I could walk into fire and be cool, I could sing and be silent, I could hold myself and yet not be there. . . . I smelled a breath that was of nowhere but rising in my nostrils sank back into me, and found death was at my door. I woke up and found death had passed by, telling me I had no business to be there. Then where was I? (1965: 113–14)

Narasimhaiah has an interesting explanation to offer for the use of the dash in 'His heart is so big, it builds a wall lest it run away with everything . . . In fact he himself is – running.' He remarks: 'And the last sentence is the most deceptive in its simplicity, for the word 'running' after a dash denotes a state of being, not becoming, that is, 'he' and 'running' are interchangeable; running itself is he and he, it.'

I suspect Rao's penchant for the finite verb 'to be' in both *The Serpent and the Rope* and *The Cat and Shakespeare* has a philosophical basis. It denotes existence, reality. And since both novels attempt to probe the nature of reality, it is frequently used: 'I do not believe that death is', 'God after all is', and 'So what is real ever is'. The highly reductive style of *The Cat and Shakespeare* is in strong contrast to the expansiveness of the earlier novels.

The English language doesn't have sufficiently deep roots in South Asia. It is therefore important for the writer to find his own individual style through which to express his world-view. The reader on his part, if he is not to misread the text, must get to know the writer's general epistemological viewpoint or the sum total of beliefs, preconceptions and values which the writer shares with others within a socio-cultural context.

References and further reading

CHAKRAVARTI, PRABHATCHANDRA (1933) *The linguistic speculations of the Hindus*. Calcutta: Calcutta University Press.

COHEN, ARTHUR, A. (1974) *Osip Emilievich Mandelstam*: *an essay in antiphon*. Ann Arbor: Ardis.

DASGUPTA, SURENDRANATH (1922) *A history of Indian philosophy*, vol. I. Cambridge: Cambridge University Press.

DUMONT, LOUIS and DAVID POCOCK (eds) (1959) *Contributions to Indian sociology*, vol. 3. The Hague: Mouton.

GEMMILL, JANET (1974) The transcreation of spoken Kannada in Raja Rao's *Kanthapura*. *Literature east and west* **18**(2–4): 191–202.

The Hindu (Madras), 18 April 1978, p. 8.

KACHRU, B. (1982) South Asian English. In *English as a world language*, edited by Richard W. Bailey and M. Gorlach. Ann Arbor: University of Michigan Press.

KACHRU, B. (1983) *The Indianization of English*: *the English language in India*. Delhi: Oxford University Press.

MALINOWSKI, B. (1923) The problem of meaning in primitive languages. In *The meaning of meaning*, edited by C. K. Ogden and I. A. Richards. New York: Harcourt Brace.

NAIK, M. K. (1972) *Raja Rao*. New York: Twayne.

NAKAMURA, HAJIME (1964) *Ways of thinking of eastern peoples*: *India, China, Tibet, Japan*, edited by Philip P. Wiener. Honolulu: East-West Center Press.

NARASIMHAIAH, C. D. (1968) Indian writing in English: an introduction. *Journal of Commonwealth literature* **5**: 3–15.

NARASIMHAIAH, C. D. (1973) *Raja Rao*. New Delhi: Arnold-Heinemann.

PARTHASARATHY, R. (ed). (1976) *Ten twentieth-century Indian poets*. Delhi: Oxford University Press.

PARTHASARATHY, R. (1982) Whoring after English gods. In *Writers in east-west encounter*: *new cultural bearings*, edited by Guy Amirthanayagam. London: Macmillan.

PATIL, CHANDRASHEKAR B. (1969) The Kannada element in Raja Rao's prose: a linguistic study of *Kanthapura*. *Journal of Karnatak University* **13**.

RAGHAVAN, V. (1956) Variety and integration in the pattern of Indian culture. *Far Eastern Quarterly* **15**(4): 497–505.

RAO, RAJA (1938) *Kanthapura*. London: Allen & Unwin. Reprinted (1963) New York: New Directions.

RAO, RAJA (1960) *The serpent and the rope*. London: Murray.

RAO, RAJA (1965) *The cat and Shakespeare*. New York: Macmillan.

RAO, RAJA (1965) The writer and the word. *Literary Criterion* **7**(1): 229–231.

RAO, RAJA (in press) *The chessmaster and his moves*. New Delhi: Vision Books.

REDFIELD, R. (1956) *Peasant society and culture*: *an anthropological approach to civilization*. Chicago: University of Chicago Press. pp. 67–104.

SRINIVAS, M. N. (1956) A note on Sanskritization and westernization. *Far Eastern Quarterly* **15**(4): 481–496.

STAAL, J. F. (1963) Sanskrit and Sanskritization. *Journal of Asian Studies* **22**(3): 261–275.

SUBRAMANIA IYER, K. A. (1965) *The Vākyapadīya of Bhartrhari with the vrtti, chapter I*: *English translation*. Poona: Deccan College Postgraduate and Research Centre.

SUBRAMANIA IYER, K. A. (1969) *Bhartrhari, a study of the Vākyapadīya in the light of the ancient grammarians*. Poona: Deccan College Postgraduate and Research Centre.

PART V

Culture and the Language Classroom

INTRODUCTION

THE inclusion of a single chapter in this section is not unintentional: it underscores the importance of cross-cultural research for the classroom. This is an area which is generally ignored in ESL or is discussed in a peripheral way. Strevens recalls the basic assumptions that underlie the study of discourse patterns in the context of EIL. He argues that such barriers are highly variable: sometimes cultural differences are of little account, while in other circumstances they produce a total blockage in the learner's mind. The variables, of course, lie in the cultures themselves, in the learners and their attitudes towards cultural presuppositions, and also in the attitude of the teachers. What are some of the cultural presuppositions? Strevens provides a tentative list: philosophical and religious beliefs, concepts of nature, notions of government, concepts of science, literature, and the society's ultimate myths.

The concept of 'ultimate myths' is discussed with relation to Anglo-American society, seeing the principal elements as: Aristotelian logic, Roman organization and public virtues, Cartesian logic, mathematics and scientific method, Judaeo-Christianity, and the impact of the scientific, technological and industrial revolutions. Strevens, of course, does not suggest that the presuppositions which, in his view, are inherent in native speaker English are, or should be, the presuppositions of non-native speakers. Instead, he makes it clear that cultural presuppositions differ across cultures and will be reflected in the discourse of people from different cultures even when they are speaking fluent English.

This final chapter, then, provides an applied perspective to the volume and demonstrates the relevance of the major issues discussed in the volume to the teacher and learner.

13

Cultural Barriers to Language Learning

PETER STREVENS

THERE is a growing realization that the massive growth and spread of the English language, into fresh areas and populations and purposes of usage, carries with it an array of unpredicted changes and consequences, both for those for whom English is the mother tongue and for non-native users of English. During recent years a number of publications have discussed this aspect of English (e.g. Bailey and Görlach (eds), 1982; Brumfit (ed.), 1982; Kachru, 1983a, b; Platt *et al.*, 1984; Quirk, 1982; Smith (ed.), 1981, 1983; Strevens, 1980, 1983a & b).

Some manifestations within this field of study have been concerned with description: with describing forms and varieties of English which earlier would have been ignored, or derided, or regarded as the province of the dialectologist. Some have also been concerned with countering 'linguistic neo-imperialism': that is to say, with establishing parity of value, in linguistic and human terms, of all Englishes, whether 'native' or 'non-native'. Thanks largely to this work (especially associated with the names of Braj Kachru, Randolph Quirk, and Larry Smith) it is now firmly accepted that English can no longer be offered, or received, as a 'possession' of the native speakers which foreign learners must aspire to. Nor is it any longer true that any and every learner should try to speak English like a Britisher or an American: the choice of model will vary from place to place and may often appropriately be that of the local, educated population.

Other manifestations of this programme of study have taken as their starting-point the repeated experience of difficulties and barriers to learning or teaching English commonly experienced by particular groups of learners or teachers, notably but not exclusively from Thailand (Sukwiwat, 1983) and India (Kachru, 1983a) on the one hand, and from America or Britain on the other. The difficulties concerned have been noticed and studied not in the linguistic perspective of 'common difficulties', or error-analysis, or contrastive analysis: they have been perceived and expressed on a different plane – that of cultural differences in the context of language communication. A number of chapters in this volume clearly demonstrate the importance and usefulness of such approaches to English.

In one sense this preoccupation with cultural aspects of language contact, or linguistic aspects of cultural contact (the elements are double-sided), harks back to the era when anthropological linguistics seemed to promise a bi-disciplinary explanation for newly perceived, intercultural influences. And of course, at the beginning of its modern history, linguistics was indeed rooted in the social and anthropological sciences, with Frank Boas and Edward Sapir in the United States, and with Bronislaw Malinowski, John Firth, and the members of the Prague School of Linguistics in Europe.

There has from the beginning been a particular outlook on the problems that is distinct from the outlook of theoretical approaches to linguistics, or anthropology, or any other solely theoretical discipline. In these studies the awareness of the existence of important, unresolved, and unexamined problems stems from the shared experience of those responsible for teaching English, for the preparation of teachers of English as a foreign or second language, and for the academic administration of EFL/ESL programmes. It is in the universe of these activities that there emerges most clearly the existence of cultural barriers to language communication – shifting, elusive, and variable, yet persistent and rather intractable – which repeatedly diminish the success of learners' and teachers' efforts to impart a command of English. This aspect has been emphasized in the introduction to this volume, by Larry Smith. The area of language most affected by these problems is that of discourse.

This concern on the part of applied linguists and specialists in language learning and teaching to understand better the cross-cultural operation of discourse patterns is in line with general developments in the theory of language teaching. After a period of some forty years, during which language teaching concentrated on an atomistic approach, itemizing the vocabulary and grammar of the target language into discrete teaching-points and drilling them as separate items, in the past decade language teaching has paid increasingly greater attention to meaning – especially situational meaning, social and varietal meaning – and more recently still to discourse patterns as examples of a more holistic approach to the learning and teaching of languages.

SOME UNDERLYING ASSUMPTIONS

The study of discourse patterns in a cross-cultural setting is potentially a vast undertaking, since each culture possesses such a great number of features, some or all or none of which may be present, to a greater or lesser degree, in the particular cultures being contrasted – perhaps that is a main reason why anthropological linguistics has been slow in developing. On the other hand, in a framework of comparison where one element is always 'the learning of English', the spread of varieties becomes much easier to handle, even though the observations cannot be assumed to have universal validity for all pairs of cultures.

In making these observations certain fundamental assumptions or pre-suppositions are made, including, at least, the following:

First, language is but one element of the complex, seamless fabric of the total culture of a society. Of course language is an immensely important element which informs and shapes other elements, yet is in turn shaped by them. It is not possible to say how far languge influences the rest of culture, and how far culture influences language. What is clear is that there are deep and indissoluble links between the two.

Second, 'language' in this context embraces much more than vocabulary, grammar, and phonology. It includes also the subtle and only partly comprehended mechanisms for interpersonal communication which are grouped under the general rubric of discourse. These mechanisms are partly linguistic, partly paralinguistic, and partly non-linguistic; they include the individual's rules for social comportment; they are subject to individual variability.

Third, difficulties of understanding in cross-cultural circumstances are often cultural as much as – or more than – linguistic in nature.

Examples of cross-cultural impediments to communication are of many kinds. The following may be representative of a wide range of possibilities:

(a) *Where the purposes for which English is being taught/learned are absent in the learner's culture*. e.g. for mathematics and science, in a number of societies in Africa, South America, and elsewhere. The problem is most acute when mathematics and science are taught, in English, in pre-industrial societies. This example well illustrates why cross-cultural barriers to communication are not usually best described in language-specific terms: they relate to cultural differences that transcend and are independent of particular languages. Primary school mathematics in English faces the young child with conceptual problems whether his family languge is Igbo, or Ndebele, or Quechua. Quantitative precision in discourse, for instance in learning to speak about numbers with decimals or fractions, may be a puzzling concept if your culture uses a unit of number based on the number of cocoa beans that can be piled onto a cloth of a given size. Learning to talk or read about geometry in English is difficult in a special way if one's own culture builds houses in which walls need to be only approximately vertical, and in which right-angles are not highly valued.

(b) *Where rational argument is not revered*. English, in common with all European and Graeco-Roman-derived languages and many others, makes frequent use of notions of logicality, causality, and rationality. *If*, *unless*, *whatever*, *because* and a host of other linguistic devices in English proclaim the need to give reasons, to justify, to be precise. Yet in very many cultures, particularly in the Orient, the virtues of rationality and precision in concepts, and thus in discourse, are not self-evident and may even be rejected. Again, the differences apply in several cultures and within many languages, some of which have been discussed in various chapters in this volume.

(c) *Where ideology outweighs everyday 'reality'*. Religion and politics provide many examples, such as the customary use, in English translations emanating from China, of expressions such as *paper tiger*, *running dog*, *lackey of the imperialists*, etc. Cheng (1983) provides further examples of such translations in Chinese English. To observe that these are direct translations from Chinese political imagery is not sufficient to bridge the cultural divide. On the one side, native speakers of English who find the expressions unfamiliar and bizarre wish to find alternative ways of stating the slogans. But on the other side, the Chinese resist paraphrases more accessible to the native speaker of English, insisting (in effect) that they are more interested in retaining the Chinese political imagery than in producing an acceptable translation. (Brumfit (1978) on this topic is of considerable interest.)

(d) *Where personal comportment plays a role.* Every society has rules and customs about personal behaviour while the individual is speaking or listening to others. The rules relate to at least the following:

(i) *loudness of voice* – apart from indicating the speaker's emotional state, loudness may be regulated by social and hierarchical relationships with others present;

(ii) *speaking/non-speaking, and turn-taking* – the antiquated slogan 'children should be seen and not heard' reflects a change in native English-speakers' rules about who may speak, who to, and when; in many societies these social rules are complex and rigid, while 'only speak if you are spoken to' can be unbreakable rule in some circumstances;

(iii) *simultaneity of speaking* – in some societies it is normal for two or three participants to speak at once, or at least to overlap their conversational turns, but in other societies or situations such behaviour would be regarded as rude, discourteous, vulgar;

(iv) *eye contact, sight-lines* – where, in some societies, in some circumstances, it can be interpreted as forward behaviour to look directly at the person one is addressing, in other cultures such averted eye behaviour may be seen as 'shifty', or dishonest, while yet other cultures regard it as highly discourteous for a person to interpose himself or herself across the sight-lines of others engaged in conversation;

(v) *head-levels* – some cultures set great store by the relative height (above floor level) of particular individuals, so that certain speakers are expected always to keep their head above or below that of other people present;

(vi) *facing, abasing, prostrating* – in extreme cases there may be rigid rules of body posture when greeting, communicating, or leave-taking;

(vii) *posture, contact* – such postures as pointing the foot, displaying the instep to other people, touching the head of another person, or indeed making any bodily contact whatever, may be culturally unwelcome in some societies, as a concomitant of personal inter-communication.

Having deliberately illustrated a wide range of different types of cross-cultural barriers out of an even greater range of possibilities, we need to point out that not all these or other examples always become barriers, and that when they do impede communication, it is not always to the same extent. Indeed, where the learners of English belong to a culture with rather few obvious differences from, say, 'British Isles' culture, neither learners nor teachers may be aware of any cultural barriers to communications, for example between British teachers and Dutch learners. Cultural contrasts vary according to the particular cultures observed.

We should recognize that quite weighty cultural differences exist even between different, native English-speaking usage. I am indebted to Ellen Shaw, of Cambridge University Press (New York), for information about her work in taking a British English dictionary and producing an American English version. She found not only the anticipated lexical differences (*petrol-gasoline*, *lift-elevator*, *trousers-pants*, etc.) but also that dictionary citations and examples were heavily culture-bound. In the British dictionary she found large numbers of citations drawn from the game of cricket, from growing flowers and grass in a domestic garden, and from small pet animals. By contrast she found American dictionaries to contain many citations concerning an individual's state of health, about the law, and about food. These contrasts can puzzle and confuse those who learn English in one culture, then move to another.

The extent to which cultural differences affect the learning of English depends also on the individual learner, the individual teacher, and the overall educational aims of the teaching.

Some learners perceive the slightest cultural innuendo and react strongly against the unfamiliar; other individuals are more easily receptive, either not perceiving or at any rate not reacting against unfamiliar patterns. This variability seems to stem partly from temperament and psychological make-up, and partly from the extent of previous foreign-language-learning experience. No doubt the culture shock of learning one's fourth foreign language is damped down by the experience of three previous encounters with different cultures.

Similarly, teachers vary in the extent to which they magnify or diminish the cultural content of language learning. The tendency to magnify – or at least to dwell upon – cultural differences is frequently present when literature is an important component of an English course. In one sense this is not surprising: literature is closely identified with the deliberate manipulation of cultural symbols and stereotypes. But for some teachers of English, both native speakers and non-native speakers, literature is important precisely because it is heavily loaded with culture. For many other teachers of English, probably the great majority, it is the *language* that needs to be taught, for communicative and other purposes not directly related to culture. And in speaking here of 'teachers', we must include also those who design teaching syllabuses, write course books and teaching materials, and construct examinations. In all these activities there may be a greater or lesser concentration on cultural content.

So, too, with overall educational aims. These may vary from teaching English in order to achieve an awareness of British or American culture, life and institutions, to the opposite extreme, in which the aims are to provide the learners with a command of the language for purposes within their own culture, whether or not the same learners may also be offered a separate course in 'British life and institutions'.

In sum, cultural differences can present severe barriers to communication or they can be negligible, depending on a range of variable factors.

A PRELIMINARY ANALYSIS OF CULTURAL PRESUPPOSITIONS

It can be argued that the cultural presuppositions of a society, when they are transmitted through language, relate especially to the expression of culture through its basic mechanisms and value-systems, including the domains of:

   (i) philosophy
  (ii) concepts of nature
 (iii) notions of government
 (iv) concepts of science
  (v) literature
 (vi) the society's 'ultimate myths'.

Each of these contributes a degree of 'cultural loading', in ways briefly discussed below. In the circumstances of particular contrasts between the culture of a native speaker of English and the culture of the learner of English, this quality potentially offers cultural barriers to language learning.

(i) Philosophy and religion

Cultural differences in this domain relate to issues such as the following:

(1) *Animism and theism*. People speak and behave differently, at least on certain occasions, if they believe in a number of gods within the universe, or only one – in which case a range of specific, further beliefs may follow – or indeed none.

(2) *The relation of man to God*, of man to man, of man to nature. Philosophical and religious beliefs of this type often regulate the response of the individual to other people of the same or different beliefs, for instance sometimes dissuading a person from associating too closely with others of a different persuasion.

(3) *Views on life and death, peace and war, an after-life*. Ideas on these issues are often deeply embedded in language and other forms of cultural expression. Violence and death are often discussed in terms which do not overtly refer to the consequences of death, the degree of blame or merit attached to causing the death of others, whether death is to be feared or welcomed, and so forth. But, for example, the phrase *a Holy War* has fundamentally different connotations for some Christians and some Moslems.

(4) *Ethics and morals*. During the long period of time over which a student's experience of learning English normally extends, it is certain that learner and teacher will encounter a number of occurrences of contrasting – and perhaps opposing – ethical and moral standpoints. Ideas of right and wrong, the balance of good and evil in personal behaviour,

the nature and importance of 'truth', and many related issues, may intrude into the learner's learning process and perhaps challenge his personal willingness to learn.

(ii) Concepts of nature

Each society tends to take for granted its own views of man's place in the universe, and of whether man is simply a passive participant or whether he can influence or dominate his condition. Such views can change over time, within a culture, as happened in Europe with the rise of 19th-century Romanticism. And the concepts of nature embrace also a culture's views of animals: contrast Buddhist, Hindu, Moslem, and Christian attitudes today. In some instances the existence of forces of a supernatural kind is accepted without question or analysis in circumstances (for instance in accounting for natural disasters) where native English-speaking peoples will tend to invoke scientific factors.

(iii) Notions of government

The nature of the highest levels of social organization and control inevitably affects people's beliefs and values, and is often expressed, or inherent, in communication. Ideas such as whether control is determined by heredity, or by force, or by group decision; kingship; caste and class; democracy; even whether government needs to be 'efficient' (compare the 'efficient' regimes of the Aztecs and the Chaldeans on the one hand, and the 'efficiency-ignoring' organization of Romany (Gypsy) society on the other), find frequent expression in language and personal comportment.

(iv) Concepts of science

It is essential to realize that what is often called 'Western science' is not the *only* science. Every society has its mathematics, its agriculture, its architecture. So the cultural contrast which emerges – for instance when primary schoolchildren in rural Zambia learn science in a foreign language, English – is not between 'science' and 'no science', but between different kinds of science. 'Western science' is highly codified and self-aware, supported by a very great deal of intellectual scaffolding which pervades Western schooling and is taken for granted, even among non-scientists. It is concepts *about* science whose textual presuppositions often provide shocks for learners of English from other societies and cultures.

(v) Literature

Even the idea of literature, taken so much for granted by native speakers of English – or at least by their education systems – is culture specific. Language-based art forms and creative artistry seem to be universal, but their nature is varied. Some societies, especially the pre-literate and recently literate, assign no value to written literature, but have an oral tradition of literature, often closely linked to music, drumming, and dance. In many cultures, too, literature is closely bound up with religion, as indeed English literature has been on occasion.

One large class of examples of authoritarian, cultural insensitivity is to be seen in many instances of the translation of *hymns* into tone languages, by native English-speaking missionaries. Retaining the *tune* of the hymn, they frequently thereby impose variations of tone which have lexical and grammatical significance – and which frequently produce nonsense, gibberish, or obscenity.

(vi) Society's 'ultimate myths'

It has been known, at least since the publication of Sir James Frazer's *The Golden Bough* in 1922, that mankind in every part of the world has evolved explanations for natural and supernatural phenomena, for the origins of men and women, for the shaping of the continents, for the progression of the seasons and the success or failure of the harvests, and so forth. To a surprising extent similar myths, such as that of a flood, are found among widely separated peoples. But there are also differences between cultures, particularly in the matter of belief in magic and the magical properties or effects of plants, animals, or special individual human beings.

To summarize this section of the argument, value-systems powerfully influence the rules of discourse in communication, and thus help to determine whether and to what extent there may be a cultural barrier between learner and target language. An obvious illustration of these differences occurs when the teacher of English assumes and places high value upon *persuasion by logical argument* and the importance of having a reason for everything, while the Eastern student of English favours *gaining merit by literary style*.

It has already been pointed out that cultural barriers of this kind are immensely variable. When they occur, how can they best be eliminated, or at least minimized? The answer can only be through greater understanding and wisdom on the part of the teacher, who can thereby assist the learner to accept the existence of cultural differences while reducing their negative effect on his learning.

In attaining this degree of understanding it may help the teacher of English, whether or not English is his or her mother tongue, to be aware of the origins of some at least of the principal cultural presuppositions conveyed in discourse in native speaker English. Briefly outlined, they include the following:

(i) *Aristotle's rhetoric.* Modern European ways of thoughts retain an underlying assumption that education seeks 'the truth' by intellectual effort – by observing and describing and classifying and deducing and inferring. It is perhaps from ancient Greek thought in particular that the notions are most clearly devised which encourage the ordering of thoughts for purposes of argument, the search for explanation and the centrality of cause and effect, the distinction between 'knowledge' and 'belief', the need to seek out recurrent patterns. From Greece, too, come the first ideas of democracy as a pattern of social government.

(ii) *Roman organization and public virtues.* It may be that it is from Rome that European thought has imbibed an assumption of the need for organization in public affairs, together with a number of qualities on virtues: bravery, fortitude, honour, pride, duty, and the merit of ordering one's individual life according to lofty principles. (Not that all native English-speakers practise these virtues, but the language continually proclaims their existence and value.)

(iii) *Descartes' logic; mathematics; scientific method.* Native speaker English constantly makes use of the refinements of logic, and of the need for language to express precisely the truth or falsity of the propositions it contains. It may be from the ferment of ideas in the 17th and 18th centuries that English assimilated its attitudes towards fact, observation, hypothesis, theory. That is not to say that English (or any other language) is 'logical', but there is no doubt that the possibility exists in English to express logical relationships with great precision.

(iv) *Judeo-Christianity* (especially as presented by the Bible). To a considerable extent the 'ultimate myths' of native English-speaking peoples are derived from the Old Testament – from the semi-literary history of the Jewish peoples, which also enshrined their system of moral values. Again, this is not to say that British or American culture subscribes today to the ethics of the Old Testatment. But many of our deepest images of good and evil, ideas of sin, concepts of heaven and hell, etc. are still heavily influenced by ancient Hebrew writings. From the New Testament the language takes expressions about God among men, self-sacrifice as a means of overcoming evil, redemption of sin, and other deep and emotional concepts.

(v) *The scientific and industrial revolutions.* In the past two centuries English has absorbed means of expressing scientific, mechanical, engineering, mathematical and other concepts. The language has gone through stages of enabling its users to conceptualize aspects of human life in the metaphor of a machine, or of electrical circuits, or of electronic devices, or of space engineering, or of computers.

The teacher of English, then, can more easily help the learner to overcome cultural barriers in discourse if he or she is aware of the presuppositions inherent in native speaker English. Without falling into the error of assuming that these ideas are necessarily in any way superior – or inferior – to those of his students' culture, the teacher assists the learner to compare them with his own presuppositions, and to come to terms with the essential diversity, yet equality, of human society.

References

BAILEY, RICHARD W. and M. GÖRLACH (eds) (1982) *English as a world language*. Ann Arbor: University of Michigan Press.

BRUMFIT, CHRISTOPHER J. (1978) The English language, ideology and international communication: some issues arising out of English teaching for Chinese students. *English Language Teaching Documents*, London: British Council.

BRUMFIT, CHRISTOPHER J. (ed.) (1982) *English for international communication*. Oxford: Pergamon Institute of English.

CHENG, CHIN-CHUAN (1983) Chinese varieties of English. In Kachru, 1983b.

FRAZER, SIR JAMES (1922) *The golden bough: a study in magic and religion*. London: Macmillan.

KACHRU, BRAJ (1983a) *The Indianization of English: the English language in India*. Delhi: Oxford University Press.

KACHRU, BRAJ (ed.) (1983b) *The other tongue: English across cultures*. Oxford: Pergamon Press.

PLATT, JOHN, H. WEBER and M. L. HO (1984) *The new Englishes*. London: Routledge & Kegan Paul.

QUIRK, RANDOLPH (1981) International English and the concept of nuclear English. In *English for cross-cultural communication*, edited by L. Smith. London: Macmillan.

SMITH, LARRY (ed.) (1981) *English for cross-cultural communication*. London: Macmillan.

SMITH, LARRY (ed.) (1983) *Readings in English as an international language*. Oxford: Pergamon Institute of English.

STREVENS, PETER (1980) *Teaching English as an international language*. Oxford: Pergamon Institute of English.

STREVENS, PETER (1983a) What is standard English? *RELC Occasional Papers*, No. 23. Singapore: SEAMEO Regional Language Centre.

STREVENS, PETER (1983b) The localized forms of English. In Kachru, 1983b.

SUKWIWAT, MAYURI (1983) Interpreting the Thai variety of English: a functional approach. In *Varieties of English in southeast Asia*, edited by R. B. Noss. Singapore: SEAMEO Regional Language Centre.

Index